ARRAYS, FUNCTIONAL LANGUAGES, AND PARALLEL SYSTEMS

ARRAYS, FUNCTIONAL LANGUAGES, AND PARALLEL SYSTEMS

Edited by

Lenore M. R. Mullin
University of Vermont

Michael Jenkins
Queen's University

Gaétan Hains
University of Montreal

Robert Bernecky
Snake Island Research

Guang Gao
McGill University

SPRINGER SCIENCE+BUSINESS MEDIA, LLC

Library of Congress Cataloging-in-Publication Data

Arrays, functional languages, and parallel systems / edited by Lenore Mullin ... [et al.].
p. cm.
"Representative of talks given at the First International Workshop on Arrays, Functional Languages, and Parallel Systems held 12-15 June 1990 in Montréal, Québec" - - Perf.
Includes index.
ISBN 978-1-4613-6789-5 ISBN 978-1-4615-4002-1 (eBook)
DOI 10.1007/978-1-4615-4002-1
1. Functional programming languages - - Congresses. 2. Parallel processing (Electronic computers) - - Congresses. 3. Array processors - - Congresses.
I. Mullin, Lenore. II. International Workshop on Arrays, Functional Languages, and Parallel Systems (1st : 1990 : Montréal, Québec)

QA76.7.A7 1991
004'.35 - - dc20 91-27527
CIP

Printed on acid-free paper.

Dedication

Alan J. Perlis
1922 - 1990

We dedicate this workshop to the memory of
Alan J. Perlis and his commitment to research in
arrays and programming languages.
The Organizing Committee:
R. Bernecky, G. Gao, G. Hains, M. Jenkins, L. Mullin

A Mentor

Arrays, how you lived them
You supported their research before their time
APL and STAPL thanks to you
You advised and mentored students everywhere
Perdue, Yale, and CMU

Thank you for your encouragement, my mentor
For your help and guidance, my advisor

We will all miss you
We will all remember you

a student

Table of Contents

PREFACE

During a meeting in Toronto last winter, Mike Jenkins, Bob Bernecky and I were discussing how the two existing theories on arrays influenced or were influenced by programming languages and systems. More's *Array Theory* was the basis for NIAL and APL2 and Mullin's *A Mathematics of Arrays*(MOA), is being used as an algebra of arrays in functional and λ-calculus based programming languages. MOA was influenced by Iverson's initial and extended algebra, the foundations for APL and J respectively.

We discussed that there is a lot of interest in the Computer Science and Engineering communities concerning formal methods for languages that could support massively parallel operations in scientific computing, a back-to-roots interest for both Mike and myself. Languages for this domain can no longer be informally developed since it is necessary to map languages easily to many multiprocessor architectures. Software systems intended for parallel computation require a formal basis so that modifications can be done with relative ease while ensuring integrity in design. List based languages are profiting from theoretical foundations such as the Bird-Meertens formalism. Their theory has been successfully used to describe list based parallel algorithms across many classes of architectures.

We decided that it would prove fruitful to get together the research community investigating formalisms for array based languages designed for parallel machines with the community actually building and using functional parallel languages. Many of the colleagues we know individually did not know each other's work, yet they were addressing topics with much commonality.

For example, some of our colleagues that have worked with language communities such as FORTRAN, NIAL, and APL, have developed arrays for scientific computation since the early 60's. The language development groups in these areas have spent years investigating design methodology, efficient implementations, and compiler technology for array operations and recently, parallelizing compilers to classes of multiprocessor architectures. Although issues of functional programming and constructive derivations are not the focus of these communities, issues on array compilation to various architectures, performance and scientific applications are.

Other colleagues have been directly involved in the design and extension of list-oriented functional programming languages to include array mechanisms. There has been very little communication between the language design and implementation groups in these different communities. As a result many ideas in the functional programming community have been rediscovered independently.

We decided to hold an invitational workshop in Montreal as a first step to bring these communities together. The list of attendees was drawn up from colleagues who had an interest in array and list algebras, functional languages, parallel algorithms, multiprocessor architectures, *intelligent* compilers, and scientific applications. The papers presented herein are representative of the talks given at the First International Workshop on Arrays, Functional Languages, and Parallel Systems held 12-15 June 1990 in Montréal, Québec.

We are very grateful to everyone who helped us achieve our goals, in particular, CRIM(*Centre de recherche informatique de Montréal*), ITRC(*Information Technology Research Centre*), NSERC, and IBM Corporation for financial support. We would like to thank Kluwer for its assitance in publishing this record of the conference.

Lenore Mullin

ARRAYS, FUNCTIONAL LANGUAGES, AND PARALLEL SYSTEMS

1

ARRAYS AND THE LAMBDA CALCULUS

Klaus Berkling
CASE Center
and
School of Computer and Information Science
Syracuse University
Syracuse, NY 13244-1190
May 1990

Keywords: Array processing, functional programming, lambda calculus, reduction machines.

INTRODUCTION

Why do functional languages have more difficulties with arrays than procedural languages? The problems arising in the designing of functional languages with arrays and in their implementations are manifold. They can be classified according to 1) first principles, 2) semantics, 3) pragmatics, and 4) performance. This paper attempts to give an outline of the issues in this area, and their relation to the lambda calculus. The lambda calculus is a formal system and as such seemingly remote from practical applications. However, specific representations and implementations of that system may be utilized to realize arrays such that progress is made towards a compromise of 1) adhering to first principles, 2) clear semantics, 3) obvious pragmatics, and 4) high performance. To be more specific, a form of the lambda calculus which uses a particular representation of variables, namely De Bruijn indices, may be a vehicle to represent arrays and the functions to manipulate them.

PROBLEM

Serious computational problems come almost always in terms of arrays. Nothing seems to be more appropriate to array processing than the von Neumann Computer Architecture. Its linear memory structure, its addressing methods (absolute address + offset + index, base registers, offset registers, index registers), and its instruction set obviously constitute a perfect base to implement arrays. Together with language features originating from FORTRAN, the system indeed fills basic needs in all four categories stated above. Why would or should one try to improve on it? Because only very basic needs are filled.

For the sake of efficiency, the higher level concepts of programming languages had to be compromised. Real problems are dealing with very large matrices and/or very frequently used matrices, for example for pointwise transformations in image processing. There is no time (or space!) for costly procedure or function entries (prologues) and exits (epilogues), for scoping of variables and blockstructures, but there is a tendency for rather flat programs and code. This becomes manifest in terms of complicated nests of DO-loop constructs and difficult to follow GOTO's. A premium is on the removal of code from more frequently executed innermost DO-loops to less frequently executed outer DO-loops or initialization pieces by program transformations.

The combination of flat code, flat name space, static memory layout, and the assignment statement as basic programming tool causes very unpleasant properties. Since index variables are usually considered first class citizens, occurrences of, for example, $A[I, K]$ may refer to different matrix elements depending on the code executed between these occurrences. Assignments to I and K may destroy the referential transparency. The scope structure is intricately mapped onto sequencing. As a consequence, variables can be easily confused, alterations become a costly, error prone, and time consuming enterprise.

It is particularly difficult to transform such flat programs into "parallel" programs, which make inherent concurrency explicit. Obviously, scoping cannot be expelled without penalty. If it is not part of the language, the compiler must symbolically execute the code to reconstruct dependencies.

Many of the problems to produce efficient and accurate code without the base of higher level concepts arise from the utilization of memory locations. The conventional viewpoint of a memory location is best described as a "box-variable," as opposed to a "place-holder-variable," which is the viewpoint taken by functional languages. This difference makes it difficult for functional languages to adopt easily array features from conventional languages. Four operations are associated to box variables: allocate (a name to refer to the box is created), deallocate, fill the box, read the contents of the box. In contrast to this, place holder variables are either attached to an expression by function application, or an occurrence of the place holder variable is replaced by the attached expression. After this replacement, neither the place nor the expression is any longer accessible through the variable name. Replacements of several variable occurrences by atomic expressions are not difficult to implement. However, a compound expression has to be shared among several occurrences of the place holder variables, each of which is replaced by a pointer rather than by a copy of the expression. The complexity of copying just cannot be afforded.

The computational problems are rarely such that matrices and vectors can be treated as conceptual units only without ever accessing single elements explicitly. The worst case to consider is the change of one element. While a straight forward functional approach would create a copy of the old matrix with one element changed, the conventional solution simply stores a new value into the appropriate location treating it as a box variable. Conceptually the old place holder variable has been replaced by a new one, although there is still the same identifier and the same pointer to the same memory area. Because of sharing as explained above, however, the change may be more globally effective than planned. The scope of variables has been mapped onto the time scale.

One might take the position to create always new matrices in new memory areas because it is compatible with place holder variables, conceptually clean, and there is enough memory. But the challenge remains to overwrite matrices which are not accessed anymore. It just seems more rewarding to solve problems requiring larger matrices when larger memories become available.

The problems of embedding consistent and elegant array processing into a functional language do not preclude pragmatic solutions. LISP and LISP-like programming languages already incorporate assignment statements and the program feature. One needs only to extend these concepts by functions and "pseudo" functions to make an array, to set a selected element of an array, and to reference a selected element. All arguments may be expressions in accordance with functional language concepts. This is a rather conventional low-level add-on.

The language which really constitutes an advance is APL. Arrays are treated as conceptual entities, functions are modified by operators and extended over the array elements. Thus the power of higher order functions is obtained and the access to array elements is delegated to the system, if possible.

There is another system originating from physics, which excels in omitting unnecessary detail, like the indication of dimension, summation signs, and bindings. We have the "Einstein" convention that equal indices indicate summation. The "inner" product of two vectors a_k and b_i, where i and k assume all index values $O \ldots n-1$ or $1 \ldots n$, is then simply denoted by $a_j b_j$. There is no free index, thus the result is a scalar. In the same spirit, $a_{ik} b_{kj}$ denotes the matrix product c_{ij}, summation over k produces the inner products of rows i and columns j. The identity matrix is denoted by δ_{ik}, the Kronecker symbol. ($\delta_{ik} = 1$ if $i = k, = O$ otherwise). There are so-called ϵ-tensors, which produce "outer products" $\epsilon_{ik} a_k = b_i$, such that $a_j b_j = O$. In general we have $\epsilon_{ijk} \ldots = +1$ for an even permutation, and $\epsilon_{ijk} \ldots = -I$ for an odd permutation of indices, and $\epsilon_{ijk} \ldots = 0$ for all other cases.

For $n = 2$ we have $a_j b_j = a_j \epsilon_{jk} a_k = a_1 a_2 - a_2 a_1 = 0$. This means b_j is orthogonal to a_i. For $n = 3$ we have $c_i = \epsilon_{ijk} a_j b_k$, which denotes a vector c_i orthogonal to a_j and b_k because the index i is free. Its first component is:

$$c_1 = a_2 b_3 - a_3 b_2$$

Finally, the determinant of a matrix a_{ik} is denoted by :

$$\epsilon_{ijk} a_{1i} a_{2j} a_{3k}$$

Since there is no free index, a scalar is denoted. While the necessary index sets are well defined, very little is given in details how to produce them. Common to APL and the above scheme is the existence of an algebra. The computation of an atomic value from an arithmetic statement can be substantially improved in terms of the number of needed steps and intermediate storage requirements by prior algebraic transformations.

The same approach using matrix algebra will yield savings in terms of intermediate storage, too. But the computation is still expressed in terms of matrices as conceptual units. Whole matrices would have to be stored intermediately, and the challenge to reuse this space by overwriting is also there.

However, by rearranging the sequence of computation in terms of of single elements, it is possible to allocate space only for the input array and the output array. Then, if the elements of the output array are denoted by an expression in terms of elements of the input array, intermediate storage is needed only for a number of single elements. Moreover, the expression denoting an output element is invariant except for index values. This concept has numerous desirable properties. The input array is only used in read-only mode, the output array is only used in write-only mode. Only the set of intermediate single element cells is used in both modes. This arrangement is very suitable to concurrent processing: Suppose a copy of the input array as well as the skeleton of the expression exists in a multitude of processors. Then each of the processors can concurrently compute a subset of elements of the output array free of interference. What is different from process(or) to process(or) is the set of index values.

The value of L. Mullin's mathematics of arrays [5] is based on the ability to transform the computation of array expressions by formal algebraic methods. The objective of these transformations is the optimal use of resources. The effect of these transformations is that elements of the result array are denoted in terms of elements of the input array. Intermediate structures are not explicitly generated.

Is there any overlap of mathematics of arrays and the lambda calculus? At first sight, the answer might be: none. But, there is certainly one application, namely, the correct implementation of scope structure for array names (and index variables?).

In the following sections we will consider other possibilities which are worth exploring. We assume familiarity with the lambda calculus. The experimental system used in the discussion is based on [3].

FIRST PRINCIPLES

The denotation of an array element like $A[IK]$ has similarity with the denotation of a function value, but only if it appears on the right side of an assignment statement. If it appears on the left side, however, it denotes a location. The denotation of a function value is compatible with the notion of a function represented by a table of ordered tuples. In terms of first principles, the occurrence of such a denotation on the left side of an assignment statement implies a resetting of a table entry, which is a function changing operation, that is, the assignment statement implies a higher order function in this context! This does not seem appropriate. Let us consider it as a datastructure. So, the question is now: What is a data structure?

Datastructures are generally input and output of programs. One may consider datastructures as code which does not require execution anymore, because there is nothing left to be done. This wording has been deliberately chosen to relate it to reduction and the lambda calculus. Reduction is a first principle and means the substitution of symbols by symbols which are equivalent with respect to a set of rules.

The result of reducing a lambda calculus expression consists of nested head normal forms. A head normal form (HNF) is an expression starting with a number of bindings, followed by a number of application nodes, and terminating with a variable. An example of a HNF is shown in tree form:

$$
\begin{array}{ll}
\lambda a \lambda b \lambda c. - & @ - \cdots \\
 & @ - \cdots \\
 & @ - \cdots \\
 & b
\end{array}
$$

Redices, which are instances of possible rule applications, are not visible. If there are any, they would be in the argument expressions (...) of the application nodes. Thus, further processing does not alter the HNF once it is constructed. This conclusion applies recursively to all lower level arguments and HNFs until a HNF degenerates to a constant or variable.

We have now recognized the result of a lambda calculus computation, or better reduction, to be a datastructure represented as nested HNFs. Can such a datastructure be the argument of a lambda expression? This does make sense only if all substructures of the datastructure can be selected once it is substituted into this lambda expression. A selector in terms of the lambda calculus is a degenerated HNF without application nodes, for example:

$$\lambda a\ \lambda b\ \lambda c\ \lambda d.\ b$$

The name "selector" is justified, because the expression above selects from 4 arguments the third one, or when counting starts at 0, the second one. Note that we count from left to right, or top down, respectively.

$$\begin{array}{l} @ - A_0 \\ @ - A_1 \\ @ - A_2 \\ @ - A_3 \\ \lambda a \lambda b \lambda c \lambda d.\ b \end{array}$$

The identifiers denoting variables do not carry any information. De Bruijn indices count the lambdas between variable occurrence and its binding. Thus, the information of the selector is completely given by

$$\lambda\lambda\lambda\lambda.2$$

or even more concisely by

$$\lambda 4.2$$

which is in terms of array accessing a pair of range and index values. In order to make the selector actually "select," it has to be substituted in place of the head variable of a datastructure. The sequence of reductions is shown here:

$$\begin{array}{lll} & @ & -\lambda 4.2 \\ \gg & | & \\ & \lambda 1. & -@ - A_0 \\ & & \;\; @ - A_1 \\ & & \;\; @ - A_2 \\ & & \;\; @ - A_3 \\ & & \;\; 0 \end{array}$$

The beta-redex ($\gg$) places the selector first into the head position. Then a sequence of beta-reductions accomplishes the selection of the argument A_2:

$$\begin{array}{lllll} @ - A_0 & @ - A_0 & @ - A_0 & @ - A_0 & A_2 \\ @ - A_1 & @ - A_1 & @ - A_1 & | & \\ @ - A_2 & @ - A_2 & | & \lambda 1.A_2 & \\ @ - A_3 & | & \lambda 2.A_2 & & \\ | & \lambda 3.2 & & & \\ \lambda 4.2 & & & & \end{array}$$

This method of applying a datastructure to a selector was discovered very early by W. Burge [4]. He coined the term "functional" datastructure. But, one can emulate the application of the selector to the datastructure by using the combinator R and write:

$$R\ \lambda 4.2 < \text{datastructure} >$$

If a datastructure consists of nested HNFs, the need for a compound selector arises. It is, of course, a HNF with simple selectors as arguments, for example:

$$\begin{array}{ll} \lambda 1.- & @ - \lambda 5.4 \\ & @ - \lambda 6.1 \\ & @ - \lambda 4.2 \\ & 0 \end{array}$$

The application of this compound selector to a nested datastructure causes the latter first to appear in its head position. Then a selection takes place in the toplevel HNF using $\lambda 4.2$. The next lower level HNF now forms a beta-redex with $\lambda 6.1$.

$$\begin{array}{ll} & @ - A\lambda 5.4 \\ & @ - A\lambda 6.1 \\ \gg & | \\ & \lambda 1. - @ - \cdots \\ & \quad \cdots \end{array}$$

This sequence of events repeats itself recursively until the primitive selectors are used up.

The dual nature of what is left subtree (operator) and what is right subtree (operand) of an application node becomes even more evident, if we look now at the construction of compound selectors. The combinator R applied to a simple selector yields an operator on datastructures:

$$\begin{array}{lll} (R\lambda m.n) \Longrightarrow \lambda 1.- & @ - \lambda m.n \\ & 0 \end{array}$$

The operation of functional composition makes a compound selector from a set of simple ones. The combinator B does it for two,

$$Bfg \Longrightarrow f \circ g$$

The generalization to $n-1$ functions is the set of combinators

$$\begin{array}{lll} B_n = \lambda n.- & @ - \cdots & @ - 0 \\ & n-1 & 1 \end{array}$$

such that

$$B_n f_{n-1} \ldots f_1 \, \mathrm{arg} = f_{n-1}(\ldots(f_1 \, \mathrm{arg}))$$

For more on sets of parameterized combinators see ABDALI [0]. The compound selector given as an example above can be constructed from the three simple ones using B_4:

$$B_4(\lambda 1.0 \; \lambda 5.4) \; (\lambda 1.0 \; \lambda 6.1) \; (\lambda 1.0 \; \lambda 4.2)$$

This expression reduces to:

$$\begin{array}{ll} \lambda 1.- & @ - \lambda 5.4 \\ & @ - \lambda 6.1 \\ & @ - \lambda 4.2 \\ & 0 \end{array}$$

which is what we expected. Dual to the "functional" composition combinators B_n, which arrange a sequence of arguments in successive operator positions, there are also "data" composition combinators T_n, which make HNFs, that is, arguments are arranged in successive operand positions. The general pattern is:

$$\begin{array}{ll} T_n = \lambda n.- & @ - 1 \\ & @ - 2 \\ & \ldots \\ & @ - n - 1 \\ & 0 \end{array}$$

The dual nature of datastructures and function makes

$$B < \mathrm{datastructure1} >< \mathrm{datastructure2} >$$

meaningful, too. However, there is a peculiar twist in the representation of expressions. The tree representation is related to the linear representation by preorder traversal. On the other hand, arguments are numbered top down in trees, because this makes it compatible with the sequence De Bruijn indices referring to them. Thus, elements of a datastructure are numbered from left to right in the linear representation.

Suppose a $n \times n$ matrix is given as a column of rows, which is a datastructure of n elements, where each element is a datastructure of n elements representing a row. Since this is not a very convenient

notion of a combinator as an abbreviation for a closed lambda expression to hide unnecessary detail. Combinators are parameterized elements of a set formed according to a common pattern [0]. We introduce the notion of parenthetical combinators, which serve to hide the particular parameter. The value of the parameter is inferred from the input either at run or compile time.

For example, the B, T, and BR combinators are used with the following syntax:

$$B_n = (BN f_{n-1} \ldots f_2\ f_1\ NB)$$

This expression is interpreted as a lambda expression with the appropriate indices filled in which are derived from the number of expressions occurring between "$(BN$" and "$NB)$."

In the next example we use the combinator pair "AT"and "TA"which denote the "apply-to-all" construct [1]. In contrast to J. Backus' version, the function to be applied to all expressions is in our case argument to the construct.

The following expression takes the last two elements (that is, drops the first three elements) from a five element structure: Every element is individually selected and the selectors placed at appropriate positions between "$(AT$"and "$TA)$." The structure enclosed in "$(T$"and "$T)$"corresponding to T_n is argument to the "apply-to-all" construct; the whole expression is abstracted from the elements.

$$\lambda 5.\ (AT(\lambda 5.4)(\lambda 5.3)TA)(T\ 4\ 3\ 2\ 1\ 0\ T) \Longrightarrow \lambda 6.0\ 5\ 4$$

This expression seems involved, but it reduces to ($\lambda 6.0\ 5\ 4$) which is much simpler and less costly to apply. The next expression takes the first three elements:

$$\lambda 5.(AT(\lambda 5.2)(\lambda 5.1)(\lambda 5.0)TA)(T\ 4\ 3\ 2\ 1\ 0\ T) \Longrightarrow \lambda 6.0\ 3\ 2\ 1$$

These expressions are the base for the implementations of drop-and-take functions which will have an additional parameter to indicate the number of elements dropped or taken. To rotate a five-element structure by two we concatenate both selections from above in reverse order with the combinator B and we obtain:

$$\begin{array}{llll} \lambda 5. & (\lambda 1.B & ((AT(\lambda 5.4) \;\; (\lambda 5.3) & TA)0) \\ & & ((AT(\lambda 5.2) \;\; (\lambda 5.1)(\lambda 5.0) & TA)0)) \\ & (T\ 4\ 3\ 2\ 1\ 0\ T) & & \end{array}$$

This expression reduces to $\lambda 6.0\ 3\ 2\ 1\ 5\ 4$. The result is not surprising, but there are more complicated compositions of APL type functions, which after reduction yield a lambda expressions which do not exhibit their operation so clearly. Also, there may be other ways of expressing the drop function. In general, two compound expressions are equivalent, if they reduce to equal normal forms. We can say equal, because the De Bruijn indices yield a unique representation of lambda expressions. An example shows the point. Through experience and intuition one might find the following solution to drop one element from a datastructure:

$$B(\lambda 1.0\ a\ b\ c)K$$

An intermediate step in the reduction sequence is:

$$\lambda 1.(\lambda 1.0\ a\ b\ c)(K\ 0)$$

The next beta-reduction step replaces the innermost variable 0 in the expression by $(K\ 0)$.

$$\lambda 1.K\ 0\ a\ b\ c$$

But $K\ 0\ a$ reduces to 0 and we finally obtain

$$\lambda 1.0\ b\ c$$

The result is again a datastructure and repetition of the $(B \ldots K)$ construct drops a corresponding number of elements. To prove equivalence we reduce

$$\lambda 5.(\lambda 1.(B(B\ 0\ K)K)(T\ 4\ 3\ 2\ 1\ 0\ T)$$

and obtain $\lambda 6.0\ 3\ 2\ 1$. This is the same result as obtained above using the element by element selection for dropping two elements from the structure.

We could now proceed to augment the system by arithmetic. However, adding arithmetic does not give any more insight in the possibilities of the lambda calculus to decompose and compose program- and datastructures.

SEMANTICS

The more difficult aspects of the semantics of the lambda calculus have not been used. Everything is finite and termination problems are not expected.

The use of reduction semantics rather than an evaluation scheme is an important point. The latter would indeed cause a semantics problem. The main reduction rule is beta-reduction. It is not necessary to consider or to refer to an alpha-rule, because there are no identifiers which could confuse variables. However, during a beta-reduction some De Bruijn indices might change in order to maintain the binding structure. Since a lambda expression is uniquely represented if De Bruijn indices are used, there is only one correct answer. Beta-reduction could be done by hand, but the mechanical assistance of an operational lambda calculus system facilitates it. As a matter of fact, all examples shown above have been verified using such a system [3].

To qualify for the task, a system has to be a full and complete, strongly normalizing implementation of the lambda calculus. A functional language implementation will generally not suffice. The system has to handle relative free variables correctly. The necessity for it becomes evident from the following argument.

A nest of DO-loops would appear in a functional language or lambda calculus representation as a nest of recursive functions. The transformations which move code from high frequency areas to low frequency areas leave free variables, which have to be used and implemented as such. The innermost, high frequency areas cannot be artificially closed. This would lead to more beta-reductions and the expected gain in efficiency is lost.

Reduction semantics has to be implemented in such a way that partial application and higher order functions are naturally available in the system. The concept of a function either insisting on the availability of all its arguments, or else generating error messages, is not very useful in this context. Partial application and higher order functions are the norm, not the exception, since input and output are represented as functional datastructures. The system has to be strongly normalizing, because functions (datastructures) have to be brought in normal form as output. When parameters are set to customize certain functions, some simplifying reductions within the function should be possible.

Equivalence of different procedures to achieve the same effect on the same input can be established by reducing both to the equal normal forms. The normal form is at the same time the most efficient, minimal representation of the procedure. Thus, the starting point can be as declarative as necessary to convince the user of its correctness. Also, the process of obtaining the normal form corresponds to a conventional compilation process.

PRAGMATICS

When comparing a bulk of assembly code with a huge lambda expression allegedly accomplishing the same task the question arises: What has been gained here? The answer is easy: The lambda expression is based on a very good mathematical theory. But, this answer barely satisfies. The deeply nested lambda expression, with no functions to discern and bindings as well as unintelligible De Bruijn indices distributed all over the expression, reveals its meaning in no way faster or easier than a bulk of assembly code. And above all, in either case the problem is, how to obtain it in the first place. A higher level programming language is a way for assembly code, without really solving the problem, however. But what is the higher level language with respect to the lambda calculus, which is in itself a higher level language? Syntactic sugaring may raise the level of appearance, but does not necessarily raise the conceptual level.

Some researchers consider combinators to be an alternate system to implement functional systems. In terms of the lambda calculus they correspond to very simple, closed lambda expressions, so simple that there is no need to implement the lambda calculus at all. (There is, of course, the need to compile functional expressions into combinator expressions.) Combinators as abbreviations of simple lambda expressions, however, fill a need to conceptualize general patterns of usage. They hide De Bruijn indices and other detail, one does not want to know about. The parenthetical combinators hide explicit parameters, which are inferred. They are more than an abbreviation, they represent a process (not necessarily part of the lambda calculus!) to create a combinator of a certain class or type.

There is an obvious need to name lambda expressions once they are created and their internal details are not of interest anymore. But don't we admit assignment statements again through the backdoor? This would certainly violate first principles. First of all, we do not fill a box variable, we associate a name to an expression so they become equivalent. (By the way, names are expanded only in head positions, there is no point to do it everywhere.) Secondly, first principles may be bent to accommodate pragmatic needs. In this case, the pragmatic need consists of defining and redefining names. An easy way to accomplish this is to make environment entries from definitions. These associations remain valid and accessible as long as the environment is not cut back. Redefinitions are shadowed, but not overwritten. This method can be characterized as uncompleted (may be over the life of the system) beta-reductions.

The interactive capabilities of modern computers offer another pragmatic advantage. The conventional, historic method first creates a large program structure, the source code, then compiles it into object code, and then "runs" it. This method is due to hardware limitations which have been overcome and is not adequate anymore. The best way to construct large, nested structures is interactive and piecemeal.

The system can guide the user, indicate at each position or state what are permitted moves, what is correct input, what are allowed structure changes. Trivial errors are prohibited at the spot. The problem of parsing can be made to disappear if only atomic tokens are permitted as input while the expression structure is system driven.

There should be means to traverse the structure once it is created to make changes where necessary. To adhere to first principles in this pragmatic context means to maintain full "recursiveness." With other words, what is available and possible at the top of the expression should be possible at every subexpression. Desirable meta-operations on expressions are:

1. Perform a predetermined number of reductions on it. (√)
2. Display it according to a selected format. (√)
3. Transform it into a combinator expression (abstraction). (√)
4. Replace it by another expression. (√)
5. Name it. (√)
6. Save it on secondary storage. ( )
7. Expand it. (√)

All these amenities do not belong to the lambda calculus, but they make it a working system. The checkmarks indicate availability in our experimental system.

PERFORMANCE

If the lambda calculus is to be used for real computing the question must be asked, does it provide real performance? The key to the possibility to reach satisfactory performance is the particular representation which can be chosen if one uses De Bruijn indices. The sequence of application nodes in the representation of vectors has to be implemented in consecutive memory locations. This is as good as any conventional method. If the sequence of application nodes becomes arguments of a function, they are now in consecutive environment locations, too. The De Bruijn index is the same as the array index, and the same as the offset when addressing the memory with the current environment as base address. Thus, the basics of hardware use are essential the same as in the conventional method and no penalty in performance has to be paid.

The issue is not as clear with respect the nests of recursive functions into which nested DO-loops get transformed. Although recursion benefits from the implementation choices, too, their automatic transformation into loops is difficult.

Some special non-lambda calculus measures are needed to permit environment changes. The environment is a shared, read-only tree structure containing arrays. Adhering to first principles permits overwriting environment entries by equivalent values only. To create a new array with only one element changed, access to the array in the environment has to be filtered for a selected index by a new environment. All other accesses are referred to the old array. This method allows the existence of different arrays, which share common elements as much as possible.

CONCLUSION

This paper investigates the suitability of the lambda calculus as a representation for arrays and the functions to manipulate them. The results show that only a full and complete, strongly normalizing implementation of the lambda calculus will suffice. Reduction semantics, De Bruijn indices, performance oriented representation and

way of storing a matrix for accessing and a row major order vector representation is preferable, we would like to transform the structure.

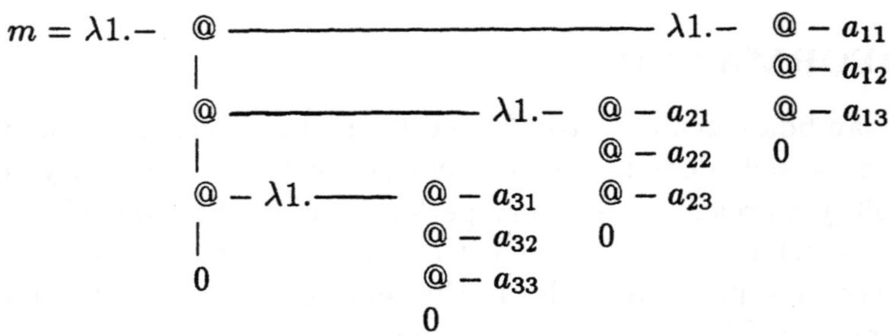

Applying this matrix representation to B_4 would place row 3 on top of the tree. To reverse the order we introduce combinators BR_n which reverse the order of their arguments:

$$BR_n = \lambda_n.- \quad \overset{}{\underset{1}{@}}- \quad \underset{2}{@}- \quad \underset{3}{@} - \cdots - \quad \underset{n-1}{@} - 0$$

Now $(m\ BR_n)$ reduces to (in linear representation, application nodes @ suppressed) which has the correct sequence:

$$\lambda 1.0\ a_{33}\ a_{32}\ a_{31}\ a_{23}\ a_{22}\ a_{21}\ a_{13}\ a_{12}\ a_{11}$$

The B_n and BR_n act as concatenators. The sequence of arguments is essential. Mathematicians use $f \circ g$ to indicate that g has to be applied first, and $f \bullet g$ to indicate that f has to be applied first.

The methods of using special lambda expression to represent and manipulate arrays are general and apply also to lists. If datastructures are restricted to two elements we get the "cons" construct, the selectors $\lambda 2.1$ and $\lambda 2.0$ correspond to "car" ("head") and "cdr" ("tail"). Compound selectors correspond to list selectors of the type "caaddar."

As a last point in this section we will demonstrate the use of the lambda calculus as a vehicle to implement the APL type functions of dropping and taking elements from arrays. Although the lambda calculus serves in this context as a very high level machine language, functions become more complicated. One might get the impression that this is due to the use of De Bruijn indices. But not using them would complicate it even more because of the many variable names and the constant worry about confusing them. We already used the implementation techniques based on proven hardware concepts, and special interactive tools have to be combined. Much further work is necessary to realize the potential power of the lambda calculus as a machine language for actual use. Particular attention has to be given to the scaling-up properties of the methods described.

BIBLIOGRAPHY

[1] Abdali S.K., "An Abstraction Algorithm for Combinatory Logic." *The Journal of Symbolic Logic*, Vol. 41, Number 1, March 1976, pp. 222-224.

[2] Backus, J. "Can Programming be Liberated from the von Neumann Style? A Functional Style and Its Algebra of Programs." CACM, V21, N8, pp613-641, (1978).

[3] Berkling, K.J., "Headorder Reduction: A Graph Reduction Scheme for the Operational Lambda Calculus," *Proceedings of the Los Alamos Graph Reduction Workshop*, Springer Lecture Notes in Computer Science, Vol 279, (1986).

[4] Burge, W.H. "Recursive Programming Techniques." Addison-Wesley, Reading Massachusetts, (1975).

[5] Mullin, L.M.R. "A Mathematics of Arrays." Ph.D. Dissertation, School of CIS, Syracuse University, (1988).

2

COMPILING APL

Robert Bernecky
Snake Island Research, Inc.
18 Fifth Street, Ward's Island
Toronto, Canada M5J 2B9
Phone: (416) 368-6944 FAX: (416) 360-4694
email: bernecky@itrchq.itrc.on.ca

Abstract

A study into the creation of efficient, portable applications for a variety of supercomputer architectures resulted in a prototype APL compiler, called *ACORN*, targeted at the Cray X-MP [1] and the Thinking Machines Connection Machine CM2 [2]. *ACORN* used a number of advanced features of APL, including recursive data structures (boxed arrays) and the rank adverb, which considerably simplified the effort required to produce the compiler. The use of APL allowed the compiler to be complete to the point of producing operational code within a week, yet allowed considerable flexibility in altering it to meet changing needs, as performance concerns came into play. Tokenization was performed in parallel, which may shed light on improving the performance of production compilers on parallel architectures.

[1]X-MP is a trademark of Cray Research, Inc.

[2]Connection Machine is a trademark of Thinking Machines Corporation.

INTRODUCTION

In 1987, discussions between the author and two scientists [3] at the Dallas Research Laboratory of Mobil Research and Development Corporation resulted in a joint project to study *the use of APL as a delivery vehicle for parallel computation.* The project was intended as no more than a feasibility study, to determine if APL could, in fact, compete with FORTRAN in the supercomputer arena.

The original project envisioned hand-compilation of two relatively simple seismic applications – convolution and Normal Move Out – written in APL, and a comparison of their performance to the production versions of the same applications, written in Cray FORTRAN. Although the applications were less than a hundred lines of APL, the tediousness of hand-compilation led to a decision to write a primitive APL to C compiler, in APL. This decision turned out to be crucial – a working compiler was operational within a week. To be fair, the majority of coding actually resided in the run-time library (the compiler does no optimization nor data flow analysis whatsoever), but the time does show that compiling APL need not be a task of monumental complexity. The remainder of this paper deals with some of the decisions made as part of the compiler design, discoveries made about performance and language design, and discusses some of the internals of the compiler.

WHICH APL SHOULD BE COMPILED?

A sensible choice of an APL dialect to compile would be ISO Standard APL [IS84]. Although this is a standard, its use was beyond the scope of our resource-limited project, and the language, like any other

[3] Stephen Jaffe and George Moeckel.

language which has evolved over time, contains a number of warts in its design. We initially decided to compile a subset of ISO Standard APL, with a number of simplifying restrictions.

System Variables

⎕*ct*, the comparison tolerance used in relational verbs to determine equality, was considered to be always zero. This reduced the effort required to code the run-time library. Like many other restrictions to be discussed, it could be easily lifted in a production compiler. Other system variables were treated similarly, being given a default value which was not alterable or accessible by the application.

Interpreted Verbs

In order to avoid the need to include an entire APL interpreter as part of the compiled code, facilities which require knowledge of the APL symbol table, such as ⍎ and ⎕*fx*, were forbidden.

Data Type Restrictions

Because we were primarily interested in the performance of numerically intensive applications, we took the liberty of making all arrays floating point. Although we expected a performance penalty in areas such as indexing and Boolean algebra, we felt that the ability to avoid all data flow analysis was a reasonable compromise for a feasibility study. If we were unable to compete in large numeric computations, we'd not have lost time writing code which would prove nugatory.

Scoping Rules

APL, like some dialects of LISP, traditionally has used dynamic scoping, in which a called verb can access or alter any variables which belong to its caller, and which are not localized within the called verb. This facility is a mixed blessing, and is more often cursed than praised by application writers who have forgotten to localize a variable, or to supply a label for a branch target. In addition, well-written APL rarely needs such crutches, particularly when recursive data structures are available for use. With this in mind, we chose to adopt static scoping rules, in which all arrays are either strictly local (to the verb which localizes them) or global to the entire execution environment. This decision had two implications.

Firstly, it meant that any APL verb could be compiled separately, with no knowledge of other verbs, calling tree, and so forth. This meant that the compiler does not have to perform global data flow analysis, and that the "compilation set" required was a single APL verb.

Secondly, it meant that the run-time environment need not contain a symbol table to allow it to be aware of the names of APL objects, altering their meaning, depending on the calling tree being invoked. An alternate approach, in which multiple copies of generated code were produced, based on all possible calling trees, was also not required.

The decisions to stick with a single data type, and to adopt static scoping were the keys which made it possible to have the compiler emitting code within a week.

DECLARATIONS AND VERB VALENCE

An early decision was the attempt to avoid declarations or other modifications to APL programs. This, combined with independent compilation of each verb, implied certain things about the interpretation of names. For example, if a name was not localized within a verb, then it could be either another verb or a global variable. Our rather arbitrary decision was to treat such names in the following manner: Niladic verbs were forbidden, except for the "main" verb required by the C language. When an expression such as `a b c` was encountered, `c` was assumed to be a variable, because of the ban on niladic verbs. `b` was therefore either a monadic or dyadic verb. If its valence could not be determined by other information (such as `a` being a local variable), it was assumed to be dyadic. If `a` and `b` were in fact both monadic verbs, this fact would not be discovered by the compiler. Presumably, running "lint" on the compiled set of verbs would pick up this error. The user would then have to establish a workaround, through use of an identity such as `a⊢b c`, parentheses, as in `a (b c)`, or introduction of a temp, as in `t1←b c ⋄ a t1`. The desirability of, and treatment of, declarations remains an open issue for APL compilation, but it is probably more of a theological issue than a practical one.

COMPILER STRUCTURE AND INTERNALS

The compiler is a model of simplicity. In fact, it is hard to believe just how simple and primitive the compiler is. It is a total of 726 lines of straightforward APL, comprising 111 verbs, in which no attempt was made to optimize performance. About half of the verbs are action verbs invoked by a finite state machine, which will be discussed in more detail later. The code contains 19 branches, of which all but two could be replaced by case constructs, such as those discussed in another paper [Be84]. The remaining two branches are used to loop over tokens and lines of source code. The latter could be replaced by a suitable invocation of the rank adverb, leaving only the finite state machine token loop.

The tokenizer examines the entire source verb in parallel, generating a token table of the same shape as the source verb. The resulting token table and source verb are then used jointly by the remainder of the compiler.

Each tokenized line is compiled independently, with a finite state machine (FSM) invoking action verbs as appropriate. The verb header is treated separately, because of its anomalous syntax. Independent compilation was done for reasons of simplicity and *workspace full* avoidance on the microcomputer. I contemplated a fully parallel compiler, but the storage limitations of the PC precluded any serious work in this area. The main problem was in the area of excessively large stacks when compiling verbs with many levels of parentheses, admittedly a rare case in APL. Irregularities in traditional APL syntax were another annoyance. The FSM (a standard APL reduction parser) is based on the current state of syntax analysis, and the class of the next token(s) to the left.

The compiler makes extensive use of boxed arrays (recursive data structures) and the rank adverb. Boxes are used to represent the symbol table as a matrix of symbol name, class, and value. The expression stack is also represented as a table, with each row containing the syntax analyzer state, and the stacked token or expression at that point. The generated code is kept as a boxed array, sometimes to several levels of nesting, for convenience. A single application of the format verb (thorn) at end of compilation produces the final character matrix result from the previously generated boxed code.

Code generation is facilitated by the use of the SHARP APL link verb, in conjunction with the rank adverb, to permit operations such as gluing fixed prefixes onto a set of declarations. The use of a verb to denote link allows application of adverbs such as rank to modify the action of the link. A typical use within the compiler is the expression `'static VAR '⊃⍤1 cons⊃⍤1 initers`, to generate declarations and initial values for constants which appear in the verb being compiled.

PORTABILITY

Our initial proposal was to compile to FORTRAN or Cray Assembler Language, CAL. A quick look at the CAL manual convinced me that life was too short to learn to write efficient code in CAL, so I sadly began to reread FORTRAN manuals after a twenty year hiatus. About this time, I discovered that the Portable C Compiler (PCC) had been ported to the Cray X-MP, so the decision was quickly made to use C as our target language. Although PCC did not perform to the same standards as the FORTRAN compiler – it did only the crudest vectorizations – its functional nature made it a much more suitable language for APL compilation. For example, the passing of data structures as arguments and results was trivial in C.

The use of C offered an added advantage in portability – we were able to perform most of our development work on other platforms, including IBM-compatible microcomputers and a SUN 386i workstation. Furthermore, the compiler was able to produce code for a variety of other machines, including mainframes and massively parallel supercomputers.

APPLICATION PORTABILITY

A major advantage of the use of APL as an application language is its portability. Because APL is an abstract language, optimizations which are required at the source level in languages such as FORTRAN can be performed by the compiler or the run-time library. APL's rich set of powerful primitives allows commonly required verbs such as set membership, sorting, searching, and matrix manipulations to be tuned appropriately to the underlying hardware by the compiler writer, rather than requiring the application programmer to change the application.

One example of this perfect portability is searching. In a traditional language such as FORTRAN, a programmer would have to specify the search technique explicitly, perhaps as a linear or binary search. In APL, the decision as to the best technique is left to the implementor of the run-time library – perhaps a binary search on a von Neumann machine, and a brute force unit time algorithm on a Connection Machine. In our work, we made extensive changes to the run-time library, but the APL application source code remained, with one exception to be noted below, unchanged.

I/O PROBLEMS

Input and output presented a major design problem for the project. PCC 4.0 did not support any record-based I/O capabilities, which we took to mean that PCC could not read the seismic files written by FORTRAN, so character-based files were used. We later learned that impedance matching routines could be written to allow FORTRAN I/O facilities to be intermixed with those native to C, but we did not have the luxury of time to make use of them.

Because APL systems tend to have component-based I/O systems, which encourage the reading and writing of arrays, rather than records, we created several utility verbs to provide these services. Dealing with files on the Cray was a problem – STDIN and STDOUT forms of I/O are acceptable, but we had no pleasant method of talking about files other than these. Lack of a character data type didn't help, either. We are going to have to come to grips with the issues of windowed I/O, data base access to the external world, and related problems.

The C language also created problems, in that the only real control over application customization lies in the execution shell's command line, a very low capacity interface. This placed C at odds with APL's traditionally functional approach to "main" programs. This was not a severe problem, yet it remains an annoyance.

COMPILER PERFORMANCE

The performance of the compiler on a mainframe is quite adequate, particularly since no thought was given at all to performance issues. Typical verbs compile in a few tenths of a second on a 3090-class machine.

On SHARP APL/PC, compile times are too slow for any serious applications – about one line per minute on an old PC/XT. This is due largely to the approach that was taken in implementing SHARP APL/PC. The interpreter is IBM/370 machine code, with a 370 emulator interpreting each 370 instruction. As a historical note, this approach was taken because it got a highly reliable and functional APL system (Six years after its introduction, SHARP APL/PC [4] remains the only APL interpreter on a PC which has boxed arrays and complex arith-

[4] SHARP APL/PC is available as shareware through various bulletin boards, and from Iverson Software Inc, 33 Major St., Toronto, Ontario M5S 2K9, Canada.

metic) to the market quickly, and because we thought that IBM would push the XT/370 technology much harder than they actually did. Without an XT/370 card in the PC, the compiler is painfully slow. On a fast AT-class machine, performance is barely acceptable. Compiling the compiler would, of course, be the ideal solution, but that is a task for the future.

Profiling the performance of the compiler showed that the majority of CPU time was spent in the FSM per-token scanner, largely in the ⍎ which invokes the actions for each state change. Function arrays [Be84] could reduce this overhead to a manageable figure.

RUN-TIME PERFORMANCE

Performance of the compiled code varies, as is traditional in the benchmark world, according to the application. On a SUN 386i workstation, the code runs two to five times faster than SAX (SHARP APL Unix) on the same machine. The factor of two applies to numerically intensive problems; the factor of five to highly iterative, scalar-oriented problems such as simple loops and Ackerman's function.

On the Cray X-MP, we initially were running PCC 3.0, which did not vectorize anything. Seismic applications ran roughly 800 times slower than hand-optimized FORTRAN. Although we were expecting problems in competing with FORTRAN, we were not exactly prepared for this sort of speed ratio. Luckily, PCC 4.0 did vectorize some relatively common constructs, and we boosted our performance into the ten to one hundred times slower arena.

Next, we looked to see where we were spending time in execution. We determined that calls to the run-time library were not significant, consuming less than one percent of the CPU time used. Several areas came to light as needing work, among them storage management and the C library functions.

The X-MP main storage appears to be quite slow compared to the speed of register operations. We found that the time spent in copying arguments to verbs was excessive, so we redesigned the storage manager to minimize the amount of data sloshing, by introducing reference counts.

We also wrote our own vectorized floor and square root functions, as the C run-time library only included non-vectorized, scalar versions of these functions. Finally, we ensured that our run-time library inner loops were as well vectorized as possible.

These changes got us to within a factor of two of hand-optimized FORTRAN for a convolution function. Since the APL convolution was written as a reduction of an outer product, and the FORTRAN version as an inner product, this factor of two makes sense. The project was terminated before we were able to time an APL convolution written using inner product.

The seismic Normal Move-out benchmark was still much slower than FORTRAN. We noted that most of the CPU time was spent in a verb which indexed one element out of each row of an array. This verb was written in traditional APL, using transpose and base value to create indices into the ravel of the array. Again, because of the slowness of main storage on the X-MP, the ravel was taking excessive amounts of time. I realized that the whole verb was performing the trivial SAX idiom "from rank 1" (`{⍤1`), and changed the source code accordingly. This simple change sped up the entire application by a factor of 28, and got us to within a factor of six of the speed of FORTRAN. Most of the remaining time was spent within a type coercion which PCC did not vectorize.

The project terminated at this point, as we felt that we had achieved our goal of proving the feasibility of compiled APL as a supercomputing tool. Recent discussions with the C compiler writers at Cray Research lend me confidence that the new Standard C Compiler (SCC), which shares a common optimizer and code generator with Cray FORTRAN, will enable *ACORN* to compete very favorably with FORTRAN.

RANK ADVERB IMPORTANCE

I have mentioned several places where the rank adverb was of value in the compiler and in applications. In addition to its value as a tool of thought, the rank adverb has practical and theoretical benefits [Be88]. In practice, it replaces expressions involving several primitives and parentheses with a single derived verb. For example, matrix-vector multiplication, normally expressed as ((⍴*m*)⍴*v*)×*m*, becomes *v*×⍤1 *m*. This can reduce the execution time of applications by a significant amount. In this example, three verbs are replaced by one, reducing the per-verb overhead, reducing storage management costs, and removing a large amount of data-sloshing which could not be avoided in older dialects of APL.

In a theoretical sense, the rank adverb offers advantages in language design, by offering a firm theoretical basis for making design decisions about the behavior of primitive verbs and adverbs. Its extensibility to the domain of user-defined verbs takes it beyond most other language constructs. The notion of independent application of the verb to each cell of the argument offers a simple and straightforward way to describe program decomposition across multicomputers.

The synergy of the rank adverb in combination with function arrays [Be84] creates a set of capabilities which allow excellent exploitation of MIMD computer architectures – problems can be decomposed to almost any granularity of parallelism desired. This will be discussed in a future paper.

NEW APL DIALECTS

A number of new dialects of APL are beginning to emerge. Two of these are "A" and "J" [Hu90]. These dialects are noteworthy in that they have taken the concept of function rank as absolutely basic to their design philosophy. The language facilities presume function rank as axiomatic, and the primitives are designed from that basis – there is a strong emphasis on application across the first axis, since function rank allows a direct way to move application to trailing axes. The APL alphabet, long decried by APL critics, is optional or gone, replaced by ASCII digraphs. The anomalous parts of APL syntax – brackets and semicolons – are replaced by verbs adhering to a simple, rigid syntax. As a result, J's parse table is a simple ten by four matrix. Control structures beyond the rank adverb have been introduced, and indexed assignment has been replaced by a side-effect free merge adverb. Finally, both dialects have adopted the static scoping rules used in *ACORN*.

It is now clear that new dialects, rather than traditional APL, should be the basis of new work in APL compilers. The new dialects are simpler to compile, and remove many of the rough edges which APL has acquired through its long history. Furthermore, the technological and psychological objections to the APL character set are neatly avoided.

ACORN ON THE CONNECTION MACHINE

Toward the end of the *ACORN* project, Walter Schwarz, then a member of the Research Department of I.P. Sharp Associates, undertook to port the *ACORN* run-time library to the Connection Machine. His report on that activity [Sc90] is contained in these proceedings. Suffice it to say that programming the Connection Machine for maximum performance is a non-trivial task, with extreme sensitivity to geometry and interprocess communication.

OPEN QUESTIONS

A number of questions remain in my mind with regard to compiled APL. What are the tradeoffs of data flow analysis versus hard declarations? Should overflow among data (Boolean to integer, integer to float, float to complex) be supported? If so, how? Is C an adequate target language, or should compilation be tied directly to an optimizer and code generator back end? Is it reasonable to share a back end with scalar-oriented languages, or will the valuable parallelism inherent in APL be lost? How should I/O and interlanguage calls be handled? Can function arrays meet all the needs of control which are otherwise missing from APL?

I am in the process of examining these questions.

References

[Be84] Bernecky, R., "Function Arrays", *APL84 Conference Proceedings*, APL Quote Quad, Vol. 14, No. 4, 1984.

[Be88] Bernecky, R., "An Introduction to Function Rank", *APL88 Conference Proceedings*, APL Quote Quad, Vol. 18, No. 2, 1987.

[Be90a] Bernecky, R., "Ergonomics and Language Design." In press.

[Be90b] Bernecky, R., "Fortran 90 Arrays." In press, SIGPLAN Notices, January 1991.

[Bu88] Budd, T.A, *An APL Compiler*, Springer-Verlag, 1988.

[Ch86] Ching, W., "An APL/370 Compiler and Some Performance Comparisons with APL Interpreter and FORTRAN", *APL86 Conference Proceedings*, APL Quote Quad, Vol. 16, No. 4, 1986.

[Cr84] Crouch, S., *An APL Compiler*, I.P. Sharp Associates internal report, 1984.

[Dr86] Driscoll, G.C., and D.L. Orth, "Compiling APL: The Yorktown APL Translator", *IBM Journal of Research and Development*, Vol. 30, No. 6, 1986.

[Dr87] Driscoll, G.C., and D.L. Orth, "APL Compilation: Where does the time come from?", *APL87 Conference Proceedings*, APL Quote Quad, Vol. 17, No. 4, 1987.

[Hu90] Hui, R., K.E. Iverson, E.E. McDonnell, and A.T. Whitney, "APL\?", to appear in *Proceedings of APL90*, ACM SIGAPL Quote-Quad. In press.

[IS84] International Standards Organization, *ISO8485: Standard for Programming Language APL.*

[Iv80] Iverson, K.E., "APL as a Tool of Thought", 1979 ACM Turing Award Lecture, *Communications of the ACM*, 1981.

[Mc80] McIntyre, D.B.,"APL in a Liberal Arts College", *APL Users Meeting*, I.P. Sharp Associates Limited, Toronto, 1980.

[Sc90] Schwarz, W., "Acorn Run-Time System for the CM-2", *Proceedings of the 1990 Arrays, Functional Languages, and Parallel Systems Workshop*, Kluwer Academic, Boston, 1990.

[Wi86] Wiedmann, C., "Field Results with the APL Compiler", *APL86 Conference Proceedings*, APL Quote Quad, Vol. 16, No. 4, 1986.

3

Acorn Run-Time System for the CM-2

Walter Schwarz
I. P. Sharp GmbH
Myliusstr. 45
6000 Frankfurt/Main, FRG

Abstract

The work described here is an extension of the work done by Robert Bernecky[Be90a,Be90b] and C. H. Brenner on the development of a prototype of an APL compiler which translates APL functions into C functions for the Cray[1] X-MP. The run-time system for the Cray was replaced by a run-time system that allows execution of the code generated by the *ACORN* compiler on a Thinking Machines Corporation CM-2.[2]

This paper describes the development of the run-time system, the results of the execution of sample programs, discusses the deficiencies of the prototype and suggests improvements.

Experimentation with the system shows that APL is a suitable language for the development of applications for

---

[1] Cray and X-MP are trademarks of Cray Research Inc.

[2] CM-2, CM, CM FORTRAN, Paris, *Lisp, and C* are trademarks of Thinking Machines Corporation. Connection Machine is a registered trademark of Thinking Machines Corporation.

massively parallel systems. In order to effectively compete with FORTRAN, significant work remains to be done in the performance area.

1 Introduction

The development of a run-time system for the execution of APL programs compiled by the *ACORN* compiler on the Thinking Machines Corporation CM-2 is a followup project to the development of the prototype of an APL compiler itself. This compiler, called *ACORN* for APL-to-C on Real Numbers, was developed by Robert Bernecky and C. Brenner. The project and the results are described in [Be90a,Be90b].

The compiler has been used to compile selected APL applications and to execute the resulting code on other machines, such as PCs, workstations (Sun-386i), IBM-compatible mainframes and the Cray X-MP.

With the opportunity to get access to a Connection Machine CM-2 through the Connection Machine Network Server (CMNS) Pilot Facility, it was a natural direction of research to evaluate the suitability of the Connection Machine as a target hardware for *ACORN* programs and the suitability of APL as a development language for the machine.

1.1 Objectives and Limitations of the Project

The objectives of the project were:

- to obtain knowledge about the CM-2 architecture, programming environment, performance, algorithmic sensitivity, and other relevant aspects,

- to obtain some experience in the development of software for this machine,
- to develop a prototype of a run-time system for execution of *ACORN* programs on the CM-2, and
- to get preliminary information about the performance of the system.

The prototype is not intended to implement a complete and general support environment for APL programs, but to provide a suitable subset of functionality that allows the execution of the examples that have been executed on other systems.

The project was subject to the same restrictions that applied for the *ACORN* project. The scope was to perform a feasibility study with extremely limited funding and time. Therefore

- only a limited subset of primitive APL functions are implemented,
- the implemented functions are restricted with respect to type, rank and shape of objects (with respect to type, only objects of type floating point are supported) and
- handling of exceptions and error conditions is usually deficient or even non-existent.

The project was intended to be a learning exercise in the first place with the goal to gain some understanding of the Connection Machine technology and to get experience with the development of applications for massively parallel machines.

An interesting aspect of the project lies in the possibility to match the Connection Machine hardware technology with the APL software technology. Our hypothesis is that the array oriented language APL is a suitable programming language for the Connection Machine and other machines with a similar architecture.

This hypothesis is suggested by the correspondence between basic concepts in the APL language and the Connection Machine system, in particular the correspondence between APL arrays and CM geometries described in section 2.3, and the correspondence between primitive and derived functions available in APL and on the CM-2.

1.2 Development Environment

The work was carried out on a machine located at Thinking Machines Corporation in Cambridge, Massachusetts, accessed through Internet-based networks. The machine is made available as part of the Connection Machine Network Server (CMNS) Pilot facility, a project sponsored by DARPA under contract DACA76-88-C-0012. It is intended for research and development of massively parallel applications. For this project access to the machine was provided by a 2400 baud dial-up connection.

The CMNS-machine is a Connection Machine Model 2 (CM-2). It is configured with 32K processors and 1K floating point coprocessors, i.e. there is one floating point accelerator for each 32 CM processors. The FP coprocessors have a word length of 32 bits. Each processor has 8K bytes of memory for a total of 256M of memory. It is configured with a DataVault which was not used in this project.

The CMNS machine is connected to two front-end computers, a Sun Microsystems Sun-4 [3] and a VAX [4], both running the UNIX operat-

[3] Sun and Sun-4 are trademarks of Digital Equipment Corporation.

[4] VAX is a trademark of Digital Equipment Corporation.

ing system.[5] The Sun system was primarily used for the development of the *ACORN* run-time system. The FORTRAN coded benchmarks were executed on the VAX.

The language used for implementation of the run-time system is C/Paris. Paris - an acronym for Parallel Instruction Set - is a low level instruction set for programming of the Connection Machine [Tm89b]. C/Paris is a C-based environment which provides a call interface to the instructions of the Paris instruction set.

2 The Connection Machine System

This section gives a brief description of the organization of the Connection Machine, its programming interface, and describes similarities between the Connection Machine hardware and APL. The description of the machine organization is restricted to the aspects that are relevant in this context. Reference [Tm89a] provides a complete overview and reference [Tm89b] specifies the Paris instruction set in full detail. A comprehensive description of the system is contained in [Ca86].

2.1 The Connection Machine Hardware

The Connection Machine is a *massively parallel system*. Depending on the configuration it can have between 4K and 64K processors. Each processor has an arithmetic-logic unit (ALU), 64K bits or 256K bits of bit-addressable memory, several 1-bit flag registers and various interfaces for interprocessor communication and general I/O. The floating point coprocessors are optional components, if present there is one coprocessor per 32 CM processors. Their word size can be either 32 or

[5] UNIX is a trademark of AT&T Bell Laboratories.

64 bits.

The system is organized as a *single-instruction stream, multiple-data stream* (SIMD) system. Instruction execution is controlled by the sequencer and all processors execute the same instruction with the restriction that execution for each processor is conditional on the value of the context-flag. The context-flag is one of the 1-bit hardware flag registers. If value of the context flag in a processor is one, this processor executes the next instruction, if the value is zero, no instruction is executed in this processor in the next cycle. Data processed by each processor are read from/written to the processor's own memory unit.

The system provides a variety of facilities for *interprocessor communication*. Processors can communicate in arbitrary patterns (each processor provides the address of the destination of a send instruction), perform next neighbour communication (each processor sends data to his neighbour to the left or right in a regular grid), or exchange data over the edges of a hypercube (each processor can directly communicate with n processors to which it is directly connected in a n-dimensional hypercube).

Programs for the CM are executed on a front-end (FE) which has a bus-connection with the CM machine hardware through which the instruction stream, data and responses are exchanged.

2.2 Connection Machine Programming

The programming paradigm for the Connection Machine is *data parallel computing*. Data parallel computing associates one processor with each data element. This makes it possible to exploit the natural computational parallelism which is inherent in many data-intensive problems.

The concept of *virtual processor* mode is introduced to avoid limiting the size of problems that can be handled by the Connection Machine by the physical configuration of the system. Virtual processor mode presents users with a larger number of virtual processors (VP) than the number of physical processors in the system, each processor with a correspondingly smaller memory. This mode hides the physical configuration and allows to write programs assuming the number of processors that is natural for the application. The number of virtual processors that are mapped on one physical processor is called the VP ratio.

Program development on the Connection Machine is supported by programming systems which allow program development based on the concept of data parallelism. High-level programming languages that have been extended for programming on the Connection Machine are

- CM Fortran, a FORTRAN 77 extension based on the draft ANSI FORTRAN 8x standard,
- C*, an extension of the C language, and
- *Lisp, a suitable extension of the Lisp programming language.

Paris – PARallel Instruction Set – is the low-level language for programming of the Connection Machine which has been used for the implementation of the *ACORN* run-time system. The language has a comprehensive set of instructions for:

- management of resources of the Connection Machine,
- execution of primitive functions, and
- communication between processors.

Resources managed by Paris programs are virtual processor sets, geometries and fields. *Virtual processor sets* (VP sets) are a collection of VPs which are required for a particular problem. *Geometries* define the organization of VP sets. A geometry defines the arrangement of the processors in rectangular processor arrays that have rank and dimension. The rank specifies the number of axes of the processor array, the dimension specifies the number of processors along each axis. The valid values for the dimensions are restricted to be powers of two. *Fields* contain the data to be operated on in parallel. They are allocated within a geometry and reserve an area in the memory of each VP. Field allocation can be either in a heap or in a stack, allocation in a stack simplifies deallocation when leaving a subroutine.

Paris provides a comprehensive set of *primitive functions* for operation on data in parallel. The main groups of primitive functions are

- move functions used for copying of data,
- functions for bitwise boolean operations (and, inclusive or, exclusive or, equivalent, nand, etc.),
- functions for the management of the hardware flags (context, test, overflow, carry) which allow a variety of operations, e.g. load, store, clear, set, invert, logical and, logical or, etc. With global reduction the flags can be and-ed, or-ed and summed; the result is returned to the front-end,
- unary arithmetic functions (e.g. negate, square root, absolute value, signum, floor, ceiling, transcendental functions, truncate, trigonometric functions, etc.), binary arithmetic functions (e.g. add, subtract, multiply, divide, max, min, power, etc.) and the relational functions (equal, not equal, less, less or equal, greater, greater or equal) operate on unsigned and signed integers or floating point numbers. The length of the operands is variable within some limits.

There are two groups of communication functions:

- general communication and
- NEWS communication.

For the purpose of general communication each processor is identified by its send-address. The send-function transmits data in a general fashion that allows any processor to communicate directly with any other processor, identified by the send-address in a field in the processor memory. If more than one processor send to the same destination, data can be combined at the destination with several logical or arithmetic functions (logical and, inclusive or, exclusive or, add, minimum and maximum).

NEWS communication is used to send data to the left or right neighbour along an axis in a geometry. In the context of NEWS communication each processor is identified by a NEWS coordinate. Functions to convert between NEWS coordinates and send-addresses are available. NEWS communication is considerably more efficient than general communication.

A special group of functions combine arithmetic functions and communication. Functions in this group are scan, reduce, spread and global reduction. The result of the scan function in every processor is dependent on the arguments in every processor which precedes the destination along a specified axis. The values can be combined with arithmetic functions (add, minimum or maximum, ...), logical functions (and, inclusive and exclusive or, ...), or be a copy of the value in the first (or last) processor along that axis. The scan can be performed on the whole axis or on partitions thereof. The reduce and spread function are useful special cases of the scan function. The global reduction functions combine values in the same way as the reduce function, but the result is delivered to the front-end.

2.3 Comparison of CM and APL Concepts

There are many similarities between the concepts of the APL programming language and the concepts implemented in the CM parallel programming system.

On the hardware level the concept of the virtual processor sets which are organized in geometries duplicates the concept of arrays in APL. Both concepts define rectangular objects with attributes of rank and dimension. Valid values for the dimension are more restricted in the CM, but otherwise not different. Fields allocated in a geometry are the direct counterpart of APL arrays.

The behaviour of the logical and arithmetic instructions of the CM is similar to the definition of the corresponding functions in APL. These functions, traditionally refered to as scalar functions, operate in parallel on all data elements of the argument arrays.

The relationship between the CM communication functions and APL is less obvious. The APL function similar to CM NEWS communication is rotate. Rotate is more general, allowing to shift data along an axis by more than one element.

The general communication mechanism of the CM does not have an immediate counterpart in APL, although the traditional indexing function allows the performance of this type of data movement. Some of APL's structural functions can be implemented by the CM send-instruction, e.g. transpose, take or drop.

There is no APL counterpart for the ability of the CM to combine the send-instruction with arithmetic functions. Roger Hui has suggested the operator "Do-by-key" or "Partition-by-key". With y being an arbitrary array and x an array of corresponding keys the expression $x\ f\ op\ y$ applies the function f to all items of y which have identical keys in x. He has provided a model of the operator in J, an APL dialect that supports user-defined operators. [Hu90a]

The concept of scan and reduction available on the Connection Machine is identical to the APL concept of the scan and reduction operator. The APL notation for the concepts is more concise and the implementation more complete (i.e. the argument range for the APL scan and reduction operators is broader). The support which the CM provides for partitioned execution of the functions makes it more useful than the APL scan and reduction operator.

The CM concept of context is used for conditional execution and selection. There is no corresponding concept in APL and it may be useful to evaluate the possibility of providing this function in APL. In his presentation on the APL conference in 1984, Robert Bernecky has shown how the conditional execution can be defined in APL based on the concept of function arrays [Be84].

3 The CM-2 Acorn Run-time System

The *ACORN* compiler translates APL programs into corresponding C code which consists mainly of data declarations and function calls to run-time routines for the execution of the APL primitive functions. For more details on the concepts, the implementation and the restrictions of the compiler, see [Be90a,Be90b].

The run-time system developed for serial machines was used as a starting point for the run-time system for the CM. However, it was necessary to reimplement the run-time system almost completely to:

- provide the memory management needed to support the different memory architecture of the CM system and to

- implement execution routines which use the CM hardware for execution of the APL primitives.

3.1 Memory Management

Each APL data object in an *ACORN* program consists of a descriptor containing information about the type of the object, its structure (rank, shape) and other information relevant for housekeeping (number of elements, reference count, etc.) and the data itself.

In the memory management scheme for serial machines, new objects are allocated dynamically with descriptor and data being adjacent in memory.

In the CM system organization, the executed program resides on the front-end (FE) and uses its memory. Data processed by the CM must reside in CM memory. In the CM run-time system, descriptors are allocated on the FE. The data are kept in the descriptor if the number of elements is one, they reside in a heap field on the CM if the number of elements is greater than one.

The following choices were considered for the mapping of the APL data into the CM memory:

- allocation of each APL object within a virtual processor (VP) set with a geometry equal to the rank of the object and dimensions in each axis that are equal or larger than the dimension of the APL entity, or
- allocation of each APL object within a virtual processor set with rank one and a length sufficient to hold all elements of the array.

The first choice exploits the similiarity between the concepts of data objects in APL and the concept of virtual processor sets in the CM. It has the potential to allow usage of NEWS communication for the implementation of primitive functions in the system. The discrepancy of the restriction of dimension in VP sets to be powers of two and the freedom which the APL language has in that respect can lead to a considerable waste of processor and memory resources if an array with rank greater than one deviates from powers of two in all dimensions. For some of the APL primitives, different algorithms are needed to execute on arrays which meet the restriction and those that do not.

The second choice replicates the allocation of APL data on machines with the traditional Von Neumann architecture. It is well understood, uses processor and memory resources as efficiently as possible, and is not affected by the limitations on the structure of CM geometries. The disadvantage is that the primitive functions will generally be unable to use NEWS communication; they have to use general communication instead.

Within this project it was decided to use the second solution, mainly because it was felt that although the first solution is superior, only the second solution was feasible with the resources available for the project.

3.2 Execution Routines

Execution routines are implemented in C/Paris and all functions for which at least one argument resides on the CM are executed on the CM. The implementation is simple and straightforward under the constraints imposed by the memory management choice described above. No attempt was made to research existing software for the CM and to evaluate the suitability of available CM-algorithms as an implementation basis for this project.

4 Performance Evaluation

Performance measurements were performed with two seismic applications that have been used for performance measurements on other systems among which the Cray X-MP. The applications are Convolution (CONV) and Normal Moveout (NMO).

Initially, the run-time system represented floating-point numbers in long (64 bit) format. However, the floating-point coprocessors installed on the CMNS machine process only short (32 bit) format. The machine will not use the floating point coprocessor if the length of a floating-point word defined in an application differs from the wordlength of the coprocessor. The run-time system was modified to support 32-bit floating point numbers. Most of the measurements were usually made with both data representations.

The execution times have been measured with the timing facilities provided by the Connection Machine. The CM timer functions report the real time used for the execution of a program and the CM-time, that is the time the CM has been active during execution. The timings are affected by the limited timer resolution of the Unix-based front-end (resolution is usually 20 msecs) and the lack of control over other activities on the front-end.

4.1 Convolution

CONV is a dyadic function that performs convolution [Ah74] on vectors using reduction of an outer product. The left argument specifies the length of the filter, the right argument the length of the data.

Execution of CONV on the Connection Machine with 32K processors gave the following results:

102 CONV d length of d, FP size	Real time (seconds)	CM Time (seconds)	Time/element (μseconds)
16000, short	14.480	14.476	900
8000, long	10.080	10.076	1200

Due to the size of intermediate results, especially the outer product, the VP set created for the first problem contains 2M processors, the VP ratio for this problem is 64. Calculation for long FP format was made with 8000 elements only since the execution for 16000 elements failed due to lack of memory resources. The size of the VP set for this problem is 1M, the VP ratio 32.

The time per element for the same problem executed on a Cray X-MP is 4.6 μsecs. The ratio between the CPU time per element on the CM-2 and the Cray is roughly 200.

4.2 Normal Moveout

NMO (Normal Move Out) is an application which is used for the analysis of seismic data [Ka88]. The function has two parameters. The first parameter specifies the number of traces; the second specifies the number of samples per trace.

NMO was executed on a machine with 16K processors. The required size of the VP set was 64K, the VP ratio 4. The following execution times were observed with long and short floating-point numbers:

TEST	Real Time (seconds)	CM time (seconds)
NMO 16 1000 (Short FP)	84.68	53.33
NMO 16 1000 (Long FP)	110.95	96.11

The execution time for the same problem on the Cray X-MP was 187 msecs. The ratio between the CPU time for the problem on the CM-2 and the Cray is more than 400.

5 Analysis of Results

The difference in performance between the execution of the *ACORN* examples on the CM-2 and the Cray X-MP is more than 2 orders of magnitude, a result which is not expected and unsatisfactory.

The observed performance difference may be attributable to one or more of the following factors:

- incorrect expectations about the performance of the CM-2 system in comparison to the Cray
- usage of unsuitable algorithms for the implementation of the execution routines which leads to poor utilization of the CM system
- poor match between the CM paradigm and the design of the run-time system for the machine exemplified by the design of the memory management

To get a better understanding of the performance characteristics of the system and to try to identify the source of the perceived performance deficiencies some more tests were performed.

The first experiment is a comparison of the performance of specific functions of the *ACORN* run-time system against the performance of an implementation of the same functions in a different programming environment. It is an attempt to calibrate the performance of the *ACORN* run-time system on the Connection Machine and is done by comparison of the performance of the inner product against the performance of an inner product implemented in CM Fortran.

The other experiment is to implement a version of the convolution algorithm which uses NEWS communication if appropriate. This is an attempt to determine the influence of the design choice in the area of memory management with its implication for the usage of interprocessor communication.

5.1 Performance Calibration

The first test was done using the inner product with +.×, i.e. matrix multiplication. The *ACORN* implementation is compared to a implementation in CM Fortran using the Cannon algorithm. [Ca69] The FORTRAN implementation was executed using 32-bit floating point numbers, the *ACORN* code was executed with 32- and 64-bit floating point.

The following tables show timings for different implementations indicated by the headings Cannon, Acorn-S and Acorn-L which denote the Cannon algorithm and the *ACORN* algorithm executed with Short and Long floating point format.

The first table shows the real-time usage. The first column is the size of the problem, i.e. the size of the square matrices which have been multiplied, the next column the number of floating operations required to generate the result, expressed in Millions (it is 5 x 2 x n*3 - the result contains n*2 elements, each of which requires n multiplications and n summations, i.e. 2 x n operations, each example was executed 5 times). The remaining columns give the elapsed time for each algorithm in seconds and the number of floating point operations executed per second, expressed in millions (Mflops).

Size	Total	Cannon time		Acorn-S time		Acorn-L time	
	Mops	Real	Mflop	Real	Mflop	Real	Mflop
16	0.04	0.81	0.05	0.73	0.56	1.12	0.37
32	0.38	1.27	0.26	1.33	0.25	2.23	1.47
64	2.62	2.98	0.88	2.38	1.10	4.44	0.59
128	20.97	4.82	4.35	7.42	2.82	15.87	1.32
256	167.77	8.41	19.95	70.34	2.39	143.72	1.17
512	1342.18	53.08	25.29	562.06	2.39	n/a	n/a

The next table shows the CM time for the same problems. The first column indicates the size of the matrices that are multiplied, and the second column shows the VP ratio in effect (The machine size on the CM-2 was 8K). The remaining columns show, for each implementation, the CM-time in seconds and the CM utilization as percent busy.

Matrix	VP	Cannon		Acorn-S		Acorn-L	
Order	ratio	sec.	%	sec.	%	sec.	%
16	1	0.18	22	0.58	80	1.10	98
32	1	0.31	25	1.15	86	2.16	97
64	1	0.86	29	2.21	93	4.32	97
128	2	1.78	37	7.06	95	15.34	97
256	8	7.62	91	67.47	96	140.46	98
512	32	52.93	100	532.13	95	n/a	n/a

For small problem sizes the elapsed time for the Cannon algorithm is dominated by the front-end execution time. The increase in CM-time for the problems with VP-ratio 1 is attributable to the increase in communication overhead. With increasing VP-ratio the CM-time grows initially linear with the VP-ratio, the increase in communication cost apparently being offset by the gains in setup time related to the increasing VP-ratio. The last problem (size 512) shows an increase which consists of the linear growth related to VP-ratio and the communications related increment.

The inner product function of the ACORN system is dominated by the CM-time for all problem sizes. The increase in CM-time shows a linear VP-ratio related growth and the increase in communication cost.

The Mflop-rate reached by the Cannon algorithm is 25, an order of magnitude more than the rate for Acorn-S. In a presentation at Supercomputing '89, Lennart Johnson et al describe a Matrix Multiplication scheme particularly designed for the Connection Machine [Jo89]. They report execution rates of 107 Mflops for the problems of size 256 and 199 Mflops for the problem of size 512, both executed on a Connection Machine with 8K processors.

5.2 NEWS vs General Communication

The second test was performed with a different implementation of the convolution algorithm. The first convolution algorithm executes without loop and uses arrays of rank greater than one.

The second algorithm loops over all elements of the filter and shifts the data elements by one position (rotate) during each pass through the loop. It uses only rank one arrays. The rotate function was modified to use NEWS communication if it is operating on vector right arguments and if their length is a power of two (and above a certain lower bound).

Timings on this algorithm were done with the following parameters

- filterlength 102 and 306
- datalength 16000 and 16384

The execution times per element (in μsecs) are as follows:

Filter Length	Execution Time Per Element (μsec)	
	Length=16000	Length=16384
102	189	23
306	565	63

The test shows that the execution time varies linearly with the length of the filter, not an unexpected result.

Although NEWS communication is not usable for a data vector with a length of 16000, it is used for the length of 16384. The execution time per element varies considerably between the two cases. For the case which uses NEWS communication it is reduced by almost an order or magnitude.

The comparison of the execution time of this algorithm to the first one shows a reduction which is even larger than expected by the observed contribution of general communication. This suggests that there is additional overhead in the execution routines related to the choice of mapping of APL objects which can be eliminated in a different implementation.

6 Discussion

The initial benchmarks provide no evidence for the hypothesis that APL is a suitable programming language for this system. However, subsequent experiments and analysis show that the performance deficiencies are to a large extent attributable to the design choice in the area of memory management. It is obvious that the decision on this topic was made with a naive view of the cost of general communication in the Connection Machine system.

The result from the comparison of the inner product implementations and from the experiment with the alternative implementation of CONV suggest that the cost of communication overhead related to the choice of linear geometries for the representation of APL objects is about 90% of the total execution cost. An implementation which uses the facilities of the machine will reduce execution cost by an order of magnitude.

It is further reasonable to assume that substantial additional gains can be made by a more careful implementation of the execution routines, usage of well-known algorithms which are suitable for the Connection Machine and usage of compilation techniques tailored to the target hardware.

Taking the potential improvements into account, the CM execution times for the examples which have been used to benchmark the prototype the system are well in the neighbourhood of the corresponding values for the Cray.

The work described here illustrates the problems associated with the development of applications for machines like the Connection Machine which have a rather different hardware architecture. Efficient usage of the available machine resources requires careful tailoring of the application code to the architecture of the hardware used for execution.

Given that the users of such system are frequently not computer scientists with in-depth knowledge of the system and its architecture, it is quite possible that they will fail in the same way that the system programmer who did this development failed. The tailoring of applications to a hardware has other disadvantages, such as the lack of portability of the code.

One way out of that dilemma is to use programming languages that can specify a computation at a high level of abstraction without reference to a specific system architecture. The responsibility to generate code that uses a target hardware efficiently can be left to the compiler.

APL is a language which has the required attributes. With a compiler that supports code generation for a variety of systems it should be a valuable tool for the development of supercomputer applications. Considering the match between the hardware concepts in the Connection Machine system and the language, it could be an particularly suitable language for this system.

References

[Ah74] Aho, A. V., J. E. Hopcroft, J. D. Ullman, *The Design and Analysis of Computer Algorithms*, Addison-Wesley, 1974.

[Be84] Bernecky, R., "Function Arrays", *APL84 Conference Proceedings*, APL Quote Quad, Vol. 14, No. 4, 1984.

[Be90a] Bernecky, R., "Compiling APL", in these proceedings.

[Be90b] Bernecky, R., C. Brenner, S.B. Jaffe, G.P. Moeckel, "*ACORN* : APL to C on Real Numbers", APL90 Conference Proceedings, APL Quote Quad, Vol. 20, No. 4, July 1990.

[Ca69] Cannon, L. E., *A Cellular Computer to Implement the Kalman Filter Algorithm*, Ph. D. Thesis, Montana State University, 1969.

[Ca86] *Communications of the ACM*, Vol. 29, No. 12, December 1986.

[Hu90a] Hui, R., *Personal Communication*, I. P. Sharp Associates Mail System, January, 1990.

[Hu90b] Hui, Roger K. W., K. E. Iverson, E. E. McDonnell, and Arthur T. Whitney, "APL\?", *APL90 Conference Proceedings, APL Quote Quad*, Vol. 20, No. 4, July 1990.

[Jo89] Johnson, S. L., T. Harris, K. K. Mathur, "Matrix Multiplication on the Connection Machine", *Proceedings Supercomputing '89*, pp. 326ff, ACM Press, 1989.

[Ka88] Kamel, L., M. Kindelan, P. Squazzero, "Seismic Computations on the IBM 3090 Vector Multiprocessor", *IBM System Journal*, Vol. 27, No. 4, 1988.

[Tm89a] Thinking Machines Corporation, *Connection Machine Model CM-2, Technical Summary*, Ver 5.1, Cambridge, Mass., May 1989.

[Tm89b] Thinking Machines Corporation, *Paris Reference Manual*, Ver 5.2, Cambridge, Mass., October 1989.

4

Compiling Issues of Monolithic Arrays

Guang R. Gao
School of Computer Science,
McGill University, 3480 University St.
Montreal, Quebec, Canada H3A 2A7

Abstract

This paper presents an efficient scheme for compiling *monolithic arrays* in scientific computation programs written in functional/applicative languages. In particular, the scheduling of code blocks (or loops) defining monolithic arrays on a pipelined dataflow computer is studied. A general framework for fine-grain code scheduling in pipelined machines is developed which addresses both time and space efficiency simultaneously for loops typically found in general-purpose scientific computation. This scheduling method exploits fine-grain parallelism through *dataflow software pipelining*. The compiler will perform loop optimization through *limited balancing* [1] of the program graph, while the instruction-level scheduling is done dynamically at runtime in a data-driven manner. Simulation results are presented for verifying the notion and power of limited balancing.

Keywords: dataflow software pipelining, monolithic arrays, code scheduling, limited balancing, fine-grain synchronization

1 Introduction

This paper presents an efficient scheme for compiling *monolithic arrays* written in functional/applicative languages for scientific computation programs [15,19]. Monolithic arrays are arrays whose

[1] Our previous work on fully balancing (see [10]) is a special case of limited balancing proposed in this paper.

elements are defined at the moment the array value is created, in contrast to *incremental arrays* whose values are defined incrementally.

In this paper, we study the scheduling of code blocks (or loops) which define monolithic arrays on a pipelined dataflow computer. Efficient loop scheduling is a challenging task facing compilers which are designed for high-performance architectures. Unfortunately, many code scheduling problems are provably NP-hard, thus discouraging further work for compile-time loop scheduling [5,16,31].

We investigate the loop scheduling problem for pipelined architectures, where *hazards* have been the main concern of maximum instruction pipelining. Such hazards can be divided into two groups:

- *data-dependent hazards*: they occur whenever data-dependence exists between two separate instructions which are close enough so that pipelining may overlap their execution [20]; and

- *collision* (or *structural*) *hazards*: i.e., two semantically unrelated instructions may attempt to use the same pipeline stage or resource (registers, memories, flags, etc.) due to the hardware structure of the pipeline. These hazards also prevent the pipeline from accepting activations (of instructions) at the maximum rate that the stage clock may support [20].

If a pipeline is free of any collision hazards, it is called a *(structurally) hazard-free* pipeline, or simply a *clean* pipeline.

There are essentially three classes of data-dependent hazards which may exist between two instructions:
(1) read-after-write hazard (RAW),
(2) write-after-write hazard (WAW) and
(3) write-after-read hazard (WAR) [20].
They correspond to the flow-, output- and anti-dependence respectively defined by Kuck et al. [21]. Branch instructions can introduce dependencies between themselves and the potential target instruction(s); although such dependencies can be classified under the above data dependencies, researchers often classify them as *control dependencies* to mark their peculiarity [21].

One basic goal of code scheduling is to find an execution order of the instructions (with possible insertion of no-ops) such that the total run time is minimized. The code scheduling problem for a pipeline with structural hazards is intractable. For completeness, we include (as an appendix) a proof of this observation based on a similar argument due to Nicholau et al. [25]. For a clean pipeline, progress has been made in finding efficient scheduling algorithms for RISC style (one-cycle) architectures, although the general problem still appears hard [4].

Recently, there has been considerable interest in a scheduling technique which exploits the repetitive nature of loops. In particular, *software pipelining* of loops was proposed to generate highly efficient code for pipelined processor architectures [23,28,30]. Under software pipelining, an iteration of a loop is activated before its preceding iteration is completed, thus multiple activations are in concurrent execution. However, the scheduling of software pipelining is NP-complete [16]. To overcome this difficulty, there have been methods which use software pipelining with expensive hardware features such as in the polycyclic architecture [28], or the FPS-164 approach where software pipelining is restricted to loops with a single Fortran statement in their bodies [30]. We also note the recent work in applying software pipelining to the Warp systolic array architecture [23]. The work most closely related to this paper is the fine-grain scheduling technique described by Aiken et al. [2,25]. However, it is not clear to us how their work will integrate with the register/memory allocation problem described below.

Another aspect which is as important as time efficiency but unfortunately often ignored is space efficiency. In most of the proposed loop scheduling schemes, register allocation is treated as a separate phase from the instruction scheduling itself. There has been no clear criteria on how the two parts can be integrated under a unified compiling framework to achieve the desired goal [4].

A fine-grain code scheduling methodology for pipelined machines, which addresses both time and space efficiency simultaneously, is presented in this paper. Section 2 introduces *dataflow software pipelining* as a compiling technique for code blocks defining monolithic arrays. . In Section 3, we briefly formulate the code scheduling problem for pipelined machines, and outline major complexity results. In Section 4, we develop a general framework for dataflow software pipelining under a realistic pipelined machine model. Section 5 establishes a set of basic results which show that the fine-grain parallelism in a loop exposed through *limited balancing* can be fully exploited by a simple greedy runtime data-driven scheduling scheme. Section 6 demonstrates that the space and time efficiency can be achieved simultaneously under a uniform loop scheduling scheme by dataflow software pipelining. Furthermore, the fine-grain synchronization overhead can also be reduced through limited balancing. Section 7 presents the simulation results of Livermore Loop7 after limited balancing. Section 8 gives hints as to how the basic framework can be generalized. Section 8 states conclusions and future work.

2 Mapping Monolithic Arrays by Dataflow Software Pipelining

Fine-grain parallelism exists in a data flow machine level program, as shown in Figure 1, which consists of seven actors divided into four stages. In Figure 1 (a), actors 1 and 2 are enabled by the presence of tokens on their input arcs, and thus can be executed in parallel. Parallelism also exists between actors 3 and 4, and between actors 5 and 6. In static data flow architecture, pipelining means arranging the machine code such that successive computations can follow each other through one copy of the code. If we present a sequence of values to the inputs of the data flow graph, these values can flow through the program in a pipelined fashion. In the configuration of Figure 2 (b), two sets of computation are pipelined through the graph, and the actors in stage 1 and 3 are enabled and can be executed concurrently. Thus, both forms of parallelism are fully exploited in the graph.

The power of fine-grain parallelism in a data flow computer can be derived from machine-level programs that form a large pipeline in which multiple actors in different stages are executed concurrently. Each actor in the pipe is activated in a totally data-driven manner,

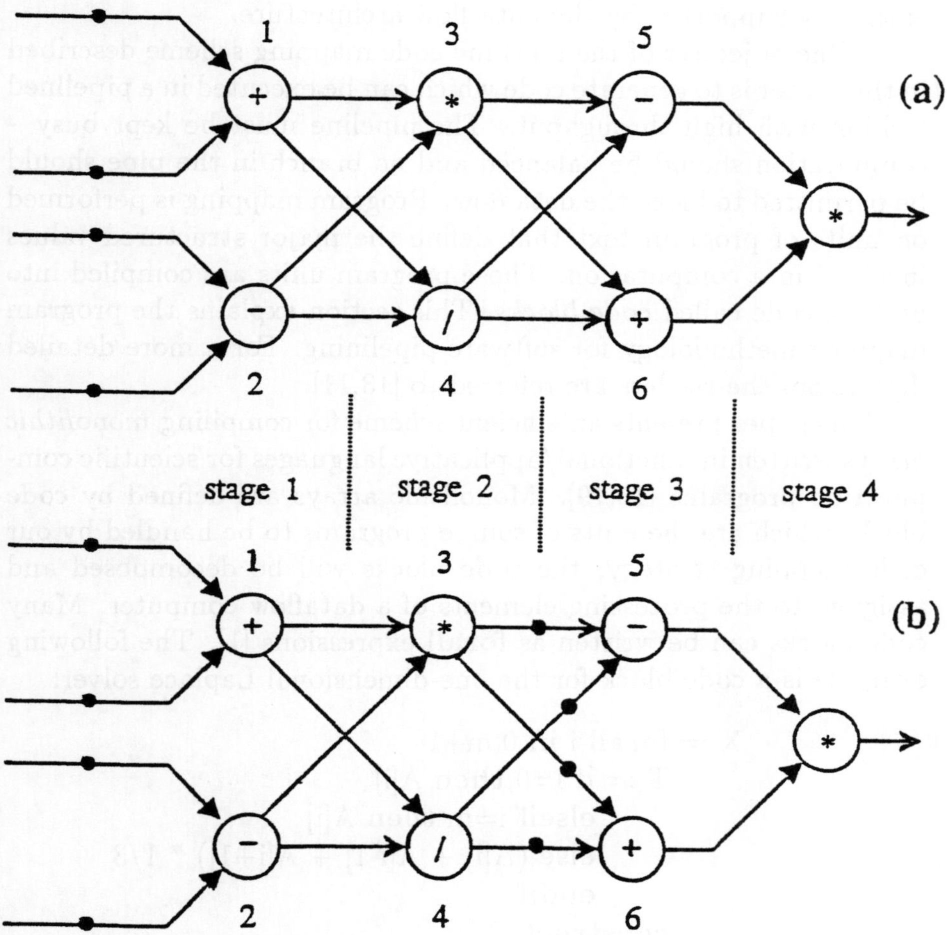

Figure 1: Pipelining of data flow programs

and no explicit sequential control is needed. With data values continuously flowing through the pipe, a sustained parallelism can be efficiently supported by the data flow architecture.

One objective of the machine code mapping scheme described in this paper is to generate code which can be executed in a pipelined fashion with high throughput. The pipeline must be kept busy – computation should be balanced and no branch in the pipe should be permitted to block the data flow. Program mapping is performed on units of program text that define the major structured values involved in a computation. These program units are compiled into units of code called *code blocks*. This section explains the program mapping methodology for software pipelining. For a more detailed discussion, the readers are referred to [13,11].

This paper presents an efficient scheme for compiling *monolithic arrays* written in functional/applicative languages for scientific computation programs [15,19]. Monolithic arrays are defined by code blocks which are the units of source programs to be handled by our code mapping strategy; the code blocks will be decomposed and assigned to the processing elements of a dataflow computer. Many code blocks can be written as **forall** expressions [1]. The following example is a code block for the one-dimensional Laplace solver:

```
X := forall i in 0,m+1
     T := if i=0 then A[i]
            elseif i=m then A[i]
            else (A[i] + A[i-1] + A[i+1]) * 1/3
            endif
     construct T
     endall
```

The main feature of a **forall** code block is that the array elements can be evaluated in parallel because there are no data dependencies among them. Typically the body expression is a conditional expression which partitions the index range of the result array into mutually exclusive and collectively exhaustive index subranges, each corresponding to an arm of the conditional expression. Such a conditional expression is called a *range-partitioning* conditional expression. In our example, it is a three-arm conditional expression.

In a data flow computation model, an array value can be regarded as a sequence of element values carried by tokens transmitted on a single data flow arc. The dataflow graph based on the pipelined mapping of the above example should contain the following constructs [12]:

1. An *index generator* subgraph (IGEN) which has two input ports for the low and high index limits and generates a sequence of "high-low+1" index values. In the above example it generates 0...m+1 at its output port. It should also generate a sequence of control values to control the progress of the iteration.

2. An *array generator* subgraph (AGEN), which takes both index and control value sequences from the corresponding IGEN and the base address of the array. The result array X is internally represented by a sequence of values presented to the output port of the body expression. The role of AGEN is to assemble these elements into a result array X.

3. The *selection* operation in the body is mapped into an array selection actor, together with an index calculation expression.

In our example, an efficient pipeline scheme can be accomplished if we arrange the mapping of the array selection operations, such that the elements of the input array A flow in a pipelined fashion into the code block in the right order and the unused values are discarded without causing jams. Figure 2 shows a dataflow graph after this optimization. The ASCATTER subgraph receives an array A and a sequence of index values from IGEN and produces a sequence of array values elements accordingly. If the elements of X are to be consumed by succeeding code blocks in the same order in which they were generated, there is no need to assemble them using AGEN and then dismantled by an ASCATTER in the succeeding code block. This optimization will avoid the overhead of storing intermediate array values in structure memory.

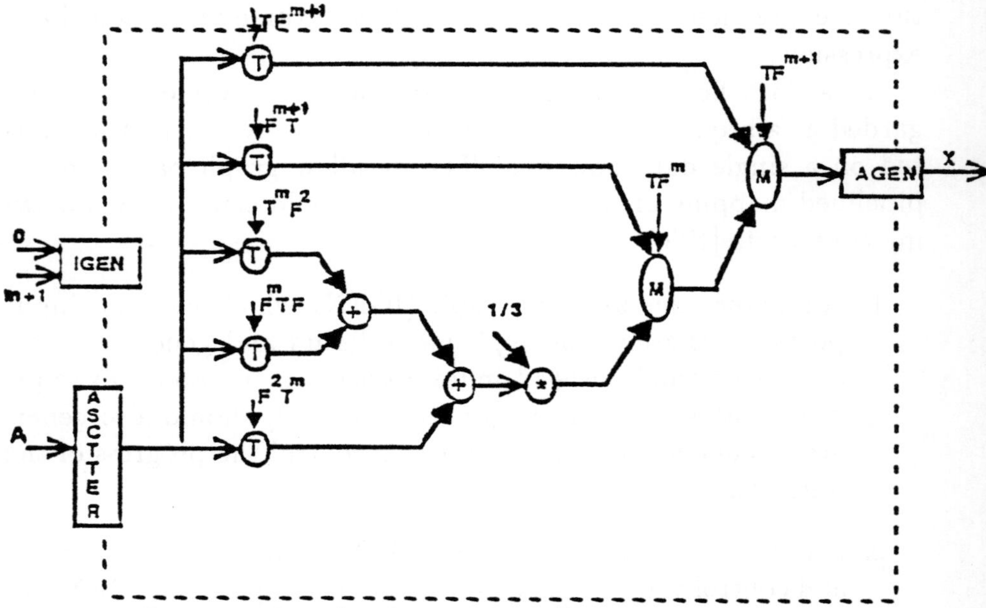

Figure 2: Result of removing all array operations

Notice that IGEN and AGEN as they are defined in this document are first introduced in our earlier work [12]. The IGEN, AGEN and ASCATTER are also similar to the corresponding RANGE-GENERATE, AGATHER and ASCATTER in IF1 representation of **forall** graphs [29].

3 The Code Scheduling Problem

The general problem of compile-time code scheduling for pipelined architectures is hard [16]. The input to such problems is usually described by a *constraint graph* — a precedence graph G such that:
(1) nodes represent operations,
(2) directed edges represent precedence relations due to data-dependent hazards, and
(3) undirected edges represent constraints due to possible collisions.
Assume an edge $e = (u, v)$ with label d exists between nodes u and v; then, in any legal schedule, node u must precede node v by at least d cycles if e is a direct edge, otherwise u and v can be executed in any order as long as they are separated by d cycles. We thus call

d the *interlock delay* between u and v, and denote it by $d(u, v)$. One basic goal of code scheduling is to find an execution order of the instructions (with possible insertion of no-ops) such that the total run time is minimized. In particular, a classical NP-complete resource constraint job-shop scheduling problem is reducible to this problem. For completeness, we include a proof of this claim in appendix A which is similar but slightly different from the argument due to Nicholau et al. [25].

3.1 Hazard-Free Pipelines

In this paper, we are interested in code scheduling problems where the hardware pipeline has no collision hazards, i.e., hazard-free. The following is the statement of the *code scheduling problem for a single clean pipeline* (CSSCP problem):

Definition 3.1 *The code scheduling problem for a single clean pipeline (CSSCP Problem) is the following:*

Input: A constraint graph G such that

1. the delay $d(u, v) = l$ for all directed edges $e = (u, v)$,
2. the delay $d(u, v) = 1$ for all undirected edges $e = (u, v)$.

Output: A sequence of operations (in G) $v_1, v_2, \ldots$, with a minimum number of no-ops such that:

- if the no-ops are deleted, the result is a topological sort of the nodes in graph G;
- any two nodes u, v are separated at least by a number of operations equal to the length of the delay $d(u, v)$ required by the constraint.

The condition on undirected edges merely states that the pipeline itself is the only resource which is shared, i.e., two instructions cannot be initiated at the same time. Therefore, we can drop this condition and G simply becomes a precedence graph (e.g., a DAG), such as those used in the study of RISC architectures [4]. In this paper, we devote our discussion mainly to the case where the DAG has a uniform edge delay of l.

In [18], it has been shown that the CSSCP problem is NP-complete if the maximum interlock delay d is unbounded. It has also been shown that, when $d = 1$, there exists a polynomial time solution to the problem [4]. Thus, the CSSCP problem for a one-cycle RISC machine may have an efficient solution. The CSSCP problem between these two extremes is still open, although the conjecture is that it is NP-hard [4].

Two approaches have been suggested to treat the register allocation problems in conjunction with pipeline scheduling. In the first approach, it is assumed that a large number of registers are available, hence the scheduling can be handled independently of the register constraints. After the scheduling is done, the global register allocation can be performed using graph coloring methods, assuming there will be enough registers [24]. In the second approach, register allocation is done before the scheduling phase. This may introduce new constraints which may limit possible reordering of the instructions, as reported in [17,18]. Neither approach is completely satisfactory.

4 Code Scheduling for Dataflow Software Pipelining

In this section, we present a unified framework for code scheduling which considers both time and space efficiency simultaneously. Our method is based on the concept of dataflow software pipelining – a fine-grain loop scheduling method for data-driven computation.

4.1 Under an Ideal Dataflow Machine Model

Consider the following example of a DOALL loop L1 :

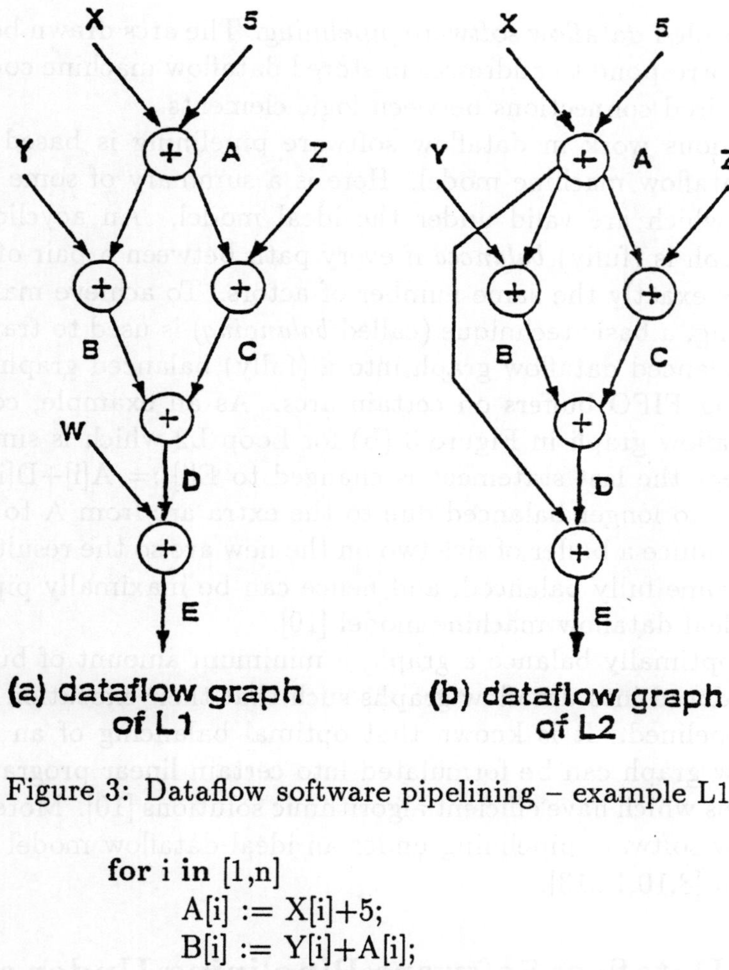

Figure 3: Dataflow software pipelining – example L1

```
for i in [1,n]
        A[i] := X[i]+5;
        B[i] := Y[i]+A[i];
        C[i] := A[i]+Z[i];
        D[i] := B[i]+C[i];
        E[i] := W[i]+D[i];
endall
```

The principle of dataflow software pipelining can be explained using the above DOALL loop which is a loop without loop-carried dependencies. The loop is translated into a pipelined dataflow graph as shown in Figure 3 (a). Successive waves of elements of the input arrays W, X, Y and Z will be fetched and fed into the dataflow graph, so that the computation may proceed in a pipelined fashion.

This is called *dataflow software pipelining.* The arcs drawn between actors correspond to addresses in stored dataflow machine code, not to the wired connections between logic elements.

Previous work in dataflow software pipelining is based on an ideal dataflow machine model. Here is a summary of some known results which are valid under the ideal model. An acyclic dataflow graph is (fully) *balanced* if every path between a pair of nodes contains exactly the same number of actors. To achieve maximum pipelining, a basic technique (called *balancing*) is used to transform an unbalanced dataflow graph into a (fully) balanced graph by introducing FIFO buffers on certain arcs. As an example, consider the dataflow graph in Figure 3 (b) for Loop L2 which is similar to L1 except the last statement is changed to E[i] := A[i]+D[i]. The graph is no longer balanced due to the extra arc from A to E. We can introduce a buffer of size two on the new arc so the result graph will become fully balanced, and hence can be maximally pipelined in an ideal dataflow machine model [10].

To optimally balance a graph, a minimum amount of buffering is introduced into dataflow graphs such that their execution can be fully pipelined. It is known that optimal balancing of an acyclic dataflow graph can be formulated into certain linear programming problems which have efficient algorithmic solutions [10]. More about dataflow software pipelining under an ideal dataflow model can be found in [8,10,12,13].

4.2 Dataflow Software Pipelining Under a Machine Model with a Single Clean Pipeline

In this section, we study how dataflow software pipelining can be applied to a more realistic dataflow architecture model with a single clean pipeline.

The goal of dataflow software pipelining is to efficiently exploit fine-grain parallelism. Under an ideal machine model, we need not be concerned with the issues of "exploitable" parallelism, because the machine is infinitely parallel. As a result, we also do not need to worry about the scheduling problem since the machine can process all enabled actors instantaneously. Under a realistic pipelined machine model, however, we must address both issues: the graph should expose the potential parallelism exploitable within the capacity of the machine, while the parallel operations should be scheduled such that the machine pipeline can be kept usefully busy.

To utilize the parallelism in the hardware pipeline of a realistic machine model, it is important that the code should be structured so that:

- the loop (or more precisely, the dataflow graph of the loop body) has "enough" parallelism;
- such parallelism is "exploitable" in a software pipelined fashion;
- no excessive parallelism is exposed which may not be efficiently utilized.

Fortunately, the model and techniques of dataflow software pipelining can be extended successfully to handle loop scheduling under a realistic machine model with a clean pipeline. In the next section, we will establish a set of results which show that the fine-grain parallelism in a loop exposed through *limited balancing* can be fully exploited on our machine model by a simple greedy runtime data-driven scheduling scheme.

5 Time Efficiency

In this section, we present some new results on the time efficiency of loop scheduling through dataflow software pipelining. We develop the basic framework on a very simple program model, i.e., we first consider loops containing no loop-carried dependencies, no conditionals and assume that all operators have the same execution time. In Section 6, we will discuss how the basic framework can be generalized.

5.1 The Basic Model

Assume that we consider the loop which has, as its body, a (static) dataflow graph G which satisfies the following conditions:

- G is acyclic;
- G is one-in-one-out (i.e., a graph with a single input node and a single output node); and
- G contains no conditionals (i.e., G consists of only regular dataflow actors[6]).

We call G a *static dataflow software pipeline*, or a SDFP. Let us also assume that G is operating under the following conditions:

- G is initially empty;
- the input/output environment for G is *maximally loaded*, i.e., it can produce input values for G and consume the output values from G without any delay; and
- the loop has a large number of iterations and the start-up and termination time can be ignored.

We assume that the abstract machine model M has the following features:

- it contains a single clean pipeline with l stages; and
- it has enough fine-grain synchronization power such that the time spent in handling the enabling signals of an instruction is negligible compared with the computation time of the instruction.

Let us consider a SDFP G as shown in Figure 4. We assume that the input node s of the graph G is driven by an input *source* which can generate a stream of input tokens as fast as the pipeline can use them. Furthermore, the output node t of the graph G is connected to a *sink* which can absorb tokens as fast as the pipeline can generate them. Figure 4 (a) shows an initial configuration where

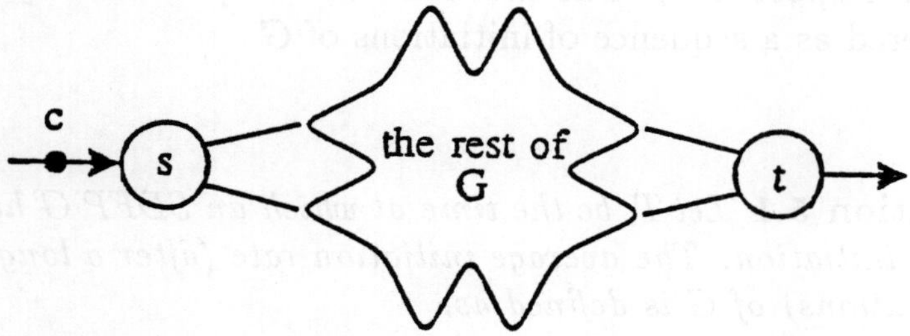

(a) before the run with respect to c

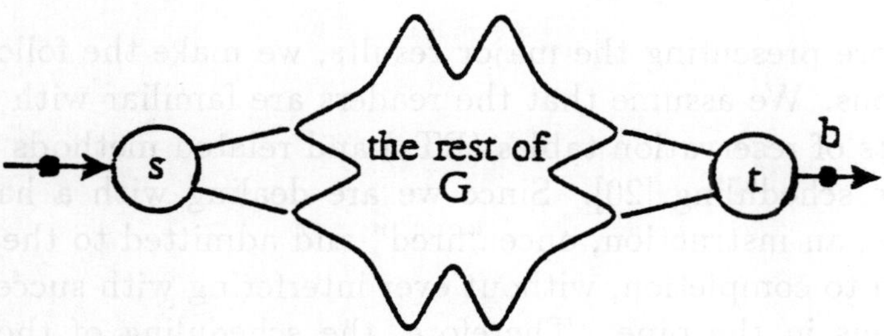

(b) after the run

Figure 4: One initiation of a static dataflow software pipeline

an input token c is presented at the input arc of G. After a finite number of cycle times, a result token b comes out from G, as in the configuration shown in Figure 4 (b). The sequence of firing of the actors in G caused by the input token c is called one *initiation* of G (with respect to c). The execution of a loop with body G can be considered as a sequence of initiations of G.

Definition 5.1 *Let T_i be the time at which an SDFP G has started its i-th initiation. The average initiation rate (after a long sequence of initiations) of G is defined as:*

$$\lim_{i \to \infty} \frac{i}{T_i}$$

Before presenting the major results, we make the following observations. We assume that the readers are familiar with the basic concepts of reservation tables (RTs) and related methods for static pipeline scheduling [20]. Since we are dealing with a hazard-free pipeline, an instruction, once "fired" and admitted to the pipeline, will run to completion, without ever interfering with succeeding instructions in the pipe. Therefore, the scheduling of the pipeline can be conceived as a reservation table RT with a single row.[2] An initiation of a SDFP, G, can be represented by putting a number of marks in the row equal to the number of nodes in G. Although the concept of RT was originally introduced to handle hardware pipeline designs, it is useful in developing some of the proofs presented below. In fact, theorem 5.1 is inspired by a similar lemma established for static pipeline scheduling [20].

Theorem 5.1 *Let G be a SDFP with n nodes. Then the average initiation rate of G on machine M is no greater than 1/n.*

[2] A pipeline may contain l identical stages, hence a complete representation will be an RT with l rows. However, since each row will have one mark (the pipeline is clean and the maximum rate is one per cycle), all rows will behave identically in our discussion. Hence we simplify the RT by only considering one row.

Proof of Theorem 5.1.
The validity of the theorem is immediately derived from the fact that the maximum utilization of the pipeline (i.e., the product of the number of marks n in the RT and the average initiation rate) cannot exceed 100%. □

Theorem 5.1 has set a bound on the maximum possible average initiation rate for a long sequence of initiations. When such a bound is achieved, the pipeline is 100% utilized. The following lemma sets up another bound on the graph initiation rate due mainly to the static dataflow graph model and the pipeline length for a machine M.

Lemma 5.1 *Let G be a SDFP. The average initiation rate of G on machine M is no greater than* $1/2l$*, where* l *is the pipeline length of the machine M.*

Proof of Lemma 5.1.
Let s be the input node of G (since G is one-in-one-out, there exists only one input node). After one firing of node s at time $\mathbf{t}$, node s cannot be activated again until the current firing of s is finished. Since the pipeline length of the machine M is l, the minimum latency between two consecutive activations of s cannot be less than $2l$. This includes the execution time of s plus the execution time of its successor to ensure that it is safe to fire again. The validity of the lemma follows immediately. □

Lemma 5.1 essentially postulates the constraints imposed by the static dataflow architecture model. Note that the structure of the graph itself may prevent the above bound to be attained, e.g., an unbalanced graph cannot achieve this bound. Furthermore, one must note that even when this bound is achieved, the pipeline is not necessarily utilized 100%. If $2l >$ n, G can never fully utilize the pipeline (theorem 5.1). However, in reality, l is usually very small (for example less than 10 - 12), so we will assume $2l \leq$ n in the rest of this section. In section 7, we briefly discuss the extension to cases where such assumptions do not hold. If $2l \leq$ n, G has the potential to keep the pipeline fully utilized under a long sequence of initiations. In order to achieve full utilization, G should be transformed (if necessary) so that it can support the maximum average initiation rate of 1/n. The main factor which restricts the maximum initiation rate of G is the degree of balancing which will be discussed below.[3]

Let us introduce the notion of *balancing ratio*, denoted by B(G), to describe the degree of balancing of a dataflow graph G. We give a definition of the balancing ratio based on the observation of token and space duality in dataflow graph models suggested by Kung et al. [22]. Let us augment G with *acknowledgement arcs* and assign one initial (dummy) token on each acknowledgement arc in G, denoting the fact that the corresponding forward (data) arc has one empty place. This is reasonable since G is initially empty under our assumptions. Then our (augmented) SDFP is similar to Kung's *augmented dataflow graph* where the acknowledgement arcs correspond to his "reverse arcs".

Definition 5.2 *Let C be any directed simple cycle in an augmented SDFP G.[4] Let the length of C (number of arcs) be K_C, and the the number of dummy tokens be D_C. The ratio $\frac{D_C}{K_C}$ is called the balancing ratio of C, denoted by $B(C)$.*

In the following lemma, we apply the results shown in *timed petri nets* [27] to establish the minimum average activation rate of nodes in a SDFP.

Lemma 5.2 *Let G be a SDFP, the activation rate of any nodes on machine M is no greater than:*

$$min\{\frac{B(C_k)}{l} : k = 1, 2, ..., q\}$$

where C_k, k = 1,2,...,q are all simple cycles in G, and B(C_k) is the balancing ratio of C_k.

[3]The outdegree of a node may also affect its maximum possible activation rate. However, we will ignore this impact as we assume the fanout of nodes in a dataflow graph are bounded by a very small constant (e.g., 2 - 4). The treatment of this factor will appear in another application.

[4]Simple cycles are cycles in which each node appears at most once. For our purpose, only simple cycles are considered.

Proof of Lemma 5.2.
Since SDFP is a dataflow graph (i.e., a decision-free petri net), the validity of the lemma is immediate from [26,27]. □

5.2 Limited Balancing

Lemma 5.2 sets an upper bound on the maximum average activation rate for any node in G. Note that this bound depends only on the cycle with the minimum balancing ratio. In other words, higher balancing ratios for other cycles in G cannot improve this bound, although a higher fine-grain synchronization cost is implied by keeping a higher balancing ratio. Based on this observation, a compiler can perform an optimization by reducing the balancing ratios of all cycles in the graph to the minimum. We begin with the following definition.

Definition 5.3 *A graph is (limitedly) balanced with balancing ratio, $B(G)$, if all directed simple cycles, C_i, in the graph have the same balancing ratio: i.e., $B(C_i) = B(G)$ for all i.*

Figure 5 gives an example to illustrate the notion of limited balancing and the concept of balancing factor. In fact, full balancing is only a special case of limited balancing where B(G)=1/2. The more the graph becomes unbalanced, the less the value of B(G). It is beyond the scope of this paper to conduct an in-depth study into the algorithmic aspect of limited balancing (which is the subject of another paper). In the following discussion, we assume that our target graph G has already been transformed into a *limited balanced graph*.

Intuitively, $l/B(G)$ determines the minimum latency between two consecutive initiations of the graph, where l is the firing time of a node (recall the fact that our machine M has l stages). According to Lemma 5.2, the maximum initiation rate of G cannot exceed $B(G)/l$.

Lemma 5.3 *Let G be a (limitedly) balanced SDFP with n nodes and a balancing ratio $B(G)$. Then the maximum average initiation rate of G on machine M is no greater than $\frac{B(G)}{l}$ where l is the pipeline length of the machine M.*

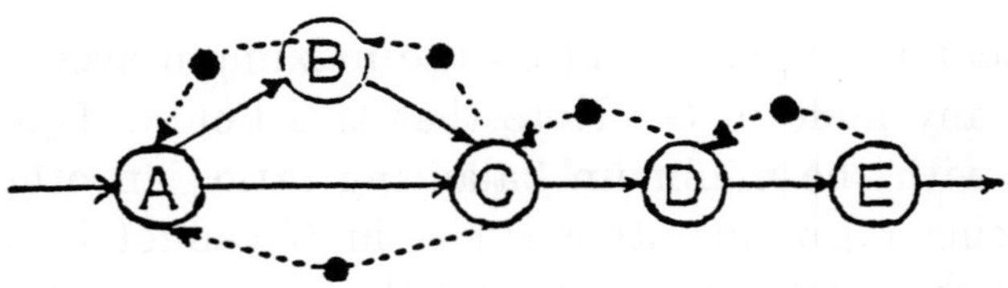

G 1

G1 is unbalanced. It has 5 simple cycles and the cycle C : A-B-C-A has the minimum balancing ratio, i.e.: B(C) = 1/3.

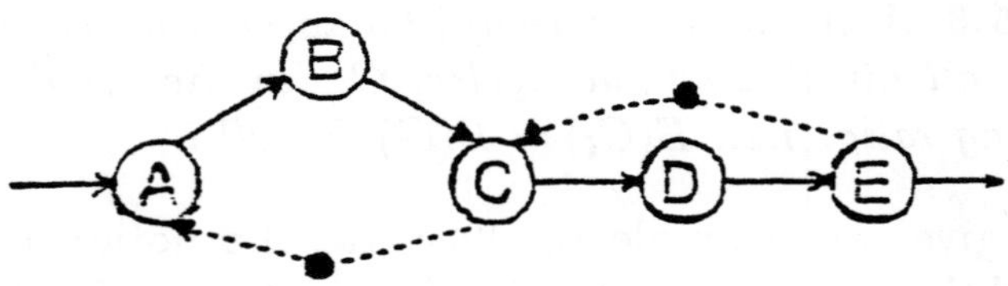

G 2

G2 is limitedly balanced with a balancing ratio B(G2) = 1/3.

Figure 5: Balancing ratio for some example graphs

Proof of Lemma 5.3
Consider the input node s of G. Since the maximum average activation rate of s is bounded by $\frac{B(G)}{l}$, the lemma follows immediately from lemma 5.2. □

With the help of lemma 5.3, we are now ready to present the following theorem as an extension of lemma 5.3.

Theorem 5.2 *Let G be a balanced SDFP with n nodes. Let $B(G)$ be the balancing factor of G. Then, under a greedy (runtime) fire scheduling of a machine M and after a sufficiently long sequence of initiations, the average initiation rate of G will be $1/n$ provided $n \geq l/B(G)$, where l is the pipeline length of the machine M.*

Before we prove the theorem, let us first state the following observation.

Observation 5.1 *Let G be a SDFP. Then, under a greedy (runtime) fire scheduling of a machine M and after a sufficiently long sequence of initiations, the average initiation rate approaches a constant.*

We now give an intuitive argument for Observation 5.1. Let the state of G be defined as a sequence of *configurations* where a configuration is an assignment of tokens to the arcs in G. A state transition is caused by the firing (activation) of an actor in G. Acute readers may immediately recognize that such configurations correspond to the concept of markings in petri net terminology. Since G is finite, and the number of tokens on each arc is bounded by one, the total number of configurations is finite. Therefore, after a long sequence of state transitions (or, initiations), the state transition sequence must be repetitive (A greedy mechanism will avoid all self-transitions). Therefore, after a sufficiently long sequence of initiations, the average initiation rate must approach a constant — we say a *steady* average initiation rate is reached. Now we are ready to prove the main theorem.

Proof of Theorem 5.2
From theorem 5.1, G can never have an average initiation rate higher than $1/n$. According to Observation 5.1, let us assume that the

steady average initiation rate is reached (after a sufficiently long sequence of initiations) which is less than 1/n. Under this assumption, the utilization of the pipeline must be less than 100%. From lemma 5.3, since $n \geq l/B(G)$ and the graph is (limitedly) balanced with a balancing ratio B(G), nothing will prevent new initiations to be made (by a greedy firing schedule) during the time slots which are not utilized, therefore the initiation rate will increase – a contradiction to the assumption that the steady initiation rate is reached. Therefore the theorem follows immediately. □

6 Space Efficiency and Synchronization Cost

Let us consider the space efficiency and synchronization cost of dataflow software pipelining. We can observe the following features:

- **Space Requirement.** Obviously, under software pipelining the storage requirement of a loop L has a constant upper bound, since only one copy of the loop is used and its storage space is shared by successive iterations. When the program graph is fully balanced, its storage requirement is maximum (at most one word for each arc in the body graph of the loop plus some buffer storage). If the graph has limited balancing, the storage requirement may be considerably less. From our experience, the bound is likely to be very small for most loops to which dataflow software pipelining may be applied.

- **Space Management.** A compiler for dataflow software pipelining does not need to perform register allocation, as a separate task from the loop scheduling (e.g., limited balancing). Instead, space allocation is performed under a unified framework with the scheduling for time efficiency. Once the limited balancing of the graph with the desired balancing ratio has been performed, we are assured of both time and space efficiency simultaneously. One attractive aspect is that the runtime storage management is totally transparent to the user (compiler). Each location (an arc, or the corresponding FIFO) is repeatedly updated and used directly under the fine-grain dataflow architecture model.

- **Reducing Synchronization Overhead**. through limited balancing, unnecessary acknowledgement signals for fine-grain synchronization can be reduced.

Of course, even with the above advantages, we still would like to know if we can minimize the space requirement under the limited balancing scheme. Recall that we are setting the balancing ratio B(G) such that it can just keep the pipeline fully busy, according to theorem 5.2. Let us call it the *critical balancing ratio* CB(G), where CB(G) = l/n. We believe that the buffer storage needed to achieve the critical balancing ratio can be minimized using techniques along the line presented in [9]. This is a subject currently under investigation.

7 Simulation Results

In this section, we apply our method of dataflow software pipelining to the McGill Dataflow Architecture Model (MDFA) – a realistic pipelined dataflow processor. The basic architecture of a processing element (PE) has two parts: a *dataflow instruction scheduling unit* (DISU) and a *pipelined instruction processing unit* (PIPU). The PIPU is an instruction processor that uses conventional techniques to achieve fast pipelined operation. The DISU holds the dataflow signal graph of the collection of dataflow instructions (actors) allocated to the processing element, and maintains a large pool of enabled instructions available for execution by the PIPU.

When an instruction is about to be executed, a *fire signal* containing a p-instruction address, say i, is presented by the DISU to the input of PIPU. The PIPU will then process it in a fashion similar to that of any conventional pipelined architecture, i.e., it goes through the normal stages such as instruction fetch, operand fetch, execution, and result store stages. The major difference is that after the execution is completed, the PIPU will deliver a *done signal* containing the instruction address (in this case, *i*) to DISU where the scheduling of instruction execution is performed. The DISU processes the *signal list* of the instruction *i* and sends a *count signal* for each instruction on the list. When an instruction receives all of its required signals, it becomes enabled. The DISU also acts as an enabled instruction scheduler and will send enabled instruction addresses to the PIPU for execution. For more information on the MDFA architecture, the readers are referred to [7].

For our simulations, we use as an example, the SISAL version of the Livermore loop 7 (loop7) which computes the equation of state fragment (a typical forall loop):

```
type OneDim = array[double];
function Loop7(m: integer; R,T:real;
                    U,Y,Z: OneDim; returns OneDim)
    for k in 1,m
        returns array of
            U[k] + R * (Z[k] + R * Y[k]) +
            T * (
                U[k+3] + R * (U[k+2] + R * U[k+1]) +
                T * (U[k+6] + R * (U[k+5] + R * U[k+4]))
            )
    end for
end function
```

This loop returns a one-dimensional array of size m. R and T are coefficients, while U, Y, and Z are input arrays that are used for the construction of the returned array. The value of m is known at compile time so that arrays are generated monolithically.

The compiler/architecture testbed that has been used throughout the simulation tests consists of a compiler and a MDFA simulator. The prototype SISAL compiler can translate the SISAL code into pipelined machine code without balancing. We perform limited balancing manually according to the need of the simulation. The fanouts of the nodes in the graph are kept under three. In each simulation run, limited balancing was only applied to one simple

PIPU: 1, DISU Signal Processing Capacity: ∞, Pipeline Stages: 8 l: 8, n: 60, CB(G) = $\frac{1}{7.5}$						
Balance Factor (B)	$\frac{1}{2}$	$\frac{1}{3}$	$\frac{1}{4}$	$\frac{1}{5}$	$\frac{1}{6}$	$\frac{1}{7}$
Avg. Init. Cycle	60	60	60	60	60	66
Avg. Instr. Delay	11.08	11.14	6.34	3.68	1.73	1.28
Run Time	12,119	12,113	12,096	12,102	12,114	13,305
Utilization	99.1%	99.2%	99.3%	99.3%	99.2%	90.3%

Table 1: Simulation results for 1 PIPU

cycle of the graph in order to ease the job of manipulating the large number of signal arcs manually.

Table 1 shows the simulation results for the machine configuration of 1 pipeline (1 PIPU) with 8 pipelined stages and infinite DISU Signal Processing Capacity.[5] The top row of the table indicates the associated machine configuration, size of the SDFP graph, n, and the predicted critical balancing ratio *CB(G)* computed with theorem 5.2. Each column of the tables gives the corresponding results of applying a distinct balancing ratio (B) to the graph. The *Average Initiation Cycle* records the average pipelining period of each node in the graph; the average initiation rate of the graph is simply the reciprocal of it. The *Average Instruction Delay* records the average time delay of the enabled instruction waiting in the fire queue, which implicitly represents the amount of parallelism exposed in the graph that has not been fully exploited by the execution pipe.

Here is a summary of the major observations from table 1 :

- In all simulation runs, we have observed that the loop initiation sequence will enter a steady state: a constant average initiation rate was reached. This confirms observation 4.1.
- Once the average initiation rate *1/n* is achieved, the pipeline

[5]The DISU Signal Processing Capacity defines the number of count signals that the DISU process per PIPU pipe beat. In the definition of the machine M, we have assumed that it has enough fine-grain synchronization power; therefore, in the simulation, the DISU Signal Processing Capacity was set to infinite.

is maximally utilized. Hence, the prediction of theorem 5.1 is confirmed.

- The critical balancing ratio predicted by theorem 5.2 for this loop is 1/7.5. Our simulation results are very close to this prediction. At B = 1/6, the pipeline is near fully utilized. The slight difference from the predicted 1/7 will be discussed below.

- The average instruction delay decreases gradually as the balancing ratio decreases. When the balancing ratio reaches the critical value, no excessive parallelism is exposed which may not be efficiently utilized, and the average instruction delay approaches its minimum.

The limited balancing scheme will reduce the amount of count signals to be handled by the DISU. In this case, if the limited balancing is applied to the entire graph, the total number of signal arcs will be reduced considerably.

As we pointed out above, we have found that there is a deviation in the observed value of the critical balancing ratio from the value predicted by theorem 5.2. This is due to the fact that, in our formal model, we have been assuming that the fanout factor is a small number (cf. section 4.1). This fanout factor cannot be ignored in reality. We have performed simulations on the code directly generated by the compiler where the largest fanout is 9. In this situation, an even larger deviation is observed. The formalization of the effects of the fanout factor is currently under investigation.

Finally, Table 2 displays the simulation results for the machine configuration of two execution pipes (2 PIPU). We can observe that the method of limited balancing can also be extended to multiple execution pipes, and the value of l is simply the multiplication of the number of PIPUs and the pipeline length. Note also that the average initiation rate is two times the original rate in this case.

PIPU: 2, DISU Signal Processing Capacity: ∞, Pipeline Stages: 8 k: 16, n: 60, CB(G) $= \frac{1}{3.75}$				
Balance Factor (B)	$\frac{1}{2}$	$\frac{1}{3}$	$\frac{1}{4}$	$\frac{1}{5}$
Avg. Init. Cycle	30	30	35	43
Avg. Instr. Delay	1.56	1.62	0.36	0.31
Run Time	6,145	6,140	7,111	8,699
Utilization	97.7%	97.8%	84.5%	69%

Table 2: Loop7 running on a 2-PIPU PE

8 Extensions

The basic framework presented in this paper can be extended in a number of ways. Here are some hints.

One way to handle graphs containing conditionals is to apply limited balancing technique to subgraphs in both branches. When each branch is considered separately, a different balancing ratio may be derived. As in our previous work on full balancing [9], we can take a somewhat conservative approach by always use the higher balancing ratio (between the two arms of the conditional) when applying theorem 5.2.

If the loop contains loop-carried dependencies, the graph may contain cycles with some back edges due to data dependencies between iterations. However, the notion of balancing ratio and limited balancing introduced in Section 4 are already based on graphs with cycles (with the augmented acknowledgement arcs as back edges). Hence, the basic framework can be extended directly to handle loops with loop-carried dependencies.

We can note that the basic framework has not excluded the possibility of having nodes with different execution times. The notion of balancing ratio can be extended straightforwardly for cycles where nodes have different execution times. The limited balancing algorithm should be modified to accommodate the new situation, and we do not expect any difficulty for such extensions.

Finally, it was pointed out to us (by Pingali, K. at Cornell) that the *percolation scheduling* techniques can be easily combined with our work to unwind the loop and compact the code so that more parallelism can be exposed. As a result, we are able to handle loops where the assumption ($2l \leq n$) does not hold (see Section 4).

9 Conclusions

This paper has outlined a general framework of compiling loops for fine-grain software pipelining under a pipelined machine model. It is interesting to compare our work with the loop "throttling" recently proposed as a powerful technique for the exploitation of loop parallelism in dynamic dataflow machines [3]. In some sense, our limited balancing suggests a way to judiciously "unravel" a loop at compile-time for pipelined execution to achieve both time and space efficiency. However, unlike loop "throttling", our scheme will use the same code and data memory space for the entire loop pipelining, avoiding the overhead for the allocation and management of space and tags.

A prototype compiler testbed is being developed to experiment with dataflow software pipelining on a newly proposed McGill Dataflow Architecture Model [14]. Work is underway to implement the limited balancing techniques in the experimental compiler for further simulation studies.

10 Acknowledgment

I would like to thank the Natural Science and Engineering Research Council (NSERC) for their support of this work and thank the Bell Northern Research Council (BNR) for their support of research in parallel processing and dataflow. I would also like to thank Herbert Hum, Philip Wong and Ning Qi for their work contributed to this paper. Ravi Shanker has helped in the preparation of the final manuscript of this paper.

Appendix A: A Proof of the CSSP Problem

The following is a formulation of the code scheduling problem for a single pipeline:

Definition 10.1 *The code scheduling problem for a single pipeline (CSSP Problem) is the following:*

Input: A constraint graph G and a positive integer k;

Output: A sequence of operations (nodes in G plus no-ops) $v_1, v_2, \ldots, v_n$ such that:

- the number of no-ops is less than or equal to k;
- if the no-ops are deleted, the result is a topological sort of the nodes in graph G;
- any two nodes u, v are separated by a number of nodes greater than or equal to the length of the delay $d(u, v)$ as required by the constraint.

The CSSP problem can be reduced to the resources-constraint job-shop scheduling problem for two processors, which is known to be NP-complete [31]. In the following, we outline a proof of the claim. Although the same conclusion was first derived in [25], here we give a proof which, we believe, is more complete.

Proof: We first state the resource-constraint two-processor job-shop scheduling problem (RC2PS problem):

Input:

1. two processors;
2. a set of jobs each taking one time unit for completion;
3. a resource R that can be accessed by at most one job at each time step;
4. a DAG G representing the precedence constraints between jobs;
5. a deadline D (a positive integer).

Output: a legal schedule for the jobs that meets the deadline D.

Now we show that RC2PS $\propto$ CSSP.

Given an instance of RC2PS, let G be the precedence constraints DAG. Let N be the number of nodes in G. We construct a constraint graph for CSSP as follows (same construction as in [25]:
(1) label all edges in the precedence graph G by "1";
(2) if u and v are jobs that require the resource, add an undirected edge (u, v) labeled "1";
(3) add a disjoint directed path of D nodes $s1, s2, \ldots, sD$, called the *s-nodes*, in which edges are labeled "2";
(4) add a start node s and edges labeled "0" from the start node to each node in the precedence graph without any ancestors, and an edge labeled "2" from the start node to the first node *s1* of the added path.

Let k equal $2D-N$. Now we show that the RC2PS has a schedule meeting the deadline if and only if the CSSP has a schedule with at most $k = 2D - N$ no-ops.

The if part. If CSSP problem has a schedule with at most k no-ops, then the two adjacent s-nodes must be separated in the schedule by exactly two nodes of G or no-ops. Otherwise the total number of no-ops in the schedule will be at least $2D - N + 1$. Therefore, the schedule for the CSSP must look like:

$s \quad n_1 \quad n_2 \quad s_1 \quad n_3 \quad n_4 \quad s_2 \ldots$

where n_1, n_2 ... are either nodes in G or no-ops. Now the following is a schedule for the RC2PS that meets the deadline:

processor	step1	step2	$\cdots$
p1	$n1$	$n3$	$\cdots$
p2	$n2$	$n4$	$\cdots$

For each processor the number of operations is at most D.

The only-if part. Assume that the following is a schedule for the RS2PS problem:

processor1 $\; n_1 \quad n_2 \quad \cdots \quad n_r, \quad r \leq D,$
processor2 $\; m_1 \quad m_2 \quad \cdots \quad m_t, \quad t \leq D,$

where n_i and m_i are the jobs to be done at time i.

Then $s \; n_1 \; m_1 \; s_1 \; n_2 \; m_2 \; s_2 \ldots \; s_D$ is a schedule for CSSP, and the number of no-ops in it is at most k. It is easy to check that the feasibility for the pipeline and the number of no-ops is at most:

$$(D-s)+(D-t)=[(s+t)-N]+(D-s)+(D-t)=2D-N.$$

This completes the proof. □

References

[1] W.B. Ackerman and J.B. Dennis. *VAL — A Value-Oriented Algorithmic Language.* Technical Report 218, Laboratory for Computer Science, MIT, 1979.

[2] A. Aiken and A. Nicolau. Optimal loop parallelization. In *Proc. of the 1988 ACM SIGPLAN Conf. on Programming Languages Design and Implementation*, June 1988.

[3] Arvind and D.E. Culler. Managing resources in a parallel machine. In J.V. Woods, editor, *Fifth Generation Computer Architecture*, pages 103–121, Elsevier Science Publishers, 1986.

[4] D. Bernstein and I. Gertner. Scheduling expressions on a pipelined processor with a maximal delay of one cycle. *ACM Transactions on Programming Languages and Systems*, 11(1):57–66, Jan. 1989.

[5] E.G. Coffman. *Computer and Job-Shop Scheduling Theory.* John Wiley and Sons, New York, 1976.

[6] J.B. Dennis. Data flow for supercomputers. In *Proceeding of 1984 CompCon*, March 1984.

[7] J.B. Dennis and G.R. Gao. *An Efficient Pipelined Dataflow Processor Architecture.* Technical Report TR-SOCS-88.06, School of Computer Science, McGill University, Montreal, Que., Feb. 1988.

[8] J.B. Dennis, G.R. Gao, and K.W. Todd. Modeling the weather with a data flow supercomputer. *IEEE Trans. on Computers*, C-33(7):592–603, 1984.

[9] G. R. Gao. *A Pipelined Code Mapping Scheme for Static Dataflow Computers.* Technical Report TR-371, Laboratory for Computer Science, MIT, 1986.

[10] G.R. Gao. Aspects of balancing techniques for pipelined data flow code generation. *Journal of Parallel and Distributed Computing*, 6:39–61, 1989.

[11] G.R. Gao. *A Flexible Architecture Model for Hybrid Dataflow and Control-Flow Evaluation.* ACAPS Technical Memo 07, School of Computer Science, McGill University, Montreal, Que., Jan. 1989.

[12] G.R. Gao. A maximally pipelined tridiagonal linear equation solver. *Journal of Parallel and Distributed Computing*, 3(2):215–235, June 1986.

[13] G.R. Gao. *Maximum Pipelining of Array Computation — A Data Flow Approach.* Technical Report TR-SOCS-87.12, School of Computer Science, McGill University, Montreal, Que., Sept. 1987.

[14] G.R. Gao and Z. Paraskevas. Compiling for dataflow software pipelining. In *Proc. of the Second Workshop on Languages and Compilers for Parallel Computing*, Illinois, Aug. 1989. To be published by Pitman in their series Monographs in Parallel and Distributed Computing.

[15] G.R. Gao, R. Yates, J.B. Dennis, and L. Mulline. An efficient monolithic array constructor. In *Proc. of the 3rd Workshop on Languages and Compilers for Parallel Computing, Irvine, CA, to be published by MIT Press*, 1990.

[16] M.R. Garey and D.S. Johnson. *Computers and Intractability: A guide to the Theory of NP-Completeness.* W.H. Freeman and Company, 1979.

[17] P.B. Gibbons and S.S. Muchnik. Efficient instruction scheduling for a pipelined architecture. In *Proc. of the ACM Symp. on Compiler Construction*, pages 11–16, Palo Alto, Calif., June 1986.

[18] J. Hennessy and T. Gross. Postpass code optimization of pipelined constraints. *ACM Transactions on Programming Languages and Systems*, 5(3):422–448, July 1983.

[19] P. Hudak. Conception, evolution, and application of functional programming languages. *Computing Surveys*, 21(3), Sept. 1989.

[20] P.M. Kogge. *The Architecture of Pipelined Computers.* McGraw-Hill Book Company, New York, 1981.

[21] D.J. Kuck, R.H. Kuhn, D.A. Padua, B. Leasure, and M. Wolfe. Dependence graphs and compiler optimizations. In *Proc. of the 8th ACM Symp. on Principles of Prog. Lang.*, pages 207–218, 1981.

[22] S.Y. Kung, S.C. Lo, and P.S. Lewis. Timing analysis and optimization of VLSI data flow arrays. In *Proc. of the 1986 International Conf. on Parallel Processing*, 1986.

[23] M. Lam. Software pipelining: An effective scheduling technique for VLIW machines. In *Proc. of the 1988 ACM SIGPLAN Conf. on Programming Languages Design and Implementation*, pages 318–328, Atlanta, Georgia, June 1988.

[24] J.R. Larus and P.N. Hilfinger. Register allocation in the SPUR Lisp compiler. In *Proc. of the ACM Symp. on Compiler Construction*, pages 255–263, Palo Alto, Calif., June 1986.

[25] A. Nicolau, K. Pingali, and A. Aiken. *Fine-Grain Compilation for Pipelined Machines.* Technical Report TR-88-934, Department of Computer Science, Cornell University, Ithaca, NY, 1988.

[26] C. V. Ramamoorthy and G. S. Ho. Performance evaluation of asynchronous concurrent systems using petri nets. *IEEE Trans. on Computers*, 440–448, Sept. 1980.

[27] C. Ramchandani. *Analysis of Asynchronous Concurrent Systems.* Technical Report TR-120, Laboratory for Computer Science, MIT, 1974.

[28] B.R. Rau and C.D. Glaeser. Some scheduling techniques and an easily schedulable horizontal architecture for high performance scientific computing. In *Proc. of the 14th Annual Workshop on Microprogramming*, pages 183–198, 1981.

[29] S.K. Skedzielewski and J. Glauert. *IF1: An Intermediate Form for Applicative Languages.* Technical Report M-170, Version 1.0, Lawrence Livermore National Laboratory, 1985.

[30] R.F. Touzeau. A FORTRAN compiler for the FPS-164 scientific computer. In *Proc. of the ACM SIGPLAN '84 Symp. on Compiler Construction*, pages 48–57, June 1984.

[31] J.D. Ullman. NP-complete scheduling problems. *J. Comput. Syst. Sci.*, 10:384–393, 1975.

5

Arrays in Sisal *

John T. Feo
Lawrence Livermore National Laboratory, L-306
P.O. Box 808
Livermore, CA 94550

Abstract

Although Sisal (Streams and Iterations in a Single Assignment Language) is a general-purpose applicative language, its expected program domain is large-scale scientific applications. Since arrays are an indispensable data structure for such applications, the designers of Sisal included arrays and a robust set of array operations in the language definition. In this paper, we review and evaluate those design decisions in light of the first Sisal compilers and runtime systems for shared-memory multiprocessor systems. In general, array intensive applications written in Sisal 1.2 execute as fast as their Fortran equivalents. However, a number of design decisions have hurt expressiveness and performance. We discuss these flaws and describe how the new language definition (Sisal 2.0) corrects them.

Introduction

Sisal 1.0 [7] was defined in 1983 and revised in 1985 (Sisal 1.2 [8]). The language definition was a collaborative effort by Lawrence Livermore National Laboratory, Colorado State University, University of Manchester, and Digital Equipment Corporation. Although Sisal is a general-purpose applicative language, its expected program domain is large-scale scientific applications. Since arrays are an indispensable data structure for such applications, the designers of Sisal included arrays and a robust set of array operations in the language definition.

---

* This document was prepared as an account of work sponsored by an agency of the United States Government. Neither the United States Government not the University of California, nor any of their employees, makes any warranty, express or implied, or assumes any legal liability or responsibility for the accuracy, completeness or usefulness of any information, apparatus, product or process herein to any specific commercial products, process, or service by trade name, trademark, manufacturer, or otherwise, does not necessarily constitute or imply its endorsement, recommendation , or favoring by the United States Government or the University of California. The views and opinions of authors

Unfortunately, defining and implementing arrays under applicative semantics is not easy. There are three major problems. First, an array, like any object, is the result of an expression. The idea of allocating storage and filling in values is alien to applicative semantics. Second, not all array definitions are legal. Since an array element can be defined at most once, any recursive definition which defines some elements more than once is illegal. Third, operations which modify arrays must first copy their operands. The cost of copying large array is prohibitive.

To solve the first problem, designers of applicative and higher-order functional languages have developed *array comprehensions* and *gather clauses*. Array comprehensions, or monolithic arrays, permit the definition of subregions of an array within a single expression. For example, a 4 x 4 block diagonal unit matrix is defined in Sisal 2.0 as

```
X := array [1..4, 1..4:
        [1..2, 1..2] 1, 1, 1, 1;
        [1..2, 3..4] 0, 0, 0, 0;
        [3..4, 1..2] 0, 0, 0, 0;
        [3..4, 3..4] 1, 1, 1, 1]]
```

Sisal 2.0 includes array comprehensions, but Sisal 1.2 does not. In Sisal 1.2, arrays are built primarily by loop expressions that deterministically assemble loop values into arrays via gather clauses. For example, vector sum is defined in Sisal 1.2 as

```
X := for i in 1, n
        z := A[i] + B[i]
     returns array of z
     end for
```

The loop body generates *n* *z*-values which are formed into an array by the returns clause.

What to do about recursive array definition is a difficult problem with no good solution. One possibility is to exclude recursive definitions all together; however, this restricts a language's ability to express certain computations and may obscure parallelism. A second alternative is to accept only those recursive definitions that can be proved legal at compile time. Recent work in this area appears promising [4]. Finally, a language designer may decide to accept all recursive definitions and rely on hardware to trap illegal expressions. This solution maximizes expressiveness, but requires special hardware and without a fine-grain implementation may introduce deadlock. Recent studies have shown fine-grain implementations to be impractical [2].

For applicative programs to execute as fast as imperative programs, copy elimination is essential. We cannot overcome the cost of copying large arrays by increased parallelism – there is simply not enough parallelism. Copy elimination in-

---

expressed herein do not necessarily state or reflect those of the United States Government or the University of California, and shall not be used for advertising or product endorsement purposes.

volves three levels of analysis: static inferencing, node reordering, and reference counting. Compile-time analysis can often identify the last user of an array. Reordering the graph to schedule read operations before write operations improves the chances of in place operations. In those instances in which analysis fails, the compiler can insert reference count operations and runtime checks to identify the last user at runtime. But if done improperly, reference counting can become a bottleneck and degrade performance [11]. In recent years researchers have made tremendous progress in the general area of copy elimination and reference count optimization in applicative and higher-order functional languages [1,5,14]. The work by Cann [1] has virtually eliminated the copy problem in Sisal.

Although conservative, the Sisal 1.2 approach has been successful. The language includes gather clauses, but neither array comprehensions nor recursive definitions (in fact, the compiler enforces a strict "definition before use" style). To eliminate copy operations, the native code compiler rearranges nodes, introduces artificial dependencies to schedule readers before writers, and inserts runtime checks when analysis fails [1]. We find that we can express most array computations easily and concisely in Sisal 1.2, and most array intensive applications execute as fast as their Fortran equivalents on shared-memory multiprocessors [3].

This paper is organized as follows. Section two describes arrays and array operations in Sisal 1.2 and discusses changes to arrays in the new language definition, Sisal 2.0 [12]. Section three presents an efficient solution for Gaussian elimination using gather operations. We compare the Sisal 1.2 code to an equivalent Fortran program on the Alliant FX/80. Section 4 discusses an array computation which is difficult to express in Sisal 1.2, but easy to express in Sisal 2.0. In section 5, we conclude by describing some of the new language directions we are pursuing.

Arrays in Sisal 1.2

Array Declaration

Sisal 1.2 includes the standard scalar types: integer, real, double precision, boolean, and character. All other types are user-defined. An array declaration specifies only the component type (any scalar or user-defined type). It does not specify size, lower or upper bound, or structure – these are specified by the expressions that create arrays. An array of integers is defined as

```
type OneDim = array[integer]
```

In Sisal 1.2, an *n*-dimensional array is an array of *(n-1)*-dimensional arrays. A two-dimensional array of integers is defined as an array of array of integers,

```
type TwoDim = array[OneDim]
```

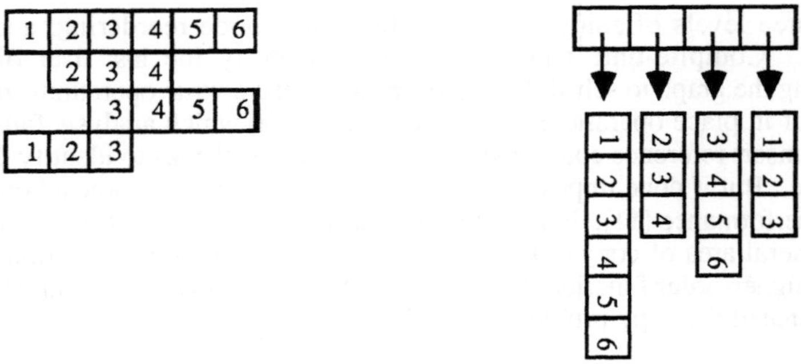

a) Logical b) Storage

Figure 1 - Hierarchial Ragged Arrays

The components of `TwoDim` can be either the rows or the columns of the mathematical array. Since the elements of an n-dimensional array are arrays, the size and bounds of each element may be different. Thus, Sisal 1.2 arrays are *hierarchical* and *ragged* [Figure 1a].

Hierarchical arrays are convenient when expressing row- or column-ordered algorithms, permit row sharing, and reduce copying costs. However, they make read operations more expensive, prevent easy access to arbitrary subcomponents (such as blocks or diagonals), and make expressing anything but a row- or column-ordered algorithm difficult. Raggedness is ideal when programming an array whose rows (columns) have different or continually changing sizes and bounds. In particle dynamics codes, an array is typically used to represent a grid of cells – each cell comprising an arbitrary number of particles. During execution, particles move from cell to cell. The continual change in cell size is easily programmed using ragged arrays. In LU-decomposition, the lower and upper triangular matrices may be stored as two ragged arrays in minimum space. However, ragged arrays do not support strides, make vectorization difficult, and require a hierarchical storage implementation [Figure 1b].

For the great majority of applications which do not need hierarchical ragged arrays, the drawbacks are severe. But, since the advantage to some applications is great, Sisal 2.0 includes both hierarchical ragged arrays and flat arrays.

Array Creation

Any expression which has type *array* creates a new array. The simplest way to create an array in Sisal 1.2 is to list the elements,

```
r := array OneDim []
s := array OneDim [1: 1,2,3]
t := array TwoDim [1: array[1:1,2,3], array[1:4,5,6]]
```

The first expression creates an empty array of integers. The type specification is mandatory. The second expression builds an array of integers with lower bound 1. The type specification is optional since it can be derived from the element list. The third expression builds a two-dimensional array (an array of arrays) of integers. *t* is similar to a flat array with two rows and three columns.

The most common way to create arrays in Sisal 1.2 is by loop expressions. The **for** expression provides a means to specify independent iterations. This expression's semantics does not allow references to values defined in other iterations. Recursive definitions are not permitted. A **for** expression comprises three parts: a range generator, a loop body, and a returns clause. Consider the expression

```
u := for i in 1,n cross j in 1,m
         z := i + j
     returns array of z
     end for
```

An instance of the loop body is executed for each *(i, j)* pair, $1 \leq i \leq n,\ 1 \leq j \leq m$. The returns clause, **array of**, deterministically gathers the *z* values into an array. The order of reduction, size, and structure of the array are specified by the range generator. Thus, *u* is a two-dimensional array with *n* rows, *m* columns, and $u[i, j] = i + j$.

For expressions are expressive, flexible, easy to implement, and exhibit good speedup on medium- and coarse-grain shared memory multiprocessors. Because the loop bodies are independent and recursive definitions are not permitted, the runtime system may execute the subexpressions in any order. Compile-time analysis inserts code to preallocate array storage where analysis or runtime calculations can determine array sizes [13]. Thus, most results are built in place eliminating useless copying [3]. **For** expressions do have one flaw – they couple the scattering of work and the gathering of result values. This is unnecessary, and results in confusion and programming errors. A common mistake is to write the transpose of an *(n x m)* matrix as

```
for i in 1,n cross j in 1,m
returns array of X[j, i]
end for
```

This expression returns an *(n x m)* matrix, not an *(m x n)* matrix. The correct expression is

```
for i in 1,m cross j in 1,n
returns array of X[j, i]
end for
```

In Sisal 2.0, the scattering of work and gathering of results are decoupled. The former governed by the range generator and the latter governed by the returns clause.

For initial expressions resemble sequential iteration in conventional languages, but retain single assignment semantics. They comprise four parts: initialization, loop body, termination test, and returns clause. The initialization segment defines all loop constants and assigns initial values to all loop-carried names. It is the first iteration of the loop. The loop body computes new values for the loop names. Unlike **for** expressions, loop values on the previous iteration are accessible – ***old*** *<name>* returns the value of *<name>* on the previous iteration. The returns clause, **array of**, gathers loop values in order into an array.

Although Sisal 1.2 prohibits recursive definitions, **for initial** expressions can build recursively defined arrays. Consider the array definition

$$X(i,\ j) = \begin{cases} 1 & i = 1 \\ 1 & j = 1 \\ X(i,\ j-1) + X(i-1,\ j) & 2 \le i \le n,\ 2 \le j \le n \end{cases}$$

A legal Sisal 1.2 expression for *X* is

```
X := for initial
       i   := 1;
       row := array_fill(1, n, 1);
     while i < n repeat
       i   := old i + 1;
        row := for initial
                 j := 1;
                 x := 1
               while j < n repeat
                 j := old j + 1;
                 x := old x + old row[j]
               returns array of x
               end for
     returns array of row
     end for
```

The expression is certainly long and obscures parallelism. It is hard to ascertain that computations along a diagonal are data independent. However, a nonstrict implementation of the loop bodies – initiate all loop bodies simultaneously and have each wait for its inputs – will realize the parallelism.

If **for initial** expressions can build recursively defined arrays and do not necessarily limit parallelism, has excluding recursive definitions cost us anything? Definitely, yes! A **for initial** expression can compute new loop values as a function of only the loop values of the previous iteration. Worse yet, **returns array of** binds the ith element of the result to the ith iteration. These two restrictions greatly complicate the programming effort and may increase copying costs. Sisal 2.0 still prohibits recursive array definitions (the performance consequences are just too great), but does allow users to specify where values computed on the *ith* iteration appear in the results.

Other Array Operations

Read operations have the form,

```
x := A[1]
```

The type of *x* is the component type of *A*. The shorthand notation, *A[i, j]*, returns the *jth* component of the *ith* component of *A*. In Sisal 1.2, you can read (access) only single elements. This is unfortunate because many array computations operate along diagonals or within blocks of an array. Sisal 2.0 permits reads to any contiguous set of elements separated by a constant stride.

Write operations have the form,

```
x := A[1: 0, 1, 2]
```

The expression preserves single assignment semantics by creating a new array, *x*, which is identical to *A* except that the first, second, and third elements are *0, 1,* and *2,* respectively. The inclusion of such explicit write operations simplifies copy elimination analysis. If the compiler can ascertain, or a runtime check can assure, that the write is the last consumer of *A*, then the update can execute in place. Although write operations can change several element values at once, the syntax is still too limiting. Values along diagonals or within blocks cannot be changed in a single expression. Like reads, Sisal 2.0 permits writes to any contiguous set of elements separated by constant stride.

Sisal 1.2 also includes operations to concatenate arrays, insert or remove values at either end of an array, set the bounds of an array, and return an array's size. Except for concatenation and array size, the more general syntax of read, write, and array creation in Sisal 2.0 supplants the other operations. It remains to be seen whether we have overly complicated copy elimination analysis by replacing explicit array modification operations with more general expressions.

LU Decomposition

LU decomposition is a method to solve systems of linear equations of the form

$$A\,x = b$$

where A is an $n \times n$ matrix, and x and b are $n \times 1$ column vectors. The method reduces A into a lower (L) and upper (U) triangular matrix. A common solution method for LU decomposition is Gaussian elimination without pivoting. The algorithm comprises n iterative steps. At step i, rows $i + 1$ to n are reduced by row i. Row i is called the pivot row and $A[i, i]$ is called the pivot element. The reduction executes in two steps:

1. $A[k, i] = A[k, i] \,/\, A[i, i], \qquad i+1 \le k \le n$

2. $A[k, l] = A[k, l] - A[k, i] * A[i, l], \quad i+1 \le k,l \le n$

L comprises the n column vectors computed in step 1 (the multipliers) and U comprises the n pivot rows.

Since A is modified every iteration, a functional implementation of Gaussian elimination creates $n - 1$ intermediate copies of A. As the computation progresses, the number of computations decreases and the amount of computationless copying increases. Solutions have ranged from proposing new algorithms [6,10] to extending the idea of monolithic arrays [4]. However, Sisal's gather operations solve the problem naturally and efficiently.

Consider the following functions

```
type OneDim  = array[double_real]
type TwoDim  = array[array[double_real]]

function GE(n: integer; A_in: TwoDim
            returns TwoDim, TwoDim)
  for initial
    i := 1;
    P := A_in[1];
    M := Multipliers(i, n, A_in);
    A := Reduce(i, n, M, A_in)
  while i < n repeat
    i := old i + 1;
    P := old A[i];
    M := Multipliers(i, n, old A);
    A := Reduce(i, n, M, old A)
  returns array of M
          array of P
  end for
end function % Gaussian Elimination
```

```
function Multipliers(i,n:integer; A: TwoDim
                               returns OneDim)
  for k in i+1, n
  returns array of A[k,i] / A[i,i]
  end for
end function % Multipliers

function Reduce(i,n: integer; M: OneDim; A: TwoDim
                         returns TwoDim)
  for k in i+1, n cross l in i+1, n
  returns array of A[k,l] - M[k] * A[i,l]
  end for
end function % Reduce
```

In **function** GE, *P* is the pivot row, *M* is the vector of multipliers, and *A* is the reduced matrix. Notice the number of rows and columns in *A* decrease by one every iteration. There is no copying and no useless computation. Every computation is necessary and computes a new value. The vectors of multipliers and pivot rows are gathered to form *L* and *U*. Both arrays are ragged; however, it is easy to extend the code to return rectangular arrays. Because the gather operation removes *P* and *M* from the computation, the code avoids useless copying. The completed portion of *L* and *U* are not carried (i.e., copied) from iteration to iteration. Unlike the equivalent Fortran code which stores the reduced matrix back into *A*, the Sisal code preallocates new storage for *A* and deallocates the storage for ***old*** *A* every iteration. Although this is cheap, it is not an insignificant expense.

We compared equivalent Sisal and Fortran versions of Gaussian elimination on a 200 x 200 problem on the Alliant FX/80. The Sisal execution times on one and five processors were 7.53 and 2.30 seconds, respectively. The Fortran execution times were 7.09 and 1.42 seconds, respectively. Memory management operations cost Sisal 1.15 and 0.61 seconds on one and five processors, respectively. In all, Sisal was 6% slower than Fortran on one processor and 62% slower on five processors. Because memory deallocation is sequential, the speedup of the Sisal code was only 3.3.

Clearly, not reusing storage hurts performance. There are two solutions. One possible optimization is to allocate space for two *n x n* arrays outside the **for initial** expression and use the two arrays alternatively for *A* and ***old*** *A*. At the end of each iteration we would swap pointers instead of allocating and deallocating memory. A second solution is to use flat arrays. We have found repeatedly that managing hierarchical arrays is expensive. The cost of allocating and deallocating a hierarchical array is linear in the product of the sizes of the outer dimensions, and the cost of accessing the innermost component is linear in the number of dimensions. For flat arrays the cost of both these operations is constant. We expect the Sisal 2.0 version of Gaussian elimination, which will include both optimizations, to execute as fast as the Fortran code.

Segmental Recomputation

Segmental recomputation is a simplification of the second Livermore Loop [9]. Let X and V be two n element vectors (assume n is a power of 2). Compute new values for X as follows:

1. Initialize *LHS, RHS,* and *VHS* as:

$$X[1..\tfrac{n}{2}],\quad X[\tfrac{n}{2}+1..\tfrac{3n}{4}],\quad V[\tfrac{n}{2}+1..\tfrac{3n}{4}]$$

2. Compute new values for the elements of *RHS*

$$RHS(i) = LHS(2 * i) + V(i) \qquad 1 \le i \le \tfrac{n}{4}$$

3. Advance LHS, RHS, and VHS:

$$X[\tfrac{n}{2}+1..\tfrac{3n}{4}],\quad X[\tfrac{3n}{4}+1..\tfrac{7n}{8}],\quad V[\tfrac{3n}{4}+1..\tfrac{7n}{8}]$$

4. Go to step 2

Continue until X is exhausted. The algorithm comprises ***Log n*** iterative steps. Figure 2 depicts the algorithm's state after the first step. The computations at Step 2 are data independent and can execute in parallel. Moreover, since *LHS* and *RHS* are disjoint, X can be updated in place.

Since Sisal 1.2 lacks subarray operations, the *(Log n) RHS* vectors must be built independently and gathered into an array by the reduction operation

```
returns value of catenate rhs
```

The Sisal 1.2 code is

```
type OneDim = array[double_real]

function SegRec(X, V: OneDim returns OneDim)
  for initial
    n   := array_size(X) / 2;
    vhs := 0;
    rhs := array_adjust(X, 1, n)
  while n > 1 repeat
    n   := old n / 2;
    vhs := old vhs + old n;
    rhs := for i in 1, n
             returns array of
                old rhs[2 * i] + V[vhs + i]
           end for
```

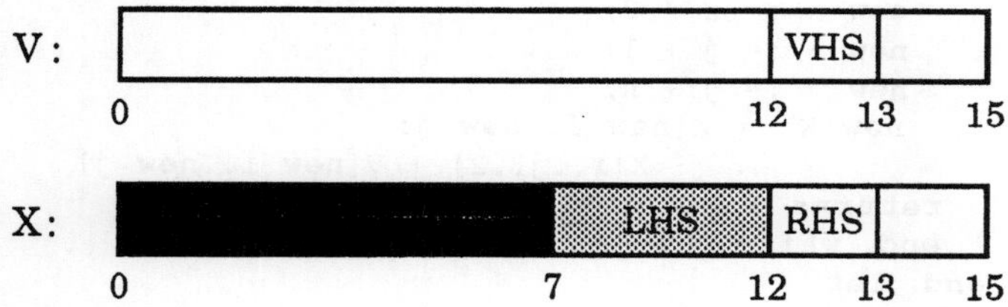

Figure 2 - Segmental Recomputation

```
      returns value of catenate rhs
      end for
   end function % Segmental Recomputation
```

Two points about the code: 1) instead of forming the subvector *VHS* every iteration, we use a pointer, *vhs,* to point to the start of the subvector; and 2) observe that *LHS* is just ***old** RHS*.

The performance of this routine is dismal; in fact, regardless of the size of *X*, computing the new values for *X* one at a time is faster. The Sisal optimizers fail completely on this code. First, the runtime system allocates new memory for *rhs* every iteration, and deallocates ***old** rhs* every iteration. Second, the optimizers fail to recognize (and who can blame them) that *X* can be updated in place. Third, the build-in-place analysis fails to preallocate memory for the result. Thus, not only do we copy *rhs* every iteration as we move it into the result, we also copy the partial result every iteration as it grows and requires more space. The optimization discussed in the previous chapter (allocate two arrays outside the **for initial** expression and switch back and forth) alleviates the first problem, and an enhanced build-in-place analyzer solves the third problem. But unless *X* is updated in place, the cost of copying *rhs* every iteration will destroy performance. The computation per loop body (one addition) is too small to recuperate much, if any, of the cost.

The problem is not weak optimizers, but poor syntax. The lack of subarray operations destroys all hope of realizing that *X* can by updated-in-place. In Sisal 2.0, which includes subarray operations, the algorithm is clean, concise, and easily optimized for update-in-place. The Sisal 2.0 code is

```
  type OneDim = array[double_real]

  function SegRec(X, V: OneDim returns OneDim)
    let
      n := size(x) / 2;
      i := 1;
      j := n
    in
      while n > 1 do
```

```
          new n := n / 2;
          new i := j + 1;
          new j := j + n;
          new X := X[new i..new j:
                        X[i..j..2] + V[new i..new j]
        returns X
        end while
     end let
  end function % Segmental Recomputation
```

Here we use *i* and *j* to point to the start and end of each subvector. The plus operation on Line 13 is an element-by-element vector addition. The update of *X* is now obvious. Moreover, it is easy for the compiler to realize that the subarray of *X* which is written, *X[**new** i..**new** j]*, is disjoint from the subarray which is read, *X[i..j..2]*, since ***new*** *i := j + 1* (Line 10).

Conclusions

In this paper we discussed the definition of arrays in Sisal 1.2 and the changes to arrays in the new language definition, Sisal 2.0. The biggest changes are: true multidimensional arrays (flat arrays), array comprehensions, and subarray operations. We showed that these changes can yield more readable code and better performance. We are hopeful that the optimization techniques developed for Sisal 1.2 are extendable to the new language definition. The goal of any functional language must be to achieve equivalent, or better, performance than Fortran; otherwise, the language will not be widely accepted. Sisal 1.2 did achieve Fortran-like speed on shared-memory multiprocessors. We believe Sisal 2.0 can achieve even better performance.

Acknowledgements

I would like to thank David Cann for helping me attain and analyze the performance data presented in Section 3. We used the Alliant FX/80 at the Northeast Parallel Architectures Center. I would also like to thank David Cann and Tom DeBoni for proofreading this paper and making a number of useful suggestions. Finally, I would like to thank the organizing committee of the First International Workshop on Arrays, Functional Languages, and Parallel Systems for inviting me to speak.

This work was performed under the auspices of the U.S. Department of Energy by Lawrence Livermore National Laboratory under contract No. W-7405-Eng-48.

References

1. Cann, D. C. Compilation Techniques for High Performance Applicative Computation. Ph.D. thesis, Department of Computer Science, Colorado State University, 1989.

2. Culler, D. E. *Managing Parallelism and Resources in Scientific Dataflow Programs.* Ph.D. thesis, Department of Electrical Engineering and Computer Science, Massachusetts Institute of Technology, 1989.

3. Feo, J. T., D. C. Cann and R. R. Oldehoeft. The Sisal Language Project. to appear *Journal of Parallel and Distributed Computing,* December 1990.

4. Gao G. R. and R. K. Yates. An Efficient Monolithic Array Constructor. in *Proceedings of the 3rd Workshop on Languages and Compilers for Parallel Computing,* Irvine, CA, August 1990.

5. Hudak, P. and A. Bloss. The aggregate update problem in functional programming systems. *Proc. Twelfth ACM Symposium on the Principles of Programming Languages.* ACM, New Orleans, LA, January 1985, pp. 300-313.

6. Hudak, P. and S. Anderson. *Haskell Solutions to the Language Session Problems at the 1988 Salishan High-Speed Computing Conference.* Yale University Technical Report YALEU/DCS/RR-627, Yale University, New Haven, CT, January 1988.

7. McGraw, J. R. et. al. *Sisal: Streams and iterations in a single-assignment language, Language Reference Manual, Version 1.1.* Lawrence Livermore National Laboratory Manual M-146, Lawrence Livermore National Laboratory, Livermore, CA, June 1983.

8. McGraw, J. R. et. al. *Sisal: Streams and iterations in a single-assignment language, Language Reference Manual, Version 1.2.* Lawrence Livermore National Laboratory Manual M-146 (Rev. 1), Lawrence Livermore National Laboratory, Livermore, CA, March 1985.

9. McMahon, F. H. *Livermore Fortran Kernels: A Computer Test of the Numerical Performance Range.* Lawrence Livermore National Laboratory Technical Report UCRL-53745, Lawrence Livermore National Laboratory, Livermore, CA, December 1986.

10. Nikhil, R. S. and Arvind. *Id: a language with implicit parallelism.* Computations Structures Group Memo 305, Massachusetts Institute of Technology, Cambridge, MA, February 1990.

11. Oldehoeft, R. R. and D. C. Cann. Applicative parallelism on a shared-memory multiprocessor. *IEEE Software* **5**, 1 (January 1988), pp. 62-70.

12. Oldehoeft, R. R., D. C. Cann, et. al. *SISAL Language Manual, Version 2.0.* in preparation.

13. Ranelletti, J. E. Graph Transformation Algorithms for Array Memory Optimization in Applicative Languages. Ph.D. thesis, Department of Computer Science, University of California at Davis/Livermore, 1987.

14. Skedzielewski, S. K. and R. J. Simpson. A simple method to remove reference counting in applicative programs. *Proc. ACM SIGPLAN '89 Conference on Programming Language Design and Implementation,* Portland, OR, June 1989.

6

Falafel: Arrays in a Functional Language

Carl McCrosky, Kanad Roy, and Ken Sailor
Department of Computational Science,
University of Saskatchewan,
Canada, S7N 0W0

Falafel, a functional programming language with first-class arrays, is being developed at the University of Saskatchewan. It is an experimental vehicle for work in language definition and implementation. This paper discusses some of the fundamental design decisions that underlie the language and its implementations. Falafel has drawn ideas from array-based programming languages (APL [Iverson] and Nial [Jenkins] [More]), functional programming languages (Miranda™ [Turner] and Haskell [Haskell]), and dataflow programming languages (Id [Nikhil] and Sisal [Sisal]). This paper discusses the nature of Falafel's value space, the structure of arrays, the role of strong polymorphic typing, the use of lazy evaluation, and a means of partial definition of arrays. A full definition of Falafel is to be published separately.

FUNCTIONAL ARRAY LANGUAGES

Programming languages can be divided into two groups: imperative languages and declarative languages. Imperative language semantics include the notion of sequencing through a list of commands which alter state variables. Declarative languages do not support mutation of state. A principal advantage of declarative languages is that their semantics are much simpler due to this lack of state. This relative simplicity enables powerful forms of reasoning about programs, and permits a wider variety of implementations.

Declarative languages fall into three categories: logic languages, term re-writing languages, and functional languages. Logic languages are based on logical relations (e.g., Prolog). Term re-writing languages are based on the ideas of universal algebras (e.g., OBJ3). Functional languages are based on the mathematical notion of functions. Although all three categories of declarative languages have compelling advantages, we are interested in functional languages because they can be mapped most directly to efficient implementations (due to the lack of backtracking) and because they support higher order functional objects.

All functional languages can be seen as syntactic sugarings of the lambda calculus. The lambda calculus gives a simple and powerful basis for the definition and implementation of functional languages [Peyton Jones].

Imperative programming languages offer arrays as a means of structuring data. Most functional languages use nested lists, or tuples, as their principal data structure. This choice seriously limits the utility of functional languages, as constant time access to large structures is abandoned. (The tree is the most efficient structure that can be constructed from nested lists, with $O(\log N)$ access time. A flat, indexable array requires only $O(1)$).

Thus it is interesting to study functional languages which incorporate arrays. Several research groups have addressed this problem. APL and Nial are array-based languages with powerful functional subsets. Sisal and Id are single assignment data flow languages which support arrays. (Single assignment languages have functional semantics). Haskell, a recent pure functional programming language, incorporates arrays.

A language has *first-class arrays* if arrays can contain any type supported by the language, and functions can map from and to arrays. We are studying semantic and implementation issues of functional languages with first-class arrays. This paper discusses the directions our research has taken, and contrasts our work with other array language projects, and with functional language research in general. In particular, we discuss the design decisions taken in the definition of our experimental language, Falafel (Functional Array Language for Experiments in Laziness).

VALUE DOMAINS

Every programming language has a domain of computable values, or universal value space, *V*. It is necessary to consider how arrays fit into these domains. We begin by examining APL and Nial. In these languages, the concept of arrays is so crucial to the domain of computable values, that the languages are said to be "array based."

APL's value domain is modelled by Equation 1. Primitive types are lumped together in the domain *Prim*, as they are not important to this paper. $array_x$ is the array domain constructor for language *x*. In APL there are two sorts (types) of values: scalars and arrays. Arrays contain only scalars. Equation 1 states that APL's arrays contain only primitive values, not other arrays. Thus, APL does not permit nested arrays. APL2 is an extension to APL that does permit nested arrays.

$$V_a = \text{Prim} + \text{array}_a(\text{Prim}) \qquad \text{(Eq. 1)}$$

Nial, based on More's *array theory* [More], has one-sorted data values. All values are arrays. Primitive values are self-containing arrays of zero dimensions, called *motes*. As the domain is one-sorted, arrays nest arrays as items. In theory, nesting is never terminated, as motes are self-containing. The value domain of array theory is modelled by Equation 2:

$$V_n = \text{array}_n(V_n + \text{motes}_n) \qquad \text{(Eq. 2)}$$

As modelled by the V_n argument to $array_n$, Nial's arrays can be nested. Nesting is a major advance in arrays, particularly in a functional language. Nested arrays permit information that might otherwise have to be coded in the program text to be contained in the data. For instance, rather than explicitly loop or recur over the rows of a table, Nial can construct a list of the rows of the table, and map an operation onto each row. In Nial, this bit of coding is done as *each f rows t*, where *f* is the function to be applied to each of the rows of the table *t*.

Although Nial is sometimes referred to as a one-sorted language, it is in fact three-sorted. Nial's three sorts are *arrays*, functions on arrays called *operations*, and functions on functions called *transformers*.

Modern functional languages such as Miranda and ML do not include arrays. Their value domains, however, are of interest. Unlike APL and Nial, which incorporate only arrays and scalars (in some form), functional languages have more general value domains based on mathematical type theory. These languages incorporate some set of primitive types and three mechanisms for constructing new types. These mechanisms are sums (+), products (*), and functions (→).

Sum types form a new type from two component types; the result type can contain values from either component type. Functional languages make use of discriminated sums, where the values in the union are tagged according to the type from which they come. The sum constructor then requires that tags be supplied for the constituent types, as in *(b Bool) + (c Char)*. Values in this sum type can be discriminated by their tag, either *b* or *c*.

Product types form tuples from component types. Thus *Int * Bool* is a two-tuple whose first item is an integer and whose second element is boolean. Sum and product types may be combined, as in Miranda, into the *sum-of-products* constructor. This constructor is universal over sum and product types in the same sense that sum-of-product forms are universal in Boolean algebra.

Function type constructors describe functions in terms of their domain and range types. For example, *Int → Bool* is a functional type which describes all functions that map from integers to truth values, such as the function *even*.

The value domains of most functional languages correspond loosely to the following domain equation:

$$V_m = \text{Prim} + (V_m + V_m) + (V_m * V_m) + (V_m \rightarrow V_m) \qquad \text{(Eq. 3)}$$

Most array-based languages are seriously limited as practical languages because they lack the general type systems of other functional languages. For instance, to represent a record, it is necessary in Nial to construct single dimensional arrays containing the fields of the record. This is a misuse of arrays, which are too general for this application. What is needed here is the simple notion of a tuple, or product type. Variant records are more difficult in array-only languages. It is necessary to distinguish one element of the array (usually the first) as a tag, and to carefully manage that value and obey its implications as to the contents of the rest of the array-record. While this can be done, the notion of sum types, or sum-of-products types, corresponds directly to the idea of variant records. Also, when using sum types, the language's type checking system can enforce the variant behaviours. This is much more satisfactory than depending on the programmer to obey artificial tagging rules. Finally, APL and Nial provide no explicit support for functional types. This aspect of functional languages is a powerful and expressive construct we are unwilling to abandon.

Falafel adopts a multi-sorted value space that include the three functional type constructors (sum, product, and function) and a nested array constructor.

$$V_f = \text{Prim} + (V_f + V_f) + (V_f * V_f) + (V_f \rightarrow V_f) + \text{array}_f(V_f) \quad \text{(Eq. 4)}$$

Id and Haskell use much the same value domain as Falafel. Differences between these two languages and Falafel are discussed in the following sections.

STRUCTURE OF ARRAYS

There are several useful categories of the structural properties of arrays. This section compares several array languages, and presents Falafel's choices.

Arrays can be structurally described by the number of dimensions *(valence)* and the extent on each dimension *(shape)*. Variety in the definitions of arrays is characterized by differing choices on these measures.

APL arrays have one or more dimensions. Empty arrays are possible by having dimensions of zero extent. Id does not support zero dimensional arrays, but it is unclear whether empty arrays are defined. Haskell arrays may have one or more dimensions. It appears from [] that empty arrays are permitted.

Sisal's arrays are implemented as nested vectors. The language's model of arrays corresponds to the implementation in that it permits varying lower and upper bounds on each vector. Thus arrays can be jagged. Sisal does not permit zero valence arrays. It is not clear whether empty arrays are permitted. Sisal's emphasis is on implementation. Sisal is the only language considered with arrays that are not rectangular [Feo].

More's array theory provides more sophistication to Nial's structure of arrays. Nial permits valences to be chosen from the natural numbers. Thus zero-dimensional arrays are permitted. These objects are included for two reasons: they permit a natural incorporation of the notion of dimensionless, self-containing atoms, and they provide smooth boundary conditions for the laws of array theory.

Nial also permits zeros in shapes. Any array with a zero in its shape is empty. Empty arrays in More's theory are present to preserve boundary conditions. To maintain certain key equations, it is necessary that empties contain information about the type of element they "used" to contain. Thus More's theory distinguishes between the empty array that contain no 3's and the empty array that contains no 2's. This aspect of Nial and More's theory is somewhat metaphysical for a practical programming language. However, the resulting mathematics are powerful and elegant.

Falafel's arrays are related to More's arrays, but the notion of information hidden in empties is avoided. Falafel's array constructor can be considered a fourth primitive type constructor, or it can be specified in terms of the product type. We take the latter course for clarity of presentation, although we do not mean for this definition to constrain implementations. The array constructor in Falafel is given in Equation 5 as a function from the values that can be contained in an array to the set of nested tuples that represent arrays:

$$\begin{aligned}
&\text{array(baseSet)} = \{ \langle\text{shape}, \text{content(baseSet)}\rangle \mid \qquad \text{(Eq. 5)}\\
&\quad \text{shape} = \langle\text{extent}_0, .., \text{extent}_{\text{valence-1}}\rangle \ \wedge\\
&\quad \text{valence} \in \text{Nat.} \ \wedge \ \ \text{extent}_i \in \text{Nat.} \ \wedge\\
&\quad \text{content(baseSet)} = \langle\text{item(baseSet)}_0 \ ... \ \text{item(baseSet)}_{\text{tally-1}}\rangle \ \wedge\\
&\quad \text{item(baseSet)}_j \in \text{baseSet} \ \wedge\\
&\quad \text{tally} = \text{extent}_0 * ... * \text{extent}_{\text{valence-1}} \ \}
\end{aligned}$$

Equation 5 specifies that Falafel's arrays permit zero dimensional arrays *(valence* $\in$ *Nat)* and empty arrays *(extent*$_i$ $\in$ *Nat)*. There is one unique empty array for each shape containing one or more zeros.

TYPE SYSTEMS

Type systems have come to be of great importance in the design of programming languages. Static type checking is so called because at compile time the expressions of a language are checked to ensure that they are well-typed: that every function is applied only to elements of its domain. Pascal is an example of a statically typed language, as the type of all variables and functions must be declared in the source code, and the declared typing is enforced by the compiler. Even in Pascal, with its relatively simple value space, static typing has worth. In languages with richer value spaces, static type checking becomes an indispensable aid to the programmer. Many common programming errors are detected and prevented by Milner style type checking. In addition, the Milner algorithm can deduce the type of an expression when no explicit typing is given. Type issues arise in several ways in the design of Falafel.

Types and Partial/Total Functions

More's development of array theory is one-sorted. Functions in his pure theory are total. These two choices are related, and relate to decisions made in Falafel. More uses total functions of the pure theory to facilitate analysis of his system. He computes the closure of the composition of functions to check the consistency of his theory. If functions were partial, it would be necessary to complicate this analysis with special cases to the point that his method would become intractable. In general, reasoning about a set of functions is much easier if they are all total.

From his pure theory, More develops an extended, more practical theory. The extended theory encounters naturally partial functions such as *divide*. More introduces *faults* to accommodate such functions. Faults are a primitive data type (self-containing arrays) that carry symbolic information about partial function applications. Thus, in Nial, *1 / 0 = ?div-by-zero*. Systematic use of faults permits many functions to remain total, as mappings to fault values complete otherwise partial functions.

Nevertheless, it is possible to construct partial functions in More's theory. It is sufficiently powerful to describe functions which do not (always) terminate. Non-termination cannot be mapped to faults in finite time. Consequently, at some point, array theory must admit partial functions. Whether it is beneficial to extend totality as far as possible, as More does, is not clear.

Falafel, however, takes a different approach. Typing is central to Falafel. The value space is divided by primitive types and all types constructable with sums, products, functions, and arrays. Functions generally do not apply to all types. For instance, integers are a distinct type. Functions on integers are meant to be partial in the sense that they do not apply to other (non-numeric) types. It would be wrong, given our Milner-style approach to types and type checking, to extend *plus* to other types and return a fault. The purpose of Milner-style type checking is to detect such domain errors during compilation.

Milner-style type checking is at odds with More's one-sorted domain with total functions. Falafel recognizes distinct types and provides type constructors to build new types. We prefer to have the compiler resolve typing issues.

Heterogeneous or Homogeneous Arrays?

Unique among the languages we are examining, Nial supports heterogeneous arrays; its arrays can mix values of different types. Thus an array could contain an integer, a boolean, and another array. Such heterogeneity extends only to data objects, not to functional objects. This choice is appropriate for Nial for several reasons.

1) Array theory constructs a one-sorted system in which types are not explicitly recognized. Types are present only in the sense of a function, *type*, that maps values to their "typical" elements (e.g. *type 1 = 0, type 2 = 0,* and *type True = Falsehood).* Thus there is no strong notion of types on which to base homogeneity.

2) Nial does not support product types; consequently, heterogeneous arrays are required to implement records.

Falafel rules out heterogeneous arrays because heterogeneity makes static type checking impossible. Consider a function on integers, *f*, applied to the *xth* element of a heterogeneous array containing integers and booleans. Only for certain values of *x* is the application of *f* well typed. Where *x* is a general expression, its value cannot be determined at compile time. Consequently, the application of *f* cannot be guaranteed to be well typed – thus static type checking is not possible. If compile time type checking is not possible, run time type checking is necessary. However, this approach has two serious drawbacks: one doesn't know until after execution whether a program is well typed, and one must pay the run time cost of maintaining and checking type information for each item of each array.

Heterogeneity also imposes a significant run time cost, because it is necessary to dynamically determine representation schemes, when as the types of items can be determined. However, this choice in the design of Nial permits a simple one-sorted view of data.

The arrays of every other language we consider are homogeneous. This decision simplifies languages and implementations.

Structural Polymorphism and Arrays

It is useful to permit functions written for use with one type to be inherited for use with other types. It is possible for inheritance to be based on either structural or behavioural aspects of types. Structural inheritance occurs when a subtype meets all the structural constraints of the supertype, and adds more constraints.

Arrays are natural candidates for structural inheritance; it is straightforward to define structurally related subtypes of arrays. Consider the following three arrays types: the set of all arrays (type *A*), the set of all *valence = 1* arrays (type *B*, or lists), and the set of all lists containing only boolean values (type *C*). *A* is clearly the most general structural type. Arrays which are lists (type *B*) meet all the constraints of type *A* (the supertype) and add the constraint that *valence = 1*. Type *C* adds the constraint that all items of the list be booleans. This view of structurally related types is developed in [McCrosky & Dutta].

Functions can be polymorphic. A polymorphic function is one which applies to more than one type, thus the function has many (poly) forms (morphic). As inheritance can be by behaviour or structure, so polymorphism can be driven by either mechanism. Structural polymorphism is where functions apply to multiple types due to the structure of the types.

A function defined on all arrays (type *A*) such as *tally* (which returns the count of items in an array) clearly applies to types *B* and *C*. *tally* is said to be structurally polymorphic; it is inherited by the two subtypes of *A* because they are structural specializations of *A*.

Functions on subtypes may not apply to supertypes. For example, *reduce* (*foldr* in some languages) is defined on one-dimensional arrays. It is not defined for general arrays. (In Nial, reduce is defined for all arrays by effectively coercing higher-dimensioned arrays to lists, and then applying reduce. In Falafel, this coercion is not automatic, but could be inserted by the programmer).

PARTIALLY DEFINED ARRAYS

Normally an array is fully defined, where a fully defined array has definite values for valence, the shape, and all the items. A partially defined array is an array that is unspecified at some or all of these places. For example, a partially defined list of length two might have its first item defined, while its second item was unspecified, or bottom. Any attempt to reference unspecified information results in bottom. Partially defined arrays have two uses: they support a useful "relational" definition form, and they permit computation with partially defined entities.

It is possible to combine partially defined arrays to form more fully defined arrays. A semantics for this, based on domains, is given in [McCrosky & Sailor]. Arrays can be combined when none of their information is contradictory (e.g., they have different valences, or first items). Equations specifying partially defined arrays are combined in a defining form in Falafel (the suchthat clause) to specify arrays by parts. For instance a fully defined list of length two could be defined as:

```
a suchthat
    shape a = [2]
    [0] pick a = 1
    [1] pick a = 9
```

Each defining equation gives a partially defined array. These may be coalesced into a single (partially or completely defined) array.

```
b suchthat [x] pick b = x mod 2 forall x in [0 ... 99]
```

This form of definition is highly appropriate for arrays. It is useful in both function definition and in application programming. For instance, the following definition of *each* (analogous to Miranda's *map*) uses this form:

```
each f a = z suchthat
    shape z = shape a
    pick x z = f(pick x a) forall x in tell (shape a)
```

It is also possible to permit computation with partially defined arrays (as opposed to insisting that all suchthat clauses completely define their arrays). When this occurs, referencing of undefined regions results in bottom. This approach is distinct from lazy evaluation, where everything must be defined, but need not be referenced. Here, everything need not be defined.

Id and Haskell include a feature called *array comprehensions* which is related to partially defined arrays. This feature permits the items of arrays to be defined by a collection of separate generators. Partially defined arrays are distinct in that they permit more general combinations of partial information.

LAZY EVALUATION Of ARRAY EXPRESSIONS

Languages based on the lambda calculus MAY take advantage of lazy evaluation. Lazy evaluation is based on normal order reduction of lambda expressions. In practice, this means that a function's arguments are substituted into the body of the function without being evaluated. During evaluation of the body of the function, the arguments are evaluated as they are required. If an argument is not referenced, then it is never evaluated. Lazy evaluation is extended to fully lazy evaluation by ensuring that no expression is evaluated more than once. This is accomplished most naturally by sharing sub-graphs in graph reduction implementations of lambda calculus reductions. If one of the references to a shared computation is demanded, the expression is evaluated and the result replaces the expression and is shared by all references.

Although lazy evaluation imposes a modest constant overhead on all computations, it is a major advance in the semantics of functional languages. Turner states that lazy evaluation is **the** natural semantics for functional languages. A principal advantage of lazy evaluation is that it allows the description of infinite objects, computing only finite parts of them. At first glimpse, this may seem rather arcane, but it turns out that many algorithms are easier to state with infinite objects. For instance, a search for the first *n* primes can just take the first *n* numbers from the infinite stream of primes selected from the infinite stream of integers.

Previous work with infinite data structures has used only nested lists, or streams. However, it is possible to perform lazy evaluation on arrays. Consider applications which involve triangular matrices. With lazy evaluation, it is possible to use rectangular array definitions, but to avoid computing regions of matrices that are not of interest (are all zero). Or image processing applications could describe exhaustive analyses of images as arrays of results, and then demand the evaluation only of parts necessary to make required deductions about the underlying image.

IMPLEMENTATION

Where imperative languages generally map only to von Neumann machines, languages based on the lambda calculus can be mapped to a wide variety of computational models, including von Neumann, graph reduction, data flow, and – for some expressions – SIMD and systolic/wavefront architectures.

The usual representation for arrays is a flat, contiguous area in linearly addressable memory. However, there are several other interesting representations for arrays. Arrays can be passed, item-by-item, along data flow links. Sparse arrays can be stored as lists of items, or hash tables. Arrays can be mapped to fine-grain SIMD machines such as the Connection Machine. Finite portions of infinite arrays can be represented using data flow or sparse array techniques.

With the great variety of approaches to the implementation of functional languages and the representation of arrays, Falafel is faced with an embarrassment of riches of implementation options. It is clear that differing implementations are appropriate for differing classes of computations, and it is doubtful that any single implementation is best, or even good, for all Falafel computations.

Our response to this wide range of options has been to choose several for preliminary exploration. This section summarizes the implementation avenues that have been explored to date.

Graph Reduction

An obvious choice for implementation of Falafel is the use of graph reduction on von Neumann machines. This approach was developed by the functional languages community. It is natural for Falafel because Falafel is at essence another functional language. Graph reduction offers straightforward solutions to some of the difficult semantic issues of higher-order functional arguments and scopes. The target machine is simple. Much useful work has been done in the optimization of graph reduction. [Peyton Jones] provides a useful summary and guide to this work. Presently, the core of Falafel is implemented in the G-Machine model by a compiler written in Miranda and YACC. The array features are theoretically complete, but unoptimized [Sailor].

Parallel, Distributed Graph Reduction

Due to the referential transparency of the lambda calculus, graph reduction can be mapped to parallel machines. We have mapped portions of Falafel to a distributed memory MIMD (eight T800 Transputers). This implementation accepts supercombinators from the sequential graph reduction work discussed above, and maps it across the distributed memory of our test bed. Reduction of the graph then proceeds in parallel.

This work is preliminary in the sense that we make no attempt to intelligently map arrays or computations to the distributed memories. In a distributed memory architecture with limited message passing bandwidth, intelligent allocation is absolutely vital (otherwise communications costs defeat the parallelism). The next phase of this work will exploit the regular structure of arrays and array operations to achieve an efficient distribution of work for some classes of problems [Chen].

Static Data Flow

Falafel expressions can be mapped to data flow models. It would be possible to map general expressions to dynamic data flow. For initial simplicity we have studied the mapping of a restricted set of Falafel expressions to static data flow. Arrays have no place in our approach! Rather, the items of arrays are mapped to scalar data flow links. Arrays remain only as conceptual bundles of data flow links, or as sequential streams of tokens down single links. This approach is feasible only where the structure of every array is known at compile time, in order that the complete data flow net can be compiled.

In this approach, there is a choice between sequential and parallel semantics for many functions. Consider the expression *eachf [a, b, c]*. This could be evaluated sequentially, with the values *a, b,* and *c* pipelined down a single data flow link to the function *f,* which passed on *f a, f b,* and *f c*. Or, one can give *a, b,* and *c* their own data flow links and have *f* act on each link. Every occurrence of a function with an option between sequential and parallel semantics provides an opportunity to tailor the resultant data flow graph to control both the size of the resultant graph and the degree of parallelism presented to the data flow machine.

A very wide degree of control over the size and parallelism of resultant graphs is possible. It remains to automate the process of choosing parallel or sequential semantics to tailor a given computation to a given machine [Roy].

Fine-Grained SIMDs

Advances in the integration of VLSI devices has made possible highly parallel, very fine grain architectures such as the Connection Machine. Such machines offer the possibility of extreme parallelism in arrays operations. When items of arrays are mapped to individual processors, parallel operations such as *eachf [a, b, c]* can occur in the time for one application, *(f a)*. There are many operations for which this paradigm is useful.

We carried out an algorithm design and simulation study of the mapping of selected array operations to very fine-grained SIMDs. The obvious parallelism described above was trivial to realize. The most interesting operations were those that required communications among items of arrays. Efficient algorithms (complexity less than or equal to $O(\log N)$) were found for a surprising number of standard array operations, including *flip*, *transpose*, and *sublist* [Gammo].

INTERMEDIATE CONTAINER REMOVAL

A primary reason for using arrays is to gain constant time access to large structures. However, the introduction of array-valued functions introduces another serious efficiency problem. Array functions map from arrays to arrays. When array functions are composed, naive implementations create intermediate containers. For instance, when functions *f* and g are composed and applied to array *A*, the naive approach is to create a container to store *g A* before *f* is applied. Because functional languages rely extensively on composition of functions, the amount of time implementations spend manipulating intermediate containers is extensive. It is doubtful that functional arrays languages can ever be competitive with imperative languages if these intermediate containers are needlessly allocated.

We have found an optimization to avoid this unnecessary work. Our solution is to compute the new function that is the composition of *f* and *g*. The shape of the the output array is computed, then for every item within that shape, the composition of *f* and *g* that produced it is computed. The result is that we produce the items of the result without ever having created the intermediate container. Usually, the items of the result share a simple common relationship with the items of the original argument, and a loop over a single expression serves to compute all of the results.

This optimization provides dramatic improvements in the execution speed of Falafel expressions [McCrosky 88]. A formal treatment of intermediate container removal is presented in [ven der Buhs].

CONCLUSIONS

Falafel is being developed as an experimental vehicle for our study of the semantics and implementation techniques of functional languages with first class arrays. Although Falafel owes large intellectual debts to the work of More, Jenkins, and Turner, it has taken a unique course. Falafel adopts much of the sophistication of More's array theory, but simplifies several areas. In particular, type-carrying empties and heterogeneous arrays are abandoned. From Miranda,

Falafel takes a more general approach to its universal value space: sum, product and function types are explicitly included. Falafel is not an "array-based" language, rather it incorporates arrays in a more general type system. Array types are related by structural polymorphism, and structural inheritance of functions applies from supertype to subtype.

Falafel introduces a form of definition based on a semantics of partially defined arrays. This form has parallels with the array comprehensions of Id and Haskell, but is more general and has a clearer semantics.

Implementation studies show there is a wide range of implementations for a functional language with arrays. Falafel can serve as a programming language for a wide range of computational models and architectures.

REFERENCES

[Chen] Chen, W. Parallel Distributed Graph Reduction of Falafel. M.Sc. Thesis, University of Saskatchewan, 1990.

[Gammo] Gammo, L. Array-Based Parallelism for Fine-Grained SIMD Machines M.Sc. Thesis, University of Saskatchewan, 1988.

[Feo] Feo, J. T., Cann, D. C., and Oldehoeft, R. R. A Report on the Sisal Language Project Submitted to the *Journal of Parallel and Distributed Computing* from the Lawrence Livermore National Laboratory, Jan, 1990.

[Hudak] Hudak, P. Report on the Programming Language Haskell, Version 1.0. Technical Report YALEU/DCS/RR-777, Yale University, April, 1990.

[Iverson] Iverson, K. E. *A Programming Language.* Wiley, New York, 1962.

[Jenkins & Jenkins] Jenkins, M. A., and Jenkins, W. *Q'Nial Reference Manual.* Brown & Martin, Kingston, Canada, 1986.

[McCrosky] McCrosky, C. The elimination of intermediate containers in the evaluation of first-class array expressions. IEEE International Conference on Computer Languages, Miami, October, 1988, pp 135-142.

[McCrosky 90] McCrosky, C. Intermediate Container Removal. *Computer Languages,* to appear, 1990.

[McCrosky & Dutta] McCrosky, C. and Dutta, D. A type-theoretic semantics of arrays. *Applied Mathematics Letters 3(1),* pp 83-87, 1990.

[McCrosky & Sailor] McCrosky, C. and Sailor, K. Partially Defined Arrays. submitted for publication, 1990.

[More] More, T. Notes on the diagrams, logic, and operations of array theory. *Structures and Operations in Engineering and Management Systems.* Bjorke and Franksen, eds., Tapir Publishers, Trondheim, Norway, 1981.

[Nikhil] Nikhil, R. S. Id Version 88.1 Reference Manual. Computation Structures Group Memo 284, M.I.T. Cambridge, August, 1988.

[Peyton Jones] Peyton Jones, S. *The Implementation of Functional Programming Languages.* Prentice-Hall, London, 1987.

[Sailor] Sailor, K. First-Class Arrays in Falafel. M.Sc. Thesis, University of Saskatchewan, 1990.

[Turner 85] Turner. D. A. Miranda: A non-strict functional language with polymorphic types. In Proceedings of IFIP Conference on Functional Programming & Computer Architecture. Springer-Verlag, LNCS #201, Berlin, 1985. {Miranda is a trademark of Research Software Ltd.}

[ven der Buhs] ven der Buhs, B. Typical Element Algebra of Arrays: A Formulation of Intermediate Container Removal. M.Sc. Thesis, Dept. of Computational Science, Univ. of Saskatchewan, 1989.

7

Arrays in HASKELL

Guy Lapalme
Département d'informatique et de recherche opérationnelle
Université de Montréal
C.P. 6128, Succ "A"
Montréal, Québec, Canada
H3C 3J7
e-mail :lapalme@iro.umontreal.ca

December 11, 1990

Abstract

This paper describes from an user point of view the array notation of the HASKELL lazy functional language. The array notation was defined in such a way as to enable an efficient implementation of indexing and updating while keeping a high level expression power. We show by means of examples how to create and use arrays.

1 What is HASKELL?

HASKELL[1] is a non-strict purely functional language defined by a committee of researchers from around the world. Their goal is to define a language suitable for teaching, research and applications; this language is described via the publication of a formal syntax and semantics and is freely available. In April 1990, Version 1.0 of the report was published under the editorship of Paul Hudak

[1] HASKELL is named after the logician Haskell B. Curry

and Philip Wadler [4] but at the time of writing (July 1990) no implementations are yet publicly available, although groups from Yale University, the University of Glasgow and the Imperial College of London have committed themselves to have one "real soon now".

HASKELL is in many ways an integration and extension of the ideas of previous functional languages in particular Miranda[2] [6, 5] from which it differs mainly in its systematic treatment of ad-hoc polymorphism (i.e. overloading) using type classes and instances. There are other important features like modules, stream and continuation based input/output and new number types. HASKELL defines arrays as a basic type and this is the aspect that we stress here. We give a user point of view by means of examples so that one can appreciate the power of the array notation of HASKELL. Anderson and Hudak[2] describe a compilation technique based on subscript analysis for the efficient implementation of the array comprehensions in HASKELL. So although the array notation of HASKELL is at a higher level of abstraction compared to other functional languages like Id and Sisal described elsewhere in this book, we can expect that its efficient implementation is possible.

2 Creation of arrays

HASKELL defines a form of array called *non-strict monolithic arrays* using *array comprehensions* which are an extension of the list comprehensions now commonly found in functional languages. A *non-strict* array can contain "undefined" elements and a *monolithic* array defines its elements all at once at the moment the array value is created.

In HASKELL, an array is a data type that has essentially the same behaviour as a function whose domain is isomorphous to contiguous subsets of integers. This enables an efficient implementation of indexing.

Arrays are created by three built-in functions `array`, `listArray` and `accumArray`:

[2]Miranda is a trademark of Research Software Ltd.

`array` *bounds list-of-associations*

is the fundamental list creation mechanism. *bounds* gives the lowest and highest indices in the array; a zero-origin vector of 5 elements has bounds `(0,4)` and a one-origin `10` by `10` matrix has bounds `((1,1),(10,10))`. The values of the bounds can be arbitrary expressions. An *association* is of the form *index* `:=` *value*. An association `i := x` defines the value of the array `i` to be `x`.

In HASKELL, a list is a series of values enclosed in square brackets and separated by commas. List can also be defined using a list comprehensions analogous to the set comprehensions in mathematics[3]:

- `[a..b]` defines a list of values from `a` to `b` inclusive. `a` and `b` have to be of the same type and define a way to get the successor and predecessor of an element of this type i.e. they must be isomorphous with a contiguous subset of integers.

- `[exp | pattern <- list]` creates a list of elements produced by evaluating `exp` in the environment produced by binding `pattern` to each matching element of `list`; this is called a generator. In the case of many generators, they are evaluated in a nested, depth-first fashion.

For example:

```
a' = array (1,4) [3 := 'c',2 := 'a', 1 := 'f', 4 := 'e']
a1 = array (0,n) [i := i*i | i <- [0..n]]
m  = array ((1,1),(2,3)) [(i,j) := (i*j)|i<-[1..2],j<-[1..3]]
```

The array is undefined if any index is out of bounds and if two associations in the list have the same index, the value at that index is undefined. As a consequence, `array` is strict in the bounds and in the indices but nonstrict in the values. We can thus use recurrences such as (as we will see in the next section `!` denotes indexing):

```
fib = array (1,10) ([1 := 1, 2 := 1] ++
                    [i := fib!(i-1) + fib!(i-2)| i<-[3..10]])
```

[3] this is a simplification of the rules of list comprehensions of HASKELL but it is sufficient for the examples presented here

`listArray` *bounds list-of-values*

is predefined for the frequently occurring case where an array is constructed from a list of values in index order. The following defines `a''` to be the same value as `a'` above.

```
a''= listArray (1,4) "face"
```

`accumArray` *f init bounds list-of-associations*

removes the restriction that a given index may appear at most once in the association list but instead combines these "conflicting indices" via an accumulating function *f*. The elements of the array are initialized with `init`. For example, given a list of values, `hist` produces a histogram of the number of occurrences of each index.

```
hist bnds is = accumArray (+) 0 bnds [i := 1 | i <- is]
```

3 Using arrays

Array subscripting is done using the `!` binary operator. Functions have also been defined for getting the bounds (`bounds`), the indices (`indices`), the elements (`elems`) and associations (`assocs`) of an array.

It is also possible to update an array in a functional style: i.e. return a new array whose values are identical to the old one except for a given index. The operator `//` takes an array and an association and returns a new array identical to the left argument except for one element specified by the right argument. For example:

```
a'//(3 := 'r')
```

redefines the third element of `a'`. Many updates can be "batched" and combined using `accum` *function array list-of-associations.* For example:

```
accum m (+) [(1,1):= 4, (2,2):=8]
```

returns a new matrix identical to m except for elements (1,1) and (2,2) to which 4 and 8 have been respectively added.

It is also possible to derive new arrays using mapping on the elements (amap *f Array*) or on the indices (ixmap *bounds f array*). For example,

```
amap (*10) fib
```

multiplies all elements of the fib array by 10 and

```
row i m= ixmap (l',u') f m
         where
         ((l,l'),(u,u'))= bounds m
         f j = (i,j)
```

returns an array comprising the elements of row i of matrix m.

The following definitions give the inner product of two vectors and the matrix multiplications of two matrices.

```
inner v w |iv==indices v = sum [v!i * w!i | i<-iv]
          |otherwise     = error "inconformable arrays"
                           where
                           iv = indices v


mult a b
    | p=p' = array ((1,1),(m,n))
                   [(i,j) := inner (row i a) (col j b)
                                     | i<-[1..m],j<-[1..n]]
           where
           ((1,1),(m,p))  = bounds a
           ((1,1),(p',n)) = bounds b

col j m = ixmap (l,u) (\i->(i,j)) m
          where
          ((l,l'),(u,u'))= bounds m
```

4 Conclusion

We have seen that the HASKELL array notation is simple and natural. It is well integrated in the language being a basic data type, the only restriction compared to an "ordinary function" is the use of "integer" indexes within fixed bounds but this enables an efficient access to the elements of the array. As [2] has shown, the monolithic array creation and controlled updating enable the optimization of the creation of lazily defined array without too much overhead (i.e. the creation of a closure for each element is not always necessary to implement lazy evaluation); it would be interesting to extend this approach for the efficient updating of arrays. We could also consider alternative ways of storing arrays using either trees or quadtrees[1]; the array notation of HASKELL gives the implementor complete freedom in this respect. In fact, the examples given in this paper were tested on a Miranda "simulator" of this array notation that uses a tree implementation of the arrays inspired by that given by [3, p 257-259].

Given that HASKELL is expected to have a wide distribution, the array comprehension notation will probably have a great impact on the array manipulation framework in the functional language world.

References

[1] S. Kamal Abdali and David S. Wise. Experiments with quadtree representation of matrices. Technical Report 241, Indiana University, Computer Science Department, February 1988.

[2] Steven Anderson and Paul Hudak. Compilation of Haskell array comprehensions for scientific computing. *Proceedings of the ACM SIGPLAN'90 Conference on Programming Language Design and Implementation, Sigplan Notices*, pages 137–149, June 1990.

[3] R. Bird and P. Wadler. *Introduction to Functional Programming.* Prentice-Hall, 1988.

[4] P. Hudak and P. Wadler (editors). Report on the programming language Haskell, a non-strict purely functional language (Version 1.0). Technical Report YALEU/DCS/RR777, Yale University, Department of Computer Science, April 1990.

[5] Research Software Limited. *Miranda System Manual, Version 2.* 1989.

[6] D.A. Turner. Miranda - a non strict functional language with polymorphic types. In P. Jouannaud, editor, *Conference on Functional Programming and Computer Architecture, Lecture Notes in Computer Science #201*, pages 1–16, 1985.

8

Array Theory and Knowledge Representation

Janice Glasgow
Department of Computing and Information Science
Queen's University, Kingston
janice@qucis.queensu.ca

1 Introduction

Representing and reasoning about real world knowledge is a fundamental research problem in the area of artificial intelligence. Many approaches to knowledge representation, such as predicate logic, semantic networks, frames and scripts, have been proposed and implemented for the purpose of solving problems using an AI approach.

Over the past several years, the Nial project at Queen's University has been investigating the use of array theory and the programming language Nial for representing and implementing existing approaches to knowledge representation. The software developed on this project includes a logic programming environment, a frame language and an integrated logic/database facility. In this paper we review some of these tools.

Array theory also provides a basis for representing and reasoning about spatial knowledge. Such a facility is particularly useful when solving problems which humans use mental imagery to solve. Examples of such problems are: recognition of complex objects, chess playing and motion planning. In this paper we present a schema for knowledge representation that provides a symbolic array depiction of the spatial relationships necessary to reason about images. This representation is currently being implemented in the programming language Nial.

2 Array Theory and Nial

Array theory is the mathematics of nested, rectangularly-arranged collections of data objects. Similar to set theory, array theory is concerned with the concepts of nesting, aggregation and membership. Array theory is also concerned with the concept of data objects having a spatial position relative to other objects in a collection.

The development of array theory was motivated by efforts to extend the data structures of APL and has been influenced by the search for total operations that satisfy universal equations [14]. In this theory, an array is a collection of zero or more items held at positions in a rectangular arrangement along zero or more axes. The items of arrays are themselves arrays. Rectangular arrangement is the concept of data objects having a position relative to other objects in the collection.

The interpretation of rectangular arrangements can be illustrated using nested, box diagrams to represent the structure. Consider the following array diagram:

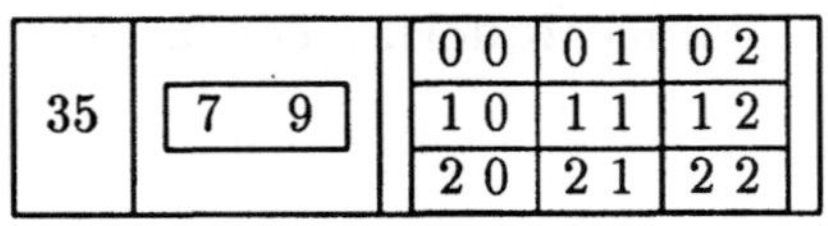

Figure 2.1 Example of an embedded array

In this array the pair formed from 7 and 9 is an array nested within the larger array. *Nesting* is the concept of having the objects of a collection be collections themselves. This is an important concept in array theory since it is this ability, to aggregate arbitrary elements in an array, that gives the theory much of its expressive power.

A first-order theory of arrays has previously been constructed [8]. The development of this theory is based on three constructors for arrays: *hitch, reshape* and *void,* and on four selectors: *first, rest, shape* and *list.* The combination of *hitch, first* and *rest* correspond to the *cons, head* and *tail* of the theory of lists, except that the axioms change slightly due to the presence of empty lists. The theory of lists based on these functions can be used to give a formal treatment to the list objects of Lisp.

The binary constructor *reshape* builds a rectangularly arranged object with the arrangement given by an addressing scheme implicitly encoded in a *shape* argument, using items provided as the second argument. The selectors *shape* and *list* retrieve the components of the construction. These functions correspond to similar ones of the same names that appear in APL.

Array theory has provided a formal basis for the development of the *N*ested *I*nteractive *A*rray *L*anguage, *Nial.* This multi-paradigm programming language combines concepts from APL, Lisp and FP with conventional control mechanisms [9]. The primitive functions of array theory have all been implemented in Q'Nial [10], a portable interpreter of Nial developed at Queen's University.

Operations in array theory are functions that map arrays to arrays. A large collection of total, primitive operations are described for the theory. These operations express fundamental properties of arrays and are defined to obey universal laws. Nial extends array theory by providing several syntactic forms that describe operations, including composition, partial evaluation of a left argument, and a lambda-form. Array theory also contains second-order functions called transformers that map operations to operations. Transformers are constructed in Nial in several ways, including composition, a lambda-form, and three juxtaposition forms [1].

3 Logic Programming With Arrays

In Nial, all data objects are arrays and hence the addition of a logic programming capability must include the ability to reason with array data structures. Our goals for the integration included the desire to minimize the need for built-in predicates, to explore the possibility of achieving true negation, and to combine the capabilities of logic and functional programming. In this section we overview the logic programming environment that has been developed using array theory and implemented in Nial. For a more detailed description of these logic capabilities, see [6].

A major goal of the research in array theory and logic programming was to provide the capability of using arrays as terms within a declarative style of programming. The approach taken is based on a first-order theory of equality of nested data structures that provides a logical basis for the data objects of Nial [8]. This theory of equality is used as the basis for extending unification to include semantic reduction. This permits the system to reason about arrays and to pass information in the form of array data structures between the logic system and the functional system.

Arrays are used to hold the representations of both the logic programs, and the state of proofs within the system. This permits the tools for the logic programming system: the parser, the unification algorithm, the provers, etc., to be written in Nial for design and experimentation purposes. Some of these have been translated to C to achieve more effective implementations.

In exploring the logic programming capability, our primary concern has been with the conceptual clarity and expressiveness of the system, although attention has been paid to developing an efficient algorithm for semantic unification and its incorporation in a variety of provers. As well, we have introduced the notion of eager variables that trigger eager reduction of function terms.

The primary motivation for implementing a logic programming system in Nial was to develop a flexible environment which integrates concepts of logic and functional programming. Rather than building a rigid system, we wanted one where we could experiment with alternative approaches to logic programs and their relationship to functional programs. Thus, we did not want to limit our scope to Horn clause logic or to a simple depth-first strategy, preferring instead to allow the users to choose their own options. In the logic system

[1]For more details on the operations and transformers of array theory and Nial see [10]

developed in Nial, it is possible to use full clausal logic (with real first-order predicate logic negation), as well as Horn clause logic, and to define new search strategies or use predefined ones.

In the remainder of this section we describe the syntax and semantics of our logic language, the interface between the logic and functional components of Nial, and the logic control strategies that have been implemented.

3.1 Nlog

In this subsection, we describe the the logic language "Nlog" that has evolved from earlier work described in [1]. We initially consider the syntax of full clausal logic as in [16]. The Horn clause logic is just a restricted version of this logic. Control strategies for both full clausal and Horn clause logic have been implemented in Nial.

In Nlog, as in Prolog, clauses have two parts separated by the symbol "$\leftarrow$". The conclusion (left hand side) of the clause and the premise (right hand side) of the clause both have zero or more literals separated by commas. A literal is a predicate name followed by a list (possibly empty) of terms. Literals may also be negated, as denoted by the symbol " $\sim$ ". A term is either a logic constant, a logic variable, or a structured term. A structured term is either a function call, a list notation, or an array notation. Finally, a goal (or a query) is a clause in which the conclusion is empty. Below is an example of a clause that defines the recursive rule for factorial

$$fact(n, x) \leftarrow fact(-(n, 1), z), unify(x, *(n, z))$$

In the context of a complete program, we would also require the axioms

$$\begin{aligned} &fact(0, 1) \leftarrow \\ &fact(1, 1) \leftarrow \\ &unify(x, x) \leftarrow \end{aligned}$$

Note that the terms including multiplication and subtraction symbols are treated as reducible expressions by the unification algorithm using Nial reduction as the theory of equality; thus, there is no need to provide special built-in predicates to effect these computations. Note also that the predicate *unify* is not a built-in predicate providing assignment; rather, it is just a predicate like *fact* and it is defined by the axiom

$$unify(x, x) \leftarrow$$

Arrays can be denoted by any regular Nial expression, surrounded by curly brackets. In this case, they are considered as logic constants. For example, the expression

$$\{\ 3\ 4\ \textit{reshape count}\ 12\ \}$$

denotes a logic constant which is a two-dimensional Nial array with items that are the atomic arrays 1 through 12. The operation *count* with the argument 12 reduces to a list of integer atoms 1 through 12. The operation *reshape* that is left-curried with the left-argument 3 4 reshapes the list into a 3 by 4 table.

If an array contains an unbound variable, it must be treated as a logic term, rather than a constant. Arrays as terms are denoted by expressions of the form

$$[< shape > : < list\_of\_terms >]$$

where $< shape >$ is a list of integers and $< list\_of\_terms >$ denotes a list of either constants, logic variables, logic arrays, or function names followed by a list of terms.

It has been demonstrated that every array can be uniquely decomposed using the operations *reshape*, *hitch* and *void* [8]. This decomposition is called the canonical form of the array. The operation *reshape* gives, as its result, an array with shape as defined by its first argument, and items as defined by its second argument. The operation *hitch* is simply a list constructor that we use to build the second argument of the *reshape* operations. The operation *void* constructs an empty list. The theory allows a variety of empty lists. A particular one, called the Null, is used as the initial list in the canonical decomposition. The canonical decomposition provides a link between the data structures of Nial and arrays as terms in logic programs. For example, in Nlog, the logic constant:

$$\{ 2\ 2\ reshape\ 1\ 2\ 3\ 4 \}$$

is equal to the Nial array of shape 2 2 :

1	2
3	4

The canonical decomposition of this array is:

$$reshape(hitch(2, hitch(2, void(0))), hitch(1, hitch\ (2, hitch(3, hitch(4, void(0))))))$$

In Nlog, the term

$$[\,2\,2\ :\ 1\ X\ 3\ Y\,]$$

denotes the Nial array

1	X
3	Y

where X and Y are logic variables. The internal form of this term is similar in structure to that of the canonical form of the array denoted by the logical constant. The unification of this term with the logical constant is done by matching their internal forms.

3.2 Logic/Functional Interface

The logic/functional interface of Nial is accomplished using the theory of equality for arrays to implement a semantic unification algorithm. There are several advantages to this approach; notably, that the prover is uncluttered by the need for special purpose predicates. We have also extended the expressibility of logic programs to include arrays and expressions involving arrays.

Semantic unification is not enough to effect an expressive logic functional interface. The functional reduction induced by semantic unification is fully lazy. However, in order to provide for efficiency and for creating side effects, the need arises to do procedural computations. To facilitate this we introduced eager variables that can only be bound to a reduced ground term, another eager variable, or an unbound variable. Semantic unification and eager variables end the need for treating predicates as procedures, as is done in many logic programming interpreters.

As discussed earlier, one of the goals of our approach is to provide a flexible environment for experimenting with logic programming ideas. For this reason, we do not restrict our reasoning to a single inferencing strategy. Instead, we provide a variety of built-in control strategies for both Horn clause and full clausal logic. The functional interface also allows user defined control strategies. In this section, we describe some of the built-in provers that have been implemented in Nial.

The oldest and simplest prover implemented in Nial is a depth-first, left-most control strategy. It was inspired by Robinson's original description of refutation search restricted to Horn clauses [15], and has none of the programming language extensions of modern provers, such as Prolog. It does not include an occurs check or semantic reduction capabilities as part of the unification step, neither does it include any special purpose predicates.

The first refinement to this original prover was the design and implementation of one that included special purpose predicates. These allowed for a rudimentary interface between the functional and logic components of Nial, by providing for the specification of functional evaluation of Nial expressions as side effects of a refutation search.

The next refinement was the design and implementation of an heuristic-based prover. The idea here is to do a localized breadth-first search combined with heuristics to choose a particular path to take next. The overall process is controlled by two parameters which limit the depth and width of the search space. If these limits are reached, a failure is returned as a result.

Another prover using simulated OR parallelism, heuristic search, and special purpose predicates, and based on full clausal logic has been implemented [3]. This prover extends the expressiveness of the logic language, incorporating true negation, disjunction and arrays as terms. Heuristics and OR parallelism are intended to solve the efficiency problem from a theoretical point of view.

Concurrent with the development of this latest prover, we have also been attempting to address the efficiency problems on a more practical level. This has resulted in a prover that is based on a non-naive implementation incorporating a multi-stack-based, structure sharing, depth-first search algorithm.

4 Array Representation for Imagery

In this section we present a knowledge representation scheme in which array theory is used as a metalanguage for describing and implementing the representations and processes that correspond to mental imagery. This metalanguage has three components: a data structure for depicting images symbolically, a set of array functions that operate on such representations, and a domain of interpretation. The embedded array data structure is used to represent both spatial and hierarchical structure of an image. The functions defined for the representation correspond to the cognitive processes that are involved in constructing, transforming and accessing images. These functions are applied in the context of world knowledge that includes a deep representation of long-term memory.

One characteristic of a good formalism for knowledge representation is that it makes relevant concepts explicit. In [6] several pertinent properties of images were identified. These include the following properties:

- Images are organized in terms of the spatial relationships of their meaningful parts.
- Complex images are hierarchically organized.
- Images can be represented in three dimensional space.
- The representation of an image can be considered from an object-centered or a viewer-centered perspective.

The array data structure provides a multi-dimensional realization of an image that satisfies the above properties. We denote an array depiction of an image as a *symbolic array.* Although such a representation is object-centered (viewer-independent), array functions such as rotate, translate and project allow an image to be viewed from a variety of perspectives. The embedded nature of the array also allows an hierarchical depiction of an image. Detailed information (lower levels of the hierarchy) can either be hidden or made explicit in such a representation. Since hierarchical structure is expressed using embedded arrays, identifying meaningful parts of an image symbolically allows the structure to be suppressed or depicted as desired.

The representation of an image is implemented using the *Nial Frame Language* [7]. In the representation model for long-term memory, primitive images are stored using literal and propositional knowledge. The literal knowledge describes the meaningful parts and their locations. From this knowledge a multidimensional array can be constructed using the procedural attachment facility of frames. The propositional knowledge provides a description of the non-spatial features of an image.

A criticism of many computational models is that they do not capture the parallelism inherent in cognitive models. Although a detailed discussion of this issue is outside the scope of the paper, it has been shown that array theory can be used to express some of the parallel processing that occurs in imagery [6].

4.1 The Data Structure

A symbolic array depiction of an image denotes the structural features of the image. This array may be depicted in one, two or three dimensions. Figure 4.1 illustrates the symbolic array data structure that would be generated using the depict slot of an island frame:

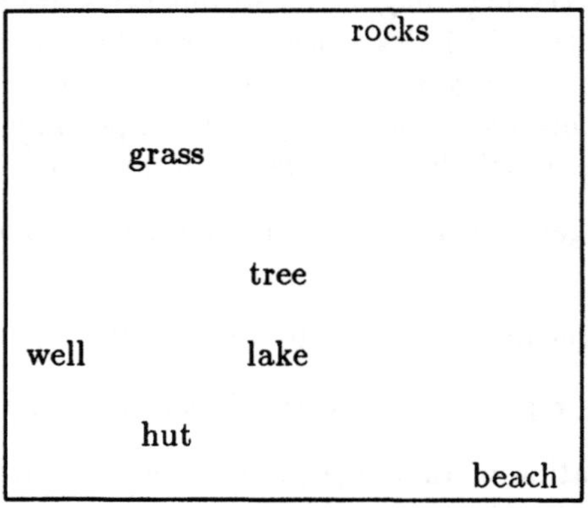

Figure 4.1 Symbolic array depiction of an island

Elements of a symbolic array correspond to the meaningful parts of an image. Such an array is interpreted in the context of some domain. For example, if we are using a two dimensional symbolic array to represent a map we may interpret the relative locations in an array in terms of the relations north, south, east and west. In a different interpretation the same spatial relations could correspond to up, down, right and left.

Hierarchical organization is a fundamental aspect of imagery. Our symbolic array representation supports a parts hierarchy by defining an image as a *recursive* data structure. A symbolic element of an array can itself denote a subimage. Consider the image of the island depicted in Figure 4.1. The symbols in this structured representation can denote structured subimages. Figure 4.2 illustrates the symbolic array depiction of the subimage "hut" of the original island image. As with the image of the island, this array would be generated using the depict slot of the image frame for hut.

roof	roof	roof
		window
	door	
	door	

Figure 4.2 Symbolic array representation of subimage hut

Note that the symbolic representation of a component of an image may occupy more than one location of an array, as in the case of the symbol "roof" in the above depiction. This is necessary to preserve the relations: *roof above door, roof above window* without implying the undesired relation *window above door.* To prevent ambiguity, if an image contains two instances of identical components, these components must be denoted using unique names. For example, the image of a hut would contain symbols for two distinct windows, which could be denoted as window1 and window2. Thus if the same symbol occurs more than once in a symbolic array it is denoting parts of the same component, not unique instances of a similar component.

4.2 Functions for Spatial Knowledge Representation

The effectiveness of a scheme for knowledge representation is measured primarily by how well it facilitates the processes that operate on the representation. Larkin and Simon argue that diagrams are computationally preferable to propositional representations, not because they contain more information but because the indexing of the information supports efficient computations [13].

A set of primitive functions have been designed and implemented to support the cognitive inferences involved in imagery. These functions on symbolic arrays are considered in three categories: functions for *constructing* images, functions for *transforming* images and functions for *accessing* images. Note that although the underlying image representation is fundamentally different, the functionality of these operations was greatly influenced by Kosslyn's computational model for imagery [12].

Images can be constructed in several ways. They can be reconstructed from a frame data structure stored in a database model of memory. In these frames, the spatial relationships are represented descriptively, rather than depictively. Images can also be constructed through perception and recognition processes. As well, users can input new images by interfacing to the frame structures of

Nial. Functions to support all of these methods of constructing images have been implemented.

Visualization often involves manipulating images through transformations. Functions that rotate, translate and vary the size of an image are included in the functions for transforming images.

Finally, it is necessary to provide an interface between a propositional representation and the symbolic array representation. Thus, functions that query or update an image based on a propositional description have been implemented. For example, a query function application *ontop box room* would return the symbolic representation of the subimage that is spatially above the subimage of the box in an image of the room. This function is domain specific since it assumes an interpretation of the relation "ontop".

4.3 Applications

A knowledge-based system for recognizing crystal structures using imagery is currently under development [4]. This application provides an ideal test case for many of the concepts described in this section. Crystal structures form a well defined domain which incorporates both spatial and hierarchical information; a crystal is depicted as a spatial relationship between molecules where a molecule is depicted as a spatial relationship between atoms. Historically, chemists have suggested that they utilized mental imagery in the identification of small molecular structures.

Other possible areas of application are visual and haptic perception and recognition. Many of the operations implemented for the crystallography system could also apply to these areas.

Also related to the vision application is the use of imagery in reasoning about motion. Psychologists have suggested that humans use imagery for solving problems related to motion. Time and motion can be added to the array model for imagery by adding another dimension to the array.

5 The Nial AI Toolkit

The design of the language Nial has been influenced by the desire to provide a multiparadigm programming environment. This feature of the language has proven useful for applications in the areas of databases and AI.

Although functional programming languages can be used to represent and reason about real world knowledge, logic programming languages do this more naturally. On the other hand, some applications in AI require the computational powers and expressive data objects of a functional language. This implies that a language that can combine these two styles of programming effectively, would provide a more powerful environment for AI problem solving than either of the individual paradigms. Nial has previously been recognized as such a language [5].

The Nial AI Toolkit [11] is a collection of programs and techniques that can be used to custom build knowledge-based systems. Unlike expert systems shells, that are typically limited to a single knowledge representation and inference engine, the Toolkit combines the flexibility of a high-level language with routines for a variety of knowledge representation and inferencing techniques.

The philosophy behind the development of the AI Toolkit was to provide building blocks from which tailored knowledge based systems are constructed [2]. In the design and development of the toolkit, several prototype knowledge based systems have been built. These include systems for chemical engineering, mechanical engineering, software testing, project management and space station applications. The AI capabilities of Nial are also currently being used for business applications in the commercial marketplace.

One of the primary tools in the toolkit, the logic programming subsystem, has already been discussed in this paper. Other tools include a database model, a frame language and a rule interpreter for reasoning about frames.

6 Discussion

In this paper we have illustrated how the array data structure can be used as a basis for knowledge representation. In particular, we demonstrated how both descriptive and depictive information can be stored and reasoned about using symbolic arrays and functions on these arrays.

An important feature of any scheme for knowledge representation is that it is computationally feasible. The programming language Nial, based on the theory of arrays, provides an implementation for the representations described in this paper.

A motivation for providing a variety of approaches for representing knowledge using a single formalism is to provide an environment from which tailored knowledge-based systems can be constructed. This goal is achieved by providing direct implementations of basic techniques that can be understood and extended by programmers constructing an application.

References

[1] Eli Blevis. A basis for effective logic programming in Nial. Master's thesis, Queen's University, Kingston, Canada, 1986.

[2] R. Chau, J.I. Glasgow, and M.A. Jenkins. A framework for knowledge based systems in Nial. In *Proceedings of the 6th Annual IEEE Phoenix Conference on Computers and Communication*, 1987.

[3] M. Feret. More expressive logic programming in Nial. Master's thesis, Queen's University, Kingston, Canada, 1988.

[4] S. Fortier, J.I. Glasgow, and F.H. Allen. The design of a knowledge-based system for crystal structure determination. In H. Schenk, editor, *Direct Methods of Solving Crystal Structures.* Plenum Press, London, 1990.

[5] J.I. Glasgow and R. Browse. Programming languages for artificial intelligence. *International Journal of Computers and Mathematics with applications*, 11(5), 1985.

[6] J.I. Glasgow, M.A. Jenkins, E. Blevis, and M. Feret. Logic programming with arrays. *IEEE Transactions on Data and Knowledge Engineering*, 1990. to appear.

[7] L. Hache. The Nial frame language. Master's thesis, Queen's University, Kingston, 1986.

[8] M.A. Jenkins and J.I. Glasgow. A logical basis for nested array data structures. *Programming Languages Journal*, 14(1):35–49, 1989.

[9] M.A. Jenkins, J.I. Glasgow, and C. McCrosky. Programming styles in Nial. *IEEE Software*, 86:46–55, January 1986.

[10] M.A. Jenkins and W.H. Jenkins. *The Q'Nial Reference Manual.* Nial Systems Ltd., Kingston, Ontario, 1985.

[11] M.A. Jenkins and W.H. Jenkins. *The artificial intelligence toolkit.* Nial Systems Ltd., Kingston, Canada, 1987.

[12] S.M. Kosslyn. *Image and Mind.* Harvard University Press, 1980.

[13] J.H. Larkin and H.A. Simon. Why a diagram is (sometimes) worth ten thousand words. *Cognitive Science 11*, pages 65 – 99, 1987.

[14] T. More. Notes on the diagrams, logic and operations of array theory. In Bjorke and Franksen, editors, *Structures and Operations in Engineering and Management Systems.* Tapir Pub., Norway, 1981.

[15] J.A. Robinson. Machine-oriented logic based on resolution principle. *Journal of the ACM*, 1, 1965.

[16] Z.D Umrigar and V. Pitchumani. An experiment in programming with full first-order logic. In *Proceedings of the Symposium on Logic Programming*, Boston, 1985.

9

A Parallel Intermediate Representation based on Lambda Expressions

Timothy A. Budd
Department of Computer Science
Oregon State University
Corvallis, Oregon
97331
budd@cs.orst.edu

November 28, 1990

Abstract

The lambda calculus has frequently been used as an intermediate representation for programming languages, particularly for functional programming language systems. We introduce two simple extensions to the lambda calculus that describe potentially parallel computations. These extensions permit us to use the lambda calculus as an intermediate form for languages that operate on large data items as single entities, such as FP or APL. We conclude by discussing how this intermediate representation can facilitate the generation of code for different types of parallel systems.

The Von Neumann Bottleneck

In his 1977 Turing Award lecture [Bac78] John Backus argued that traditional languages suffered from the "von Neumann bottleneck." This bottleneck is caused by processors which access words of memory one at a time. This results in programming languages that treat data in small units, to be processed individually. This in turn finally causes programmers to spend an inordinate amount of time dealing with the breaking up of large data items into small pieces, and the gathering together of small pieces of data into larger conceptual units. If languages dealt with data in larger conceptual units, Backus argued, not only would the programming task be simplified, but architects might be encouraged to develop machine organizations which overcome the basic word-at-a-time limitation of the conventional von Neumann design.

Backus proposed a new language, FP, which dealt with lists as large data items. Other languages, such as APL and LISP, have also been noted for dealing with large data items as a single unit, rather than one element at a time. It is certainly true that programs in these languages are often surprizingly succinct; for example Backus' two line definition of matrix multiplication, or the infamous APL one-liners [PeR79]. Some would argue, however, that brevity is not always synonymous with clarity. Regardless of how one stands on this issue, it is intuitive that a language, such as APL, that deals with operations on large data items implicitly in parallel should somehow be more easily amenable to parallel processing than, say, a language such as FORTRAN where parallelism is much less obvious in the original source code. While the intuition is clear, the practical matter of how one goes about making effective use of this parallelism is much more difficult.

Our research has been concerned with the development of compiler techniques that can be applied to languages, such as FP and APL, in which the basic elements of computation are large structures. Our approach is in many ways conventional. The compiler is divided into a number is separate stages or passes; a parser which translates the source code into an intermediate representation, various transformations on the intermediate representation, and a code generator which produces the final object code from the intermediate representation. In this paper we wish to concentrate on describing our intermediate representation, with a few brief words near the end showing how this intermediate representation simplifies the task of producing code for various types of parallel machines.

Lambda notation

The λ calculus has been studied extensively since the 1930s as a simple and elegant model of the notion of a function [Bar84]. A lambda expression is written as the symbol λ, one or more identifier (argument) names, and an expression:

$$\lambda \text{ x, y, z . } \textit{expresison}$$

It is important to note that the λ expression is a value, and can be treated as such (passed as an argument to another function for example). Various transformations can be performed on λ expressions, such as converting a λ expression of multiple arguments into a series of λ expressions each of one argument (called *curring*), applying a λ to values (so called β transformations), and so on. We will not describe these here; readers unfamiliar with λ notation are referred to any number of sources, such as [Pey86] or [Bar84].

Recently, λ notation has been adopted as a useful abstraction technique, and intermediate representation, for a number of functional languages [Pey86, Dil88]. Used in this manner various extensions to the bare λ forms are often employed. Examples of such extensions include single assignment variables and conditionals. Usually these extensions can be defined in the basic λ calculus, although this is often only of theoretical interest, since the definition may introduce unnecessary duplication or inefficiencies. This extended lambda calculus is then used as part of the internal language for describing computation.

Before describing our own extensions to the λ calculus, we note that the traditional formulation suffers from the same "von Neumann" bottleneck as conventional languages. A λ abstraction describes a function, but it is a function in which the user feeds in *one* value and obtains *one* result. If multiple values are desired, multiple invocations of the λ function must be performed. To overcome this, and to permit us to describe the computation of large data items in a convenient formal framework, we introduce two extensions to the λ calculus.

Collection (κ) forms

Our first extension is called a collection, or κ form. The collection form describes an entire group of values. It is formed by the symbol κ followed by two fields.

κ *size* (λ x . *expression*)

The first field is the *size* field, and describes the size of the object being described. The structure of the size field is different depending upon the language being compiled; in FP it can be simply a single scalar value representing the number of elements in a list, while in APL it is a pair representing a rank (number of dimensions) and a shape (extent along each dimension) for an arbitrary size array. In whatever form it takes, the expression can either be determined as a constant at compile time, or it may be maintained as a symbolic expression to be evaluated and determined at run time.

The second portion of the collection form is a λ expression. This expression, when evaluated with integer argument i, where i is between 0 and the number of elements of the item, yields the ith element of the resulting structure.

As a simple example, consider the characterization of the APL expression ⍳200. The APL function ⍳ takes a scalar argument and yields a vector where the elements run from 1 upto the argument value. Thus the result of this expression would be a vector containing 200 elements. To obtain any particular element, it is sufficient to add one (since ⍳ is one-based, and the κ form zero based) to the argument value. This is described as follows:

κ (1 (200)) (λ p . p + 1)

The κ form is a single value, and can be manipulated as a value in much the same manner as a λ form. Just as there are transformations that can be applied to λ forms, we have defined various transformations on κ forms. These include extracting the size and/or λ portion, and computing the result of the λ portion when given a specific (perhaps symbolic) argument.

It is also important to note that the κ form does not imply any specific ordering on the evaluation of each element of the result, or indeed that each element will ever be evaluated. This fact will become important when we consider the generation of parallel code for expressions containing a κ form.

Reduction (σ) forms

Our second extension to the λ calculus attempts to capture the common notion of a reduction of a vector to a single scalar quantity. The reduction form consists of the symbol σ followed by three fields. The first field is the name of a built-in function, such as addition (+), multiplication (×) or the like. The second field is an expression (perhaps symbolic) representing a scalar value indicating the size of the vector being reduced. The third field is once more a lambda expression, indicating the value to be used in the reduction.

σ *fun limit* . (λ x . *expression*)

The scalar value of a σ expression is determined by evaluating the nested λ expression on the values 0 to one less than the limit, and combining the results using the given function. It is important to note that for communtative and associatative functions no ordering on the evaluations is implied. This fact will be of importance when we describe our code generation strategy. The next section will give an example illustrating the use of a σ form.

While the σ form always produces a scalar value, this does not preclude the description of larger values being generated by a reduction, for example a two dimensional vector being reduced to a vector. Such objects can be described as a combination of κ and σ forms, as shown in the example in the next section.

An APL Compiler

Space does not permit a detailed description of the APL compiler we are constructing based around out intermediate representation; interested readers are referred to [Bud88b] and [Bud88c]. The general technique employed, however, is as follows.

- First we have defined characterizations, in terms of our extended λ calculus, for each of the many APL operations. Each of these characterizations is represented as a λ function which takes a κ form as input and yields a κ form as result.

- A parser then translates an APL expression into a concatenation of these characterizations, yielding a single large expression in our extended λ

language. (Typically each statement of APL produces a single large κ form).

- Transformation rules, chiefly β conversion on λ forms, are then applied to simplify this expression. Any computations and simplifications that can be applied at compile time are performed.

- The simplified form of the statement is then given to a code generator, producing the final object code.

While we have chosen to implement an APL system for our initial investigations, the techniques we use would be similar in any language that manipulated large data objects as single entities, such as FP (see [Bud88b]).

For the remainder of the paper we will restrict ourselves to considering only code generation for assignment statements, as this is the principle action in APL. Furthermore we will ignore details such as memory management and the storage of shape information, and consider only code that computes the value of an expression.

A typical APL assignment statement is the following, which computes a vector of length 200 containing one values in positions corresponding to primes and zero everywhere else. It accomplishes this by computing, for each value, the set of divisors for the value. If the number of even divisors is equal to two, then the value is considered to be prime. (Readers unfamiliar with APL may wish to consult a description of the language, such as [PoP75]).

$$\text{primes} \leftarrow 2 = +/0 = (\iota N) \circ.| \, \iota N$$

A detailed description of the compilation process for this expression is presented in [Bud88c]. For out purposes it is sufficient to note that this is eventually transformed into the following expression.

$$\begin{aligned}\text{primes} \leftarrow \kappa\ (1, (200))\ .\ (\lambda\ \text{p}\ .\\ 2 = \sigma +, 200\ .\\ (\lambda\ \text{q}\ .\ 0 = (\text{q}+1) \bmod (\text{p}+1)))\end{aligned}$$

The form of this intermediate representation is typical, consisting of an outermost $\kappa - \lambda$ pair surrounding zero or more $\sigma - \lambda$ or $\kappa - \lambda$ pairs. The major task during code generation is the translation of these forms into more conventional code sequences.

Code Generation

In this section we will discuss the issues involved in generating code from our extended λ expressions. Note that our basic underlying computational model corresponds to a conventional machine, perhaps augmented with parallel instructions, and thus we have little in common with systems that generate code from λ expressions using graph reduction [Pey86, Dil88].

Scalar Processors

When generating code for a conventional scalar processor, both κ and σ forms become loops. A κ form loops around a subscripted assignment generating each of the individual elements, where the variable being assigned is a temporary or, when a κ is combined with an assignment statement, the variable being assigned.

```
for i := 0 to 199 do begin
    ...
    primes[i] := ...;
end
```

A σ form becomes a loop modifying a reduction variable.

```
redvar := 0;
for i := 0 to 199 do begin
    ...
    redvar := redvar + ...;
end
```

The code is similar to that produced by other techniques [Bud88a].

Vector Machines

In the absence of conditional instructions or nested λ forms, each argument in a λ expression is acted upon in the same manner. On machines that possess vector instructions, if we can make a vector consisting of all the potential input values (that is, a vector running from zero up to the limit of the surrounding σ or κ form), then we can produce all values in parallel. This input vector can be either generated or copied from a static constant location. For example, the values generated by a innermost λ in the example of the last section might all be placed into a temporary variable *t* in parallel by the following straight-line code.

```
t(0:199) := ι 200; all inputs
t(0:199) := t(0:199) + 1;
t(0:199) := t(0:199) mod (p+1);
t(0:199) := (0 = t(0:199));
```

Conditional (**if**) forms can often be handled by generating both halves the the conditional and combining them with a mask.

SIMD Machines

Our model for a SIMD machine will be something like a Connection Machine, which has slightly more general capabilities than simple vector instructions [HiS86]. As with vector instructions, parallelism is utilized first in the innermost λ forms; with the surrounding forms either being incorporated into the parallel stream or generated as scalar code (see [Bud88c]).

On such a machine all elements of a κ form can be computed in parallel (assuming the number of elements of the array does not exceed the number of processors), since the target of each assignment is independent in each iteration.

```
for i := 0 to 199 in parallel do begin
    ...
    primes[i] := ...;
end
```

To perform a reduction a variation of Hillis' and Steels' logarithmic array summing algorithm can be employed. This produces the scalar result in time proportional to the log of the number of elements being reduced, leaving the answer in the first position of the array.

```
for j := 1 to ceil(log_2 extent) do
    for all k to extent in parallel do
            if k mod 2^j = 0 then
                if k + 2^(j-1) < extent then
                    x[k] := x[k] op x[k + 2^(j-1)]
                fi
            fi
    od
od
```

MIMD Machines

We are considering only shared memory MIMD machines. On such systems, the goal is to divide a computation into a number of roughly equivalent parallel tasks each involving a nontrivial amount of computation. Thus, in contrast to the technique used for SIMD machines, we want to parallelise around the outermost κ form of an assignment statement, giving each processor the task of generating a section of the final result. Within each processor scalar code is used to generate the values for the result. If we let *numberProcessors* represent the number of processors, and *extent* the size of an outermost loop generated for a κ form, the high level pseudo-code we could generate for a κ form would be as follows:

```
for i := 1 to numberProcessors do begin
    fork off process doing the following
    for j := i * (extent/numberProcessors)
        to (i+1)*(extent/numberProcessors) - 1 do begin
        primes[j] := ...
wait for all processors to complete
```

We have not considered the issues involved in generating code for non-shared memory MIMD machines.

Conclusions

We have introduced two simple extensions to the λ formalism for describing functional computations. These extensions permit us to describe the manipulation of large data objects as if they were single values. Our extended λ formalism is at the heart of an experimental APL system we are constructing, although the techniques are also applicable to FP or other languages that manipulate large values as single entities. Having introduced our extensions, we have discussed how these constructs, by eliminating explicit control flow requirements from the description of computations, facilitate the generation of code for a variety of parallel processors.

It is interesting to note that the technique we have outlined works best on large and complex expressions. Thus the infamous "one-liner", considered almost an art form among supports of APL [PeR79], and strongly denounced by detractors of the language [Dij72], is shown to have a useful and practical benefit.

References

[Bac78] Backus, John, "Can Programming Be Liberated from the von Neumann Style? A Functional Style and Its Algebra of Programs", *Communications of the ACM*, Vol 21(8): 613-641, (August 1978).

[Bar84] Barendregt, H.P., *The Lambda Calculus: its syntax and semantics* (2nd ed), North-Holland, 1984.

[Bud88a] Budd, Timothy A., *An APL Compiler*, Springer-Verlag, 1988.

[Bud88b] Budd, Timothy A., "Composition and Compilation in Functional Programming Languages", Technical Report 88-60-14, Computer Science Department, Oregon State University, June 1988.

[Bud88c] Budd, Timothy A., "A New Approach to Vector Code Generation for Applicative Languages", Technical Report 88-60-18, Computer Science Department, Oregon State University, August 1988.

[Dij72] Dijkstra, Edsger W., "The Humble Programmer", *Communications of the ACM*, Vol 15(10):859-866 (October 1972).

[Dil88] Diller, Antoni, *Compiling Functional Languages*, Wiley, New York, 1988.

[HiS86] Hillis, W. D. and Steele, G. L., "Data Parallel Algorithms", *Communications of the ACM*, Vol 29(12):1170-1183 (December 1986).

[Pey86] Peyton Jones, Simon L., *The Implementation of Functional Programming Languages*, Prentice-Hall, 1986.

[PeR79] Perlis, Alan J. and Rugaber, Spencer, "Programming with Idioms in APL", APL Quote Quad, Vol 9(4):232-235 (June 1979).

[PoP75] Polivka, R. and Pakin, S., *APL: The Language and Its Usage*, Prentice Hall, 1975.

10

Arrays in FIDIL*

Luigi Semenzato[†]
Paul Hilfinger

Computer Science Division
University of California at Berkeley

June 9, 1990

Abstract

The FIDIL language introduces the *map* type, an extension of the traditional array type, to simplify the programming of numerical methods for partial differential equations. This paper describes some of the obstacles to an efficient implementation of maps, and proposes techniques to circumvent them.

1 Overview of the FIDIL Language

The FIDIL language is one response to the programming difficulties caused by the increasing complexity of modern algorithms in computational fluid dynamics (CFD), and by the subtleties of achieving high performance from a diverse set of modern supercomputer architectures. When, for example, a modern two-dimensional adaptive mesh-refinement scheme, describable in a few pages of mathematics, becomes 10000 lines of FORTRAN, it becomes difficult to experiment with simple variations on the method, and nearly impossible to consider moving to three dimensions. These problems multiply if one wants to maintain such a program over a variety of architectures.

*This research was funded by the NSF PYI Award DCR-8451213, with matching funds from Sequent Computer Systems, and the NSF (DARPA) grant DMS-8919074

[†]Authors' address: 571 Evans Hall, Berkeley, CA 94720. E-mail: luigi@ginger.berkeley.edu and hilfingr@ginger.berkeley.edu

To address these problems, the FIDIL language provides two extensions over languages currently popular for scientific computation. First, it incorporates modern capabilities for defining operators and for performing "higher-order" operations upon functions. Second, it extends the usual notion of array types to provide arrays with more general index sets. The result, we think, is well-suited to the needs of scientific programmers who work with finite-difference and particle methods. Furthermore, because FIDIL programs are explicitly formulated in terms of operations upon entire arrays, we believe that it will be feasible to compile FIDIL for disparate architectures with little source-code modification required.

In this paper, we will concentrate on implementation issues in the implementation of the array data structures in FIDIL. Section 2 gives a very brief overview of FIDIL's array-related features. The language is described in more detail elsewhere [6, 5]. The rest of the paper is devoted to implementation.

2 Relevant Language Features

In most ways, FIDIL is just another strongly-typed language in the Algol family. For the purposes of this paper, the essential differences arise in its treatment of arrays. In conventional procedural languages, arrays have index sets that are fixed no later than the time of their creation and that consist of rectangular sets of integer tuples. FIDIL arrays are generalized into what we call *maps*. At any time, an n-dimensional map has an index set (called a *domain*) that is an arbitrary set of n-tuples of integers. Domains are themselves legitimate data values; they (and thus the index sets of maps) may be data-dependent, computable only on execution of the program. A map variable may be *flexible*, in which case its index set may change dynamically.

The notation "`[`D`]` T" (used in variable or parameter declarations) denotes a map type with domain D and codomain (element type) T. Thus,

```
[ 1 .. 10, 1 .. 10 ] real U
```

indicates that the variable `U` is a 10×10 array of reals. The notation "`[*`n`]` T" in a parameter declaration indicates a map with any n-dimensional domain and codomain T ('`[*1]`' may be abbreviated '`[]`'). The modifier "**flex**" in front of an array type indicates that the domains of instances of that type may vary.

Maps and domains may be stored in variables, passed as parameters,

Expression	Meaning
$D_1 + D_2$	Union of D_1 and D_2.
$D_1 * D_2$	Intersection of D_1 and D_2.
$D_1 - D_2$	Set difference of D_1 and D_2.
p **in** D	a logical expression that is **true** iff p is a member of D.
lwb(D), upb(D)	Lower and upper bounds of D. For multidimensional domains, these are vectors (one-dimensional maps).
shift(D, S), $D << S$	Where D is an n-ary domain and S is a vector of n elements, these denote the shifted domain $\{d + S \mid d \text{ in } D\}$.
arity(D)	The arity of domain D.
contract(D, S)	The domain $\{d \text{ div } S \mid d \text{ in } D\}$. Here, when D has an arity greater than 1, the integer division operator (**div**) applies to corresponding pairs of elements in d and S.
expand(D, S)	The domain $\{d * S \mid d \text{ in } D\}$.
accrete(D)	The set of points that are within a distance 1 in all coordinates from some point of D.
boundary(D)	accrete(D) $- D$.
$[\ L_1..U_1, \cdots, L_n..U_n\ ]$	The rectangular domain containing all integer n-tuples whose i^{th} members are both between L_i and U_i for all i.

Table 1: Some representative operators on domains.

returned as values, or stored as fields of structures. The language contains a rich set of generic operations upon maps and domains, some of which are summarized in tables 1 and 2.

For computational purposes, one of the most significant operations is the functional operator '`@`'. If F is a function on reals that produces real values, for example, then F`@` denotes a function operating on maps of reals and producing maps of reals, defined by extending F to apply pointwise to the elements of a map. Technically, F`@` is overloaded to denote a family of such functions, one for each possible arity of the map arguments. If G takes two arguments, then G`@` takes two maps and returns a map. To resolve the issue of what to do when the domains of the two arguments to G`@` differ, FIDIL defines G`@ (`X`,`Y`)` to

Expression	Meaning
domainOf(X)	The domain of map X.
upb(X) lwb(X) arity(X)	upb(domainOf(X)) lwb(domainOf(X)) arity(domainOf(X))
[p **from** D: $\mathcal{E}$] [$E_1, \ldots, E_n$]	The map with domain D whose elements, for each p, are computed by evaluating expression $\mathcal{E}$ (which will generally involve p). The vector whose elements are the E_i.
X # Y	Map composition: (X#Y) [p] is equivalent to X [Y [p]] for any p.
shift(X, S), X << S contract(X, S) expand(X, S)	These operations correspond to the similarly-named ones on domains. That is, $op(X, S)$ produces a map whose domain is op(domainOf(X),S) and whose elements are "carried along."
X **on** D	The map X restricted to domain $D \cap$ domainOf(X).
F@	Assuming that F takes arguments of type T_i and returns a result of type T, F@ is a (generic) function that takes arguments of types $[*n]\ T_i$, that returns a result of type $[D]\ T$, where D is the intersection of the domains of the T_i. The result of applying this function is the result of applying F pointwise to the elements at the same indices.

Table 2: Representative operators on maps.

produce a map whose domain is the intersection of those of X and Y. We have found this to be the most convenient definition in practice. The standard arithmetic operators are all overloaded with instances that behave as if '@' had been applied. Thus, given the variables

```
[ 1..10, 1..100 ] real    A;
[ 1..100, 1..10 ] real    B;
```

the expression A+B produces a 10×10 map value containing the sums of corresponding elements of A and B whose indices are between 1 and 10. As a further convenience, the arithmetic operators will also take a mixture of scalar and map arguments, with the obvious meaning.

The array features of FIDIL are similar to those of several other languages that have been proposed for scientific computation. APL is perhaps the best-known example of a language that allows the direct manipulation of arrays as complete entities, and provides functional operators that can in principle be applied simultaneously over all elements of an array. FORTRAN 8X [1] and Actus [7] are two languages that also provide for concise descriptions of operations over entire arrays. Both of them, like standard APL, concentrate on rectangular data structures. Connection Machine Lisp [8] has an even more general array structure than ours (the index sets may be arbitrary sets of Lisp objects). It is not clear, however, what effect this generality will have on performance. For CFD algorithms, at least, it is reasonable to restrict ourselves to uniform sets of integer tuples.

3 Implementation Issues

For the initial version of the FIDIL compiler, we have concentrated on producing a retargetable run-time structure and executable code of acceptable quality for serious use. The initial target is a uniprocessor vector architecture, more specifically a single processor Cray-XMP. For ease of retargeting, the compiler outputs C code. We initially considered FORTRAN as the target language, but switched to C as the quality of vectorizing C compilers (in particular those for the Cray family) improved. Moreover, we are employing run-time data structures that have potential for being reused in future multiprocessor implementations.

Naive implementations of FIDIL maps have some obvious sources of inefficiency. We developed techniques to reduce or eliminate them. One source is present in many instances of elementwise map operations; we deal with it with an extension of the live-variable analysis technique, as described in section 4. Other sources are introduced by the generality of the map type and our need to implement it efficiently, as explained in sections 5, 6 and 7.

4 Live-domain Analysis

Languages with elementwise operations on arrays give programmers many opportunities to introduce unnecessary computation. It is often simpler, as well as correct, to evaluate some expressions on a larger domain than the one subsequently used. This is made even easier in FIDIL by the implicit intersection rule. Consider the following elementwise statement in FIDIL, where A, B and C are maps:

```
let A = B ** 2 + 1 / B ** 2 + C;
```

A compiler can analyze this statement is isolation to see that the computation need only be carried out on the intersection of the domains of B and C. However, a programmer would like to consider the statement above equivalent to the following statements:

```
let Bsquared = B ** 2;
let A = Bsquared + 1 / Bsquared + C;
```

Here, analysis of the first statement in isolation computes Bsquared over the entire domain of B. The value of A will be the same in both cases, but if the domain of B and the domain of C are not identical, part of the computation of Bsquared is wasted.

To minimize these effects we have designed and implemented a data-flow analysis technique, *live-domain analysis*, which is an extension of the traditional live-variable analysis for scalars. Live-domain analysis has also an important impact on vectorization, as mentioned in section 7. The analysis annotates each elementwise statement with a conservative (sufficiently large) approximation of the *live domain* of each map variable appearing in that statement. The live domain of map M at statement S denotes the part of M that will be used at some point in the program after executing statement S. After the approximated live domains have been obtained, the compiler annotates each statement S with its *minimal execution domain*, a subset of the original execution domain.

In most cases it is impossible to compute the live domains at compilation time, as they depend on quantities that are not known before program execution. Instead we compute *live domain descriptors*, symbolic descriptions of domain-valued expressions that evaluate to the live domains at run time.

The following example illustrates a simple case of live-domain analysis on a program fragment. Each of the four FIDIL **let** statements declares and initializes a constant. We annotate the statements with relations between the *used domain*, $\delta_{use}(\mathrm{M})$, of the maps in the right hand side, and the live domain, $\delta_{live}(\mathrm{M})$, of the map in the left hand side. These relations are derived from local inspection of each statement:

let A = B + C; /* $\delta_{use}(\mathrm{B}) = \delta_{use}(\mathrm{C}) = \delta_{live}(\mathrm{A})$ */
let D = A + E; /* $\delta_{use}(\mathrm{A}) = \delta_{use}(\mathrm{E}) = \delta_{live}(\mathrm{D})$ */
let F = D + G; /* $\delta_{use}(\mathrm{D}) = \delta_{use}(\mathrm{G}) = \delta_{live}(\mathrm{F})$ */
let H = D + K; /* $\delta_{use}(\mathrm{D}) = \delta_{use}(\mathrm{K}) = \delta_{live}(\mathrm{H})$ */

Other useful relations are available from the implicit intersection rule in FIDIL; for instance, $\delta(\mathrm{A}) = \delta(\mathrm{B}) \cap \delta(\mathrm{C})$, where $\delta(\mathrm{M})$ stands for the domain of map M according to FIDIL semantics.

Global analysis lets us derive the following relations (among others) for the live domains of maps after their definition. For simplicity, $\delta_{live}(\mathrm{M})$ indicates the live domain of M at the statement that defines M. We assume that A, B, C, D, E, G, and K have no further uses after the program fragment, and F and H are fully used:

let A = B + C; /* $\delta_{live}(\mathrm{A}) = \delta_{live}(\mathrm{D})$ */
let D = A + E; /* $\delta_{live}(\mathrm{D}) = \delta_{live}(\mathrm{F}) \cup \delta_{live}(\mathrm{H})$ */
let F = D + G; /* $\delta_{live}(\mathrm{F}) = \delta(\mathrm{F})$ */
let H = D + K; /* $\delta_{live}(\mathrm{H}) = \delta(\mathrm{H})$ */

From these we can calculate the minimal execution domains in terms of values of domains that are known before the statements:

let A = B + C; /* $\delta_{\mathrm{ME}} = \delta(\mathrm{B}) \cap \delta(\mathrm{C}) \cap \delta(\mathrm{E}) \cap (\delta(\mathrm{G}) \cup \delta(\mathrm{K}))$ */
let D = A + E; /* $\delta_{\mathrm{ME}} = \delta(\mathrm{B}) \cap \delta(\mathrm{C}) \cap \delta(\mathrm{E}) \cap (\delta(\mathrm{G}) \cup \delta(\mathrm{K}))$ */
let F = D + G; /* $\delta_{\mathrm{ME}} = \delta(\mathrm{D}) \cap \delta(\mathrm{G})$ */
let H = D + K; /* $\delta_{\mathrm{ME}} = \delta(\mathrm{D}) \cap \delta(\mathrm{K})$ */

The analysis does not make any assumptions on the actual values of the domains. Although this is useful, since the values are often not known at compilation time, it makes it difficult to extend this method to expressions containing *reshaping* operators, such as **shift**. A description of the data-flow equations and the lattice employed for their solution is beyond the scope of this paper.

5 Domain Representation

Compactness of descriptors and efficiency of domain operations is not the primary issue in the design of a run-time representation for domains. More important is the impact this design has on vectorization (and, in future implementations, parallelization) of operations on maps. With this in mind, we have identified three shapes for the kinds of domains that are likely to appear in FIDIL programs: the *boxy* shape, the *thin* shape, and the *thick* shape [3]. The boxy shape corresponds to conventional arrays or other simple, compact sets, such as the boundary of a rectangular array (see fig. 1). Representing it as a list of disjoint boxes (n-dimensional rectangles) facilitates vectorization on maps with that shape.

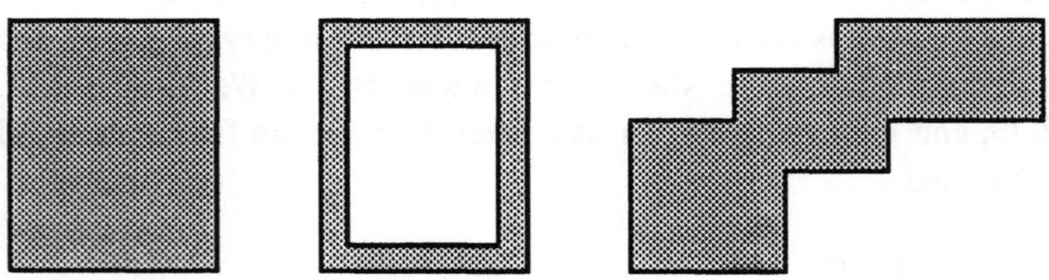

Figure 1: Examples of *boxy* domains

The thin shape corresponds to a set of mostly isolated points, or other shapes that are neither boxy nor thick. The thick shape is a boxy shape with thin "holes" in it, and it arises in situations in which a grid has some singular points that should be skipped in an elementwise computation (see fig. 2).

Each of these shapes uses a different run-time representation. A thin descriptor is a list of all the points in the domain in lexicographic order. A

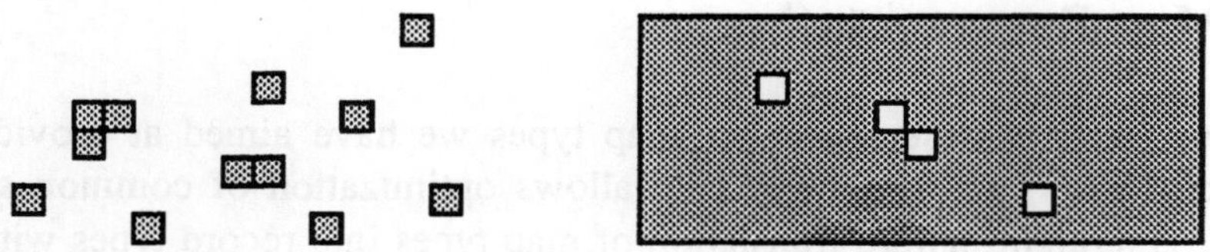

Figure 2: Examples of *thin* and *thick* domains

thick descriptor consists of a boxy descriptor plus a thin descriptor for the holes. A boxy descriptor is a list of disjoint boxes in *canonical form.*

The main idea behind the canonical form consists of assigning a priority to each dimension, and insuring that boxes extend as much as they can along the dimensions with higher priority. In other words: a box should extend as much as possible along dimension i, as long as that does not preclude maximum extension along dimensions $(i-1), \ldots, 1$ (see fig. 3).

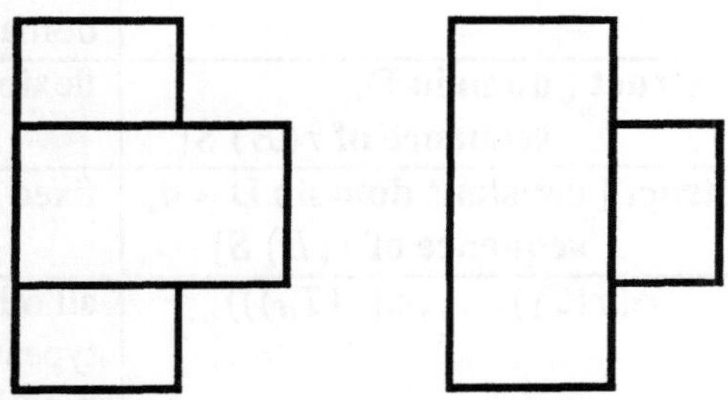

Figure 3: Canonical form of a boxy domain

Using a canonical form speeds up several domain operations (e.g. checking for equality), and even though it does not guarantee the smallest possible number of boxes for a given domain, it helps avoiding excessive fragmentation. More importantly, it insures that maps with the same domain also have the same layout, thus improving vectorization.

6 Map Representation

In choosing a representation for map types we have aimed at providing a uniform, fully general scheme that allows optimization of common simple cases. A straightforward translation of map types into record types with two components, one for the map's domain and one for the map's data, is adequate for maps with scalar elements (e.g., [D] **real**), and nested maps with a flexible codomain (e.g., [D] **flex** [*2] **real**), but it is inefficient for nested maps with a fixed codomain: for instance, every element of a map with type [D1] [D2] **real** must maintain its own copy of the value of D2.

To remedy this problem, we apply two type transformations to a FIDIL program during its compilation. The first one translates map types into record types, and it can be described by a recursive function τ that takes a type T and returns its transformation, as in the following table:

T	$\tau(T)$	comments
simple type	T	number types, logical, domain, etc.
flex [ ] E	**struct [domain D; sequence of** $\tau(E)$ **S]**	flexible map type
[d] E	**struct [constant domain D** = **d; sequence of** $\tau(E)$ **S]**	fixed map type
$\alpha(T_1, \ldots, T_n)$	$\alpha(\tau(T_1), \ldots, \alpha(\tau(T_n)))$	all other aggregate types (record, function)

If the map has a fixed domain, the first field is constant. The second field has the type **sequence of** .... A sequence is just a one-dimensional array with a lower bound of 0; the definition of the sequence type does not require that all its elements be stored in consecutive memory locations, as explained in section 7.

As an example, τ transforms a nested map type as shown:

```
[D1] [D2] real   ⇒   struct [
                         constant domain D = D1;
                         sequence of struct [
                            constant domain D = D2;
                            sequence of real S;
                         ] S;
                     ]
```

The example shows how every element of the nested map must store a copy of D2. To exploit the fact that all elements have the same domain, the second transformation, called *sequence-record flipping*, changes sequences of records into records of sequences. A function ϕ describing this transformation is shown here:

T	$\phi(T)$	comments
simple type	T	number types, logical, domain, etc.
sequence of struct [$T_1\ f_1$; ⋮ $T_n\ f_n$]	struct [ϕ(sequence of T_1) f_1; ⋮ ϕ(sequence of T_n) f_n]	
sequence of E, $E \neq \phi(E)$	ϕ(sequence of $\phi(E)$)	
sequence of E, $E = \phi(E)$	T	
$\alpha(T_1, \ldots, T_n)$	$\alpha(\phi(T_1), \ldots, \phi(T_n))$	all other aggregate types (record, function)

This transformation exposes sequences of identical elements, whose representation can be optimized. The type in the example above becomes then:

```
struct [
   constant domain D = d1;
   struct [
      constant sequence of domain D = constSeq(d2);
      sequence of sequence of real S;
   ] S;
]
```

When this transformation is performed, appropriate conversion operations must be inserted to preserve the original program semantics. Most of the conversions disappear in a following simplification phase. However, an element of a map A with type [D1] [D2] **real**, such as A[i], is no longer described by a single pointer after the sequence-record flipping. The occurrence of A[i] in a context requiring a location (lhs of an assignment, actual reference parameter, or location returned by a selector) is classified as a *generalized location* and requires further rewriting.

Both domains and sequences are represented as pointers to structures. These structures can be shared at run-time: in fact, every assignment of a domain or a sequence causes the object to be shared by creating one additional pointer to it. A reference count is kept for each object for the purposes of garbage collection and *delayed copying* of sequences. FIDIL is not a purely functional language, so individual elements of a sequence can be modified by the assignment operation. Every time this happens, the run-time system checks if the sequence being modified is shared, and if necessary it makes a new, private copy of the sequence before the assignment.

7 Elementwise Operations on Maps

The implementation of maps, and elementwise operations on them, must obey two constraints: good vectorization and efficient use of memory. The typical application that FIDIL targets runs for a long time on supercomputers, spends most of its time doing vector floating point computation, and it does a lot of dynamic allocation of large data structures. To make it easier to optimize the use of memory, a sequence (the part of a map that contains its data) is not stored sequentially in memory, but it is broken in *chunks* with a fixed maximum size.

The technique we use to implement elementwise statements is called *chunk-by-chunk evaluation.* The compiler identifies groups of consecutive elementwise statements with the same execution domain[1], and it translates them into two nested loops: an outer loop that iterates over chunks, and a vectorizable inner loop that iterates over all elements of a chunk. In the general case (e.g. the operands have domains with different shapes), the outer loop aligns the operands' elements by copying them into *temporary chunks* with calls to run-time library routines. The run-time system recognizes several opportunities for optimizing this scheme by eliminating the extra copy: for instance when the operands have the same domain as the statement domain of execution; or when they have simple shapes, and the alignment can be achieved by fiddling with the iteration bounds.

We are considering a future improvement to this scheme that would handle several *reshaping* operators better, such as the scaling operators **contract** and **expand**. The improvement consists in combining the chunk-by-chunk evaluation with delayed evaluation techniques proposed for the compilation of APL programs [4, 2]. We call the resulting combination *lazy chunk-by-chunk evaluation*.

8 Implementation Status and Remarks

Our version of the compiler is currently compiling small programs for a Cray X-MP/14. The back-end is written in Common Lisp and it implements the techniques described above. A limited form of lazy chunk-by-chunk evaluation has already been introduced for the **shift** operator. Regrettably, we have not yet been able to measure the performance of these techniques on realistic programs. The following observations, however, lead us to believe that good performance can be achieved:

1. the typical application spends a very large percentage of the total running time performing floating point computation. Therefore, we believe that there is room for a considerable amount of run-time support to dynamically analyze and set up various parameters of the vector operations;

2. in many instances of elementwise statements, the number of floating point operations per element, plus loads and stores caused by vector register spills, is large. In these cases the overhead of an extra load and

[1] Live-domain analysis often has the effect of assigning the same minimal execution domain to statements that would otherwise have different execution domains.

store per element, for the purpose of aligning corresponding elements in consecutive memory locations, seems tolerable.

In the near future, we plan to experiment with larger programs implementing modern CFD algorithms. Experience with these programs will indicate where to concentrate our efforts.

9 Conclusion

We have presented the main issues arising from the implementation of FIDIL maps, and the techniques we propose for their solution. We have aimed at optimizing execution on a vector processor, based on the typical use of maps in CFD algorithms. For this purpose we have developed a data-flow analysis algorithm for map variables, a type transformation technique for map types, and an adaptive run-time system for elementwise operations.

References

[1] AMERICAN NATIONAL STANDARDS INSTITUTE, I. Draft Proposed Revised American National Standard Programming Language FORTRAN. ANSI, 1987. ANSI X3.9-198x edition.

[2] BUDD, T. A. An APL compiler for a vector processor. *ACM Transactions on Programming Languages and Systems 6*, 3 (July 1984), 297–313.

[3] COLELLA, P. Private communication, 1988.

[4] GUIBAS, L. J., AND WYATT, D. K. Compilation and delayed evaluation in APL. In *Conference Record of the Fifth ACM Symposium on Principles of Programming Languages* (1978), pp. 1–8.

[5] HILFINGER, P. N., AND COLELLA, P. FIDIL reference manual (draft release 4). University of California, Department of Electrical Engineering and Computer Sciences, internal working document.

[6] HILFINGER, P. N., AND COLELLA, P. FIDIL: A language for scientific programming. In *Symbolic Computing: Applications to Scientific Computing*, R. Grossman, Ed., Frontiers in Applied Mathematics. SIAM, 1989, ch. 5, pp. 97–138.

[7] PERROT, R. H., CROOKES, D., AND MILLIGAN, P. The programming language Actus. *Software Practice & Experience 13* (1983), 305–322.

[8] STEELE, JR., G. L., AND HILLIS, W. D. Connection machine Lisp: Fine-grained parallel symbolic processing. In *Proceedings of the 1986 ACM Conference on LISP and Functional Programming* (1986), pp. 279–297.

11

Structured Data-Types in the Reduction System π-RED

C. Schmittgen, H. Blödorn and W. Kluge
Department of Computer Science
University of Kiel
West–Germany
Email: {hb,wk}@informatik.uni-kiel.dbp.de

July 28, 1990

Introduction

Modern functional languages [6, 7, 8, 11, 14, 15] provide elegant means of concisely specifying operations on structured data. Unfortunately, the efficient implementation of these operations remains a considerable problem. Conceptually, they must create new result objects rather than update existing ones in order to keep functional computations free of side effects. Copying repeatedly large arrays which need merely be restructured without changing their entries is extremely costly in terms of both memory space and processing time expended. Though some of these difficulties can be overcome by manipulating structured data objects as conceptual entities rather than incrementally, there is no generally satisfactory solution to the complexity problems inflicted by copying. Trying to find out by a static program analysis which operations may overwrite their operands without introducing side effects shifts the complexity in large parts from program execution to compiling [2].

In this paper we will discuss an APL-like approach of supporting structured data types in the reduction system π-RED [9, 10], an applicative order graph reducer equipped with a high-level user interface for interactive syntax-directed program design and execution. Rather than compiling functional programs into executable code of a conventional machine, π-RED truly performs meaning-preserving program transformations following the reduction rules of a full-fledged applied λ-calculus.

Programs written as sets of (recursively nested) function equations and function applications are reversibly converted into graph representations of λ-expressions for execution. Partially or completely (to normal form) reduced λ-expressions are re-converted into equivalent high-level language representations for inspection and modification by the user. Due to the Church-Rosser-property of the λ-calculus, reductions may be carried out under user-control in any part of a large program.

Since π-RED supports an untyped λ-calculus, programs require no type declarations and need not even be well-typed. Types are dynamically checked and inferred (and appropriate memory space is dynamically allocated) at run-time based on type descriptions carried along with all computational objects. Applications of primitive functions to type-incompatible arguments are considered constant and left as they are, and reductions may continue elsewhere in the program.
It may be argued that the absence of a rigid typing discipline is a considerable deficiency when it comes to writing correct programs. We prefer to consider it an asset which enhances the expressive power of a functional language beyond that of polymorphically typed languages such as MIRANDA and ML [6, 7, 14, 15]. We may have self-applications, the component expressions of lists and conditionals may have different types, and primitive as well as user-defined functions may be highly generic, allowing for a wide variety of argument types. Of course, this flexibility can be had with competitive performance only at the expense of tailor-made machinery which provides effective hardware support for dynamic type checking and type inference, dynamic memory management, and for the traversal of array structures. These features are a major design objective of a π-RED machine architecture.

Data Types in π-RED

High-level program expressions for π-RED are usually specified in the reduction language KIR (for Kiel Red Language [3]) or in OREL/2 [12], a variant of KIR whose syntax resembles that of ML and MIRANDA. They typically have the form

```
expr = DEFINE
             .
             f [x_1,..,x_n] = f_expr
             .
             h [y_1,..,y_m] = h_expr
             .
             IN g_expr
```

All component expressions of this construct may be recursively defined in the same way. Other expressions relevant in this context include

- function applications, denoted as `func [arg_1,...,arg_n]`, where `func` is the name of a defined function or a symbol for a primitive function, and `arg_1,...,arg_n` are argument expressions;
- linearly ordered sequences of expressions, denoted as `< expr_1 ,..., expr_n >` which are the basic vehicles for defining, generating and manipulating structured objects.

The basic data types of KIR are numbers, booleans and character strings. Legitimate structured objects of KIR fall into one of the following type classes [1, 9]:
VALue is an atomic expression of one of the basic types;
VECtor is a (possibly empty) sequence of values of the same basic type;
MATrix is a (possibly empty) sequence of vectors, all of which have the same number of values of the same basic type;
TUPle is a (possibly empty) sequence of KIR expressions (including sequences), which may have heterogeneous types (or type classes).
Reasonably complete sets of primitive generic structuring and value-transforming functions are available as well. The former are applicable to objects of the classes **VECtor**, **MATrix**, **TUPle**, and the latter are applicable to objects of the classes **VALue**, **VECtor** and **MATrix** with numerical or boolean elements.
Applications of structuring functions generally have the form

struc_func[{coord}, par, arg]

where

- **arg** specifies the argument object;
- **coord** specifies only in the case of matrices the coordinate along which the structure is to be changed;
- **par** denotes a structuring parameter.

The primitive structuring functions include

SELECT which returns the component ({**coord**,} **par**) and discards all other components of the argument object;

CUT which deletes the first or last **par** components of the argument object along **coord** (depending on whether **par** has a positive or negative value, respectively);

ROTATE which rotates the argument object along coord by **par** positions to the left (if **par** < 0) or to the right (if **par** > 0)

In addition, we have a function **APPEND** which concatenates n argument objects of the same type class (including **VALue**) along a specified coordinate.
Applications of value-transforming functions to objects of the classes **VALue**, **VECtor** and **MATrix** include

- elementwise arithmetic and relational unary and binary operations;
- summation, multiplication, minimum, maximum etc. over all elements of a vector or over all row/column-vectors of a matrix;
- inner- and cartesian products;

These applications can only be reduced if the arguments conform to the functions with respect to class, element type and structural specifications. For instance, in the case of a matrix multiplication, the number of columns of the first argument matrix must match the number of rows of the second argument matrix, and both matrices must have the same element type.
Since KIR is an untyped language, structured objects may be specified only as sequences (of sequences). A pre-processor which converts KIR programs into executable λ-expressions also converts sequences into objects of the type classes to which they syntactically conform, and annotates them accordingly. In addition to class and type of elements, this annotation also includes object shapes (e.g. row and column dimensions of matrices).

Other Operations on Structured Data

A powerful concept used in almost all functional languages is pattern matching. The basic idea is to specify operations which extract substructures from a given structural context and substitute them for names (identifiers) in another structural context. Pattern matching functions are in KIR specified as

```
WHEN pattern {guard} DO p_expr
```

where

pattern is either a variable or a (recursively nested) sequence whose atoms are variables;

guard is an optional guard expression defined in terms of pattern variables which is supposed to reduce to a boolean value;

p_expr may be any legitimate KIR expression in which some or all pattern variables may occur free

WHEN binds free occurrences of the pattern variables both in **guard** and **p_expr**.

The application of a pattern matching function to an argument expression **arg** is denoted as **(WHEN pattern guard DO p_expr arg)** and reduces as follows: If the syntactical structures of the pattern and of the argument expression match in that

- for each (sub-) sequence of the pattern there exists a corresponding (sub-) sequence in the argument so that
- each variable of the pattern can be associated with a (sub-) structure of the argument

then all free occurrences of the pattern variables in **guard** and **p_expr** are substituted by the respective argument substructures. If in addition the guard thus instantiated evaluates to TRUE, then the entire application reduces to the normal form of the instantiated body expression **p_expr**. Otherwise the

argument is considered not within the domain of the pattern matching function (or not of a compatible type), i.e. the application remains unchanged.
Following this interpretation, the pattern in fact defines a structured data type. It is the set of all (nested) sequences which match the pattern.
Patterns in KIR may in places of variables also have

- constants of the type class VALue;
- type or type class specifications;
- terminals of the form AS ... x.

Constants must match literally and type (type class) specifications must match in type (type class) with the corresponding argument (sub-) structures, and AS ... x binds some contiguous (sub-) sequence of matching argument components whose length is unspecified.
Several pattern matches may form a CASE expression

```
CASE x WHEN pattern_1{guard_1} DO p_expr_1
         .
         .
         .
       WHEN pattern_n{guard_n} DO p_expr_n
     {OTHERWISE q_expr}
END-CASE
```

The CASE is a unary function which, when applied to an argument, tries all pattern matches in sequence. The first successful match (including a satisfiable guard) is reduced to its normal form which, by definition, is also the normal form of the entire CASE application. If none of the pattern/guard combinations matches, then the application either reduces to the optional OTHERWISE-expression or, if this expression is not specified, it remains as it is.
A simple example in kind is a function which tests whether or not a sequence has palindrome property:

```
DEFINE
 pal [ x ] = CASE x WHEN <> DO TRUE
                    WHEN <z> DO TRUE
                    WHEN <u, AS ... y, v> (u EQ v) DO pal[ y ]
                    OTHERWISE FALSE
IN pal [ <e_1, e_2,...,e_(n-1), e_n> ]
```

The general case is covered by the third pattern: provided the argument is a sequence of at least two components, it binds its first and last component (e_1 and e_n in this particular application) to the variables u and v, respectively, and the subsequence <e_2,...,e_(n-1)> that is in between to the variable y. The guard compares literally the expressions bound to u and v for equality and, if so, the function pal is recursively applied to the subsequence bound to y. The program terminates either with the value FALSE (if the third pattern match or its guard fails) or with the value TRUE, if the sequence to which pal

is (recursively) applied is empty or contains only one element (in which case we have a palindrome).
A **CASE** function defines a structured data type which is the union of all sequences (of sequences) which match the patterns **pattern_1,...,pattern_n** and, if specified, satisfy the associated guards.
Pattern matching is made to work only on sequences for the following reason: if a new structured object is to be composed from the components of an argument object, it must be specified in the body *p_expr* of a pattern matching function in terms of pattern variables. Since neither matrices nor vectors may contain variables as entries, assembling a new object of either type class must be specified by means of sequences which must be subsequently converted.
For example, switching the first and the last row of a matrix by pattern matching may then be programmed thus:

```
TO_MAT[(WHEN <u, AS ...  x ,v > DO <v, LIFT[x], u> TO_SEQU[Z])]
```

where the primitive functions **TO_MAT** and **TO_SEQU** respectively convert a given object to a matrix or to a sequence, if syntactically possible, **LIFT**[x] lifts the elements of the sequence bound to x to the same level as v and u, and z is the place-holder for the object to be re-configured.
Another form of structural conversion is required when generating structured objects by tail-recursive functions of the form

```
f[x_1,..,x_n] = IF pred_expr
                THEN < >
                ELSE <e_0,f[e_1,...,e_n]>
```

where **pred_expr,e_0, e_1,...,e_n** are expressions defined in terms of the parameters **x_1,..,x_n**. This function recursively expands the tail of the binary sequence specified in its **ELSE** clause to some k nesting levels, returning **<a_0, <a_1, <a_2, ... , <a_k>> ... >**. In order to convert this nested structure to a flat object **<a_0,a_1, ... ,a_k>** of a particular type class, KIR includes primitive functions **FLAT_X**, where X stands for any of the type classes **MAT**, **VEC**, **TUP**.
Structured objects with known bounds may alternatively be generated by the higher-order primitives **MAKE_X** (where **X** again stands for **VEC**, **MAT** and **TUP**) which effect what is commonly known as comprehension. Applications of **MAKE_MAT** have the general form **MAKE_MAT**[$(i : n, j : m)$, $gen[i,j]$] where $(i : n, j : m)$ defines the indices and upper bounds for rows and columns, respectively, and $gen[i,j]$ defines the generator expression for the matrix entries. The lower bounds are always assumed to be $(1,1)$. **MAKE_VEC** and **MAKE_TUP** require just one index/bound specification.
KIR also includes the primitive higher order functions (or functional forms)

MAP which applies a given function to all expressions of a sequence:

```
MAP [func,<e_1,...,e_n>] → <func[e_1],...,func[e_n]>;
```

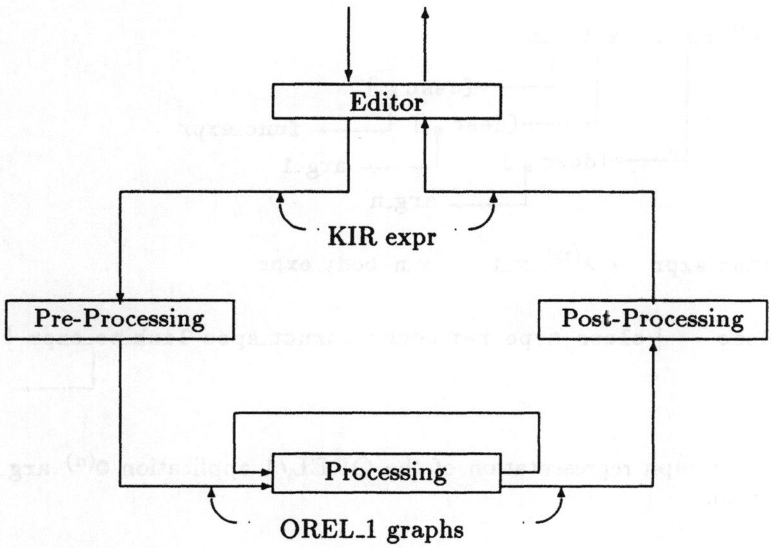

Figure 1: π-Red Basic Program Execution Cycle

FOLD which drives a given function into a sequence so that it recursively applies to the sequence and to its rest without the first component:

FOLD[func,<e_1,...,e_n>]→func[<e_1,FOLD[func,<e_2,...,e_n>]].

And there is, of course, a function **REPLACE** which replaces an index-selected subexpression of a sequence with another one:
REPLACE [i, expr, <e_1,...,e_i,...,e_n>] → <e_1,...,expr,...,e_n>.
This function conceptually creates a new object. However, in an actual implementation the representation of the argument sequence will be updated in the i-th component provided it is not shared with another part of the program.

Internal Representation of Structured Objects

π-RED uses an applied λ-calculus called OREL/1 as machine language. Program expressions of OREL/1 feature an n-place constructor syntax which translates straightforwardly into n-ary graph representations. KIR programs are by a pre-processor reversibly converted into OREL/1 graphs for execution. Partially or completely reduced OREL/1 graphs are by a post-processor reconverted into equivalent KIR programs. The transformations thus involved in executing a KIR-program are schematically depicted in figure 1. A given program may pass through this cycle several times when executing it stepwise. If the post-processed expression obtained from a partially reduced program is not changed by the user, processing continues directly with the OREL/1 graph

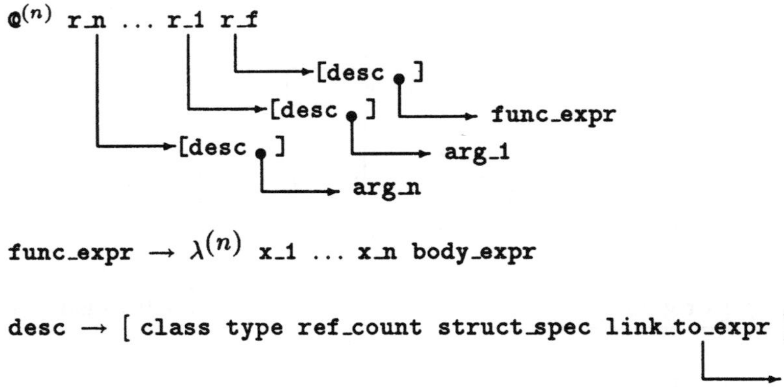

Figure 2: Graph representation of the OREL/1 application $@^{(n)}$ **arg_n ... arg_1 func**

received as output from processing. Otherwise, at least the subexpressions that are being changed at the editor level must be pre-processed again.

When transforming OREL/1 expressions into graphs, the pre-processor recursively generates descriptors for all subexpressions that are to form subgraphs referenced by graph pointers. These descriptors contain in condensed form class/type and structural specifications of the subexpressions they represent. Their primary purpose is to give effective runtime support to type compatibility checks, to the instantiation of generic operators with actual argument types (type classes), and to operations on structured objects. (Sub-) graphs are generated for all (sub-) expressions which the semantics of OREL/1 considers constant. These are basically all expressions other than applications, i.e. defined functions turned into λ-abstractions, pattern matches and `CASE`s, and of course all structured objects.

Function applications specified in a KIR-program as **func [arg_1 ,..., arg_n]** translate into the OREL/1 syntax as $@^{(n)}$ **arg_n, ..., arg_1 func**. Assuming that all component expressions of this application are constant, we get the graph structure shown in figure 2.

The root node of this graph is made up from the application of a pointer in function position to pointers in argument positions. Each of these graph pointers refers to a descriptor which in turn includes an internal link to the graph representation of the respective subexpression. We refer to subgraphs represented in this way also as heap objects.

Graph pointers are subject to orderly consumption and reproduction in the course of performing reductions. The links simply connect descriptors to the object representations. Once established, they are never copied and may only be changed if the object representations are moved in the course of compacting the heap.

In addition to the links, all descriptors have in common a `class` entry which

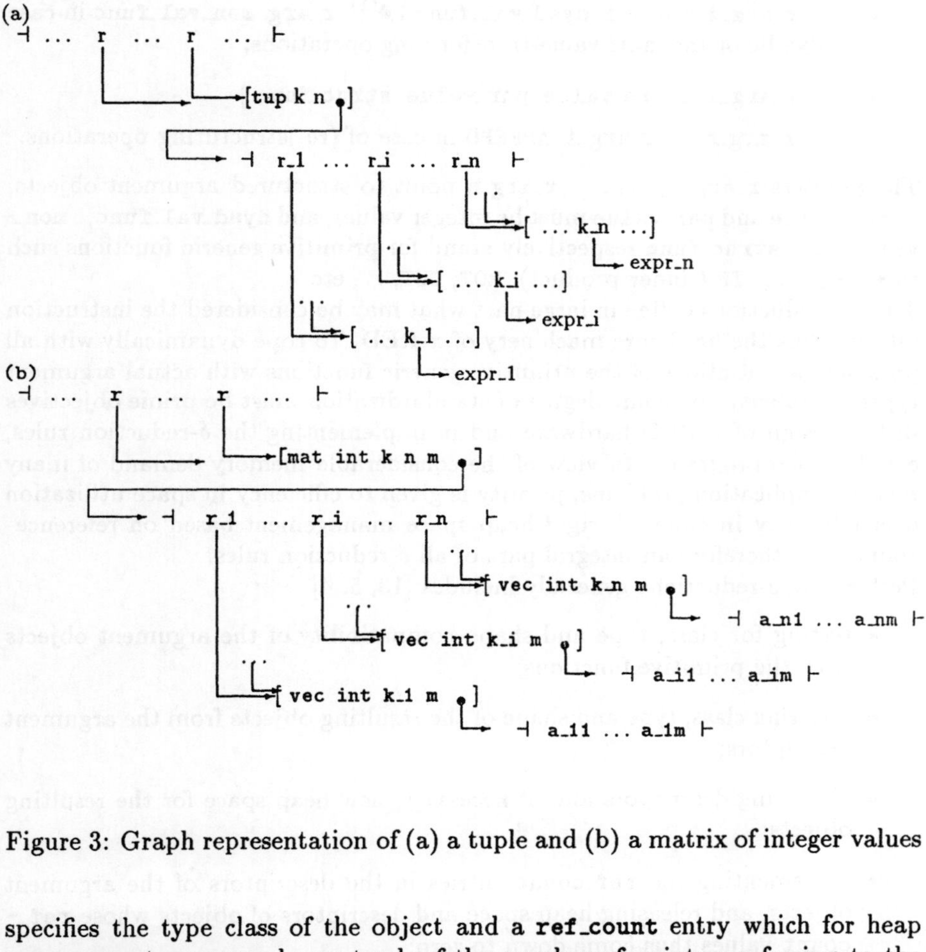

Figure 3: Graph representation of (a) a tuple and (b) a matrix of integer values

specifies the type class of the object and a **ref_count** entry which for heap management purposes keeps track of the number of pointers referring to the object. All other entries depend on the object class [4, 13].

Figure 3 shows complete graph representations for a sequence of expressions **<expr_1,...,expr_n>** turned into a tuple (3a) and for a sequence of sequences of numbers **<<a_11,...,a_1m> ,..., <a_n1,...,a_nm>>** turned into a matrix (3b). We note that in (3a) and (3b) the links to the object representations point to sequences of pointers to descriptors of subexpressions.

The subexpressions of both objects generally have reference count values $k\_i \geq 1$ for all $i \in [1..n]$ since they may be shared with more parts of an OREL/1 program in execution than with just the objects under consideration.

δ-Reductions on Structured Objects

Instances of δ-reductions may occur in OREL/1 graphs as application nodes

- $@^{(2)}$ `r_arg_2 r_arg_1 dyad_val_func` | $@^{(1)}$ `r_arg mon_val_func` in case of dyadic or monadic value-transforming operations;
- $@^{(3)}$ `r_arg_1 coord_value par_value struc_func` |

  $@^{(n)}$ `r_arg_n ...r_arg_1 APPEND` in case of (re-)structuring operations.

The pointers `r_arg_1, ... ,r_arg_n` point to structured argument objects, `coord_value` and `par_value` must be integer values, and `dyad_val_func`, `mon_val_func`, `struc_func` respectively stand for primitive generic functions such as `+`, `-`, `...`, `IP` (inner product), `ROT`, `CUT`, ... etc.
These δ-reductions define in large part what may be considered the instruction set and thus the hard-core machinery of π-RED. To cope dynamically with all possible instantiations of the primitive generic functions with actual argument types, simplicity and some degree of standardization must be prime objectives in the design of π-RED hardware and in implementing the δ-reduction rules, e.g. by microprograms. In view of the considerable memory demand of many real-life application problems, priority is given to efficiency in space utilization over efficiency in time. A rigid heap space management based on reference-counting is therefore an integral part of all δ-reduction rules.
Performing δ-reductions generally includes [13, 5, 4]

- testing for class, type and shape compatibility of the argument objects with the primitive functions;
- inferring class, type and shape of the resulting objects from the argument descriptors;
- allocating descriptors and, if necessary, new heap space for the resulting objects;
- decrementing the `ref_count` entries in the descriptors of the argument objects, and releasing heap space and descriptors of objects whose `ref_count` values thus come down to zero;
- and, if so required, generating the components of the resulting objects.

A typical example is the computation of the inner product of two matrices by δ-reduction of an application $@^{(2)}$ `r_arg_2 r_arg_1 IP`. Assuming that `r_arg_1` and `r_arg_2` point to descriptors `[mat, int, k_1, n, p, link_to ...]` and `[mat, int, k_2, p, m, link_to ... ]` , respectively, a new descriptor for the resulting matrix can be inferred as `[mat ,int, 1, n, m, link_to ...]`. To accommodate the result matrix, the memory manager must allocate

- another n vector descriptors to be instantiated with `[vec, int, 1, m, link_to ...]`;
- a linear array of n pointers to these vector descriptors,

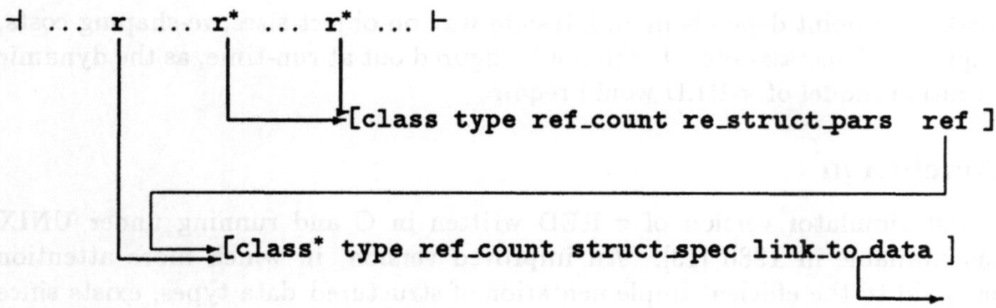

Figure 4: Re-Structuring via indirect descriptors

- n linear arrays of m integer formats each for the row vector representations.

Having inserted the base address of the pointer array into the link entry of the matrix descriptor and the base addresses of the integer arrays into the link entries of the vector descriptors, the result matrix entries may be computed by systematically traversing the rows of the first and the columns of the second matrix, using appropriate address generation schemes.
Other value-transforming δ-reductions and applications of the higher-order primitives `MAKE_X`, `MAP_X`, `FOLD_X` are carried out in a similar way. All element-wise arithmetic / logic / relational operations and applications of `REPLACE` overwrite (one of) their arguments if the respective `ref_count` values are one, i.e. the objects are not shared.
Applications of (re-)structuring functions can in many cases be reduced without creating complete new object representations. Most select operations simply return pointers to substructures of the argument objects. Rotating and cutting structured objects can often be deferred by creating indirect descriptors which specify by means of appropriate re-structuring parameters the shapes of the new objects in relation to the original ones. All accesses to objects represented via indirect descriptors thus involve modifications of the access indices by the re-structuring parameters. Indirect descriptors are linked up to the descriptors of the original objects as depicted in Figure 4. Cascading indirect descriptors is ruled out in order to avoid the complexity of repeated index modifications. Sequences of applications of the same re-structuring function (either `ROTATE` or `CUT`) can be condensed in one indirect descriptor. Otherwise, complete object representations must be generated by copying relevant parts of the argument objects. In many cases this may just be a sequence of pointers to substructures. Copying at least pointer sequences, if not complete argument objects, into contiguous heap space is also necessary when reducing applications of `APPEND`. Thus, alternatingly rotating and cutting large objects or assembling them by repeated `APPEND` operations may turn out to be rather costly in both space and time. However, the general problem that we face here is the trade-off between the costs of accessing an object whose re-shaping is deferred, possibly over a chain of several indirect descriptors, vs. paying once or several times the price of generating complete new objects which then can be accessed directly. The

break-even point depends in an intricate way on object sizes, re-shaping costs, frequency of accesses etc.. It can not be figured out at run-time, as the dynamic execution model of π-RED would require.

Conclusion

A first simulator version of π-RED written in C and running under UNIX was available in 1986 [13]. An improved version, in which more attention was paid to the efficient implementation of structured data types, exists since 1988. Performance measurements on a number of application programs which make extensive use of vector, matrix and tuple manipulations, other than revealing the expected complexity problems with re-structuring operations, are not very conclusive. This is largely due to the fact that we must simulate by lengthy instruction sequences many elementary operations which in a tailor-made hardware implementation of π-RED can be carried out in one machine cycle. Typical examples are the interpretation of descriptor entries in general, and type checking / type inference in particular. Unfortunately, there is no simple way of exactly scaling the simulation to the hardware other than by methods that would slow down by several orders of magnitude the simulator which is now trimmed to be competitive in speed with interpreted versions of ML and MIRANDA.
The development of a prototype π-RED hardware machine is presently in progress.

References

[1] P.S Abrams. *An APL Machine.* Stanford University, California, 1970.

[2] S. Anderson and P. Hudak. *Efficient Compilation of Haskell array comprehensions.* Yale University, Department of Computer Science, 1989.

[3] H. Blödorn. *The Kiel Reduction Language Users Guide.* Internal Report of the Dept. of Comp. Sc., University of Kiel, Germany, 1989.

[4] W.K. Giloi and H.K. Berg. *Data-Structure Architectures - A Major Operational Principle.* Proceedings of the IEEE, 1978.

[5] W.K. Giloi and R. Güth. *Concepts and Realization of a High-Performance Data Type Architecture.* International Journal of Computer and Information Science, Vol. 11, No. 1, 1982.

[6] R. Harper. *Introduction to standard ML.* LFCS Report Series, EC-LFCS-86-14, November 1986.

[7] R. Harper, R. Milner, and M. Tofte. *The definition of standard ML version 2.* University of Edinburgh, LFCS, August 1988.

[8] P. Hudak, P. Wadler, and (Eds.) et al. *Report on the Functional Programming Language Haskell.* Draft Proposed Standard, Yale University, December 1988.

[9] K.E Iverson. *A Programming Language.* Wiley,New York, 1962.

[10] W.E. Kluge and C. Schmittgen. *The π-System - A Concept for High-Performance Reduction Systems.* Proc. of the 1st Autumn Workshop on Reduction Machines, Ustica, September 1985.

[11] R.S. Nikhil. *ID-Version 88.1 Reference Manual.* MIT Comp. Struc. Group Memo 284, 1988.

[12] H. Schlütter and E. Pless. *The Reduction Language OREL/2.* Working Paper of the GMD, St. Augustin, Germany, 1989.

[13] C. Schmittgen. *Die Spezifikation der Architektur und Realisierung eines Reduktionssystems mit konsequenter Unterstützung strukturierter Datenobjekte und n-stelliger definierter Funktionen.* PhD thesis, Fachbereich 20 Informatik,TU Berlin, Germany, Oktober 1986.

[14] D.A. Turner. *Miranda: A non-strict language with polymorphic types.* FPLCA, LNCS 201, 1985.

[15] D.A. Turner. *An Overview of Miranda.* SIGPLAN Notices, December 1986.

12

Psi, the Indexing Function: a basis for FFP with arrays

Lenore M. Restifo Mullin
Department of Computer Science and Electrical Engineering
Votey Building
University of Vermont
Burlington, Vermont 05405
lenore@newton.uvm.edu

June 1990

Abstract

An array of arbitary components can be viewed as a variable whose value is a function from subscripts into its components[17]. The subscripts(or indices) of a 1-dimensional array are related to the system of integers, more precisely the natural numbers, which play an important role in the theory of groups. A Mathematics of Arrays(MOA)[13] builds upon these ideas to construct permutation and transformation groups into a calculus of n-dimensional arrays with the Psi function as the fundamental building block. We propose that this calculus provide a basis for Formal Functional Programming(FFP)[2] with arrays for parallel architectures.

Keywords: arrays, FFP, FP, massively parallel, formal derivation, permutation and transformation groups, parallel processing, program verification

Introduction

Since the onset of computers and computation, arrays have been the primary data structure used for scientific problem formulation. FORTRAN, one of the first and most widely used programming language for scientific computation, is used by scientists desiring an efficient and readily available tool to describe problems transcending various domains. FORTRAN, a procedural language, was designed for von Neumann machines and is therefore highly sequential in its expression of arrays. With the advent of parallel computers, the desire to perform operations on arrays in their entirety in a massively parallel way has been a major research topic in computer science. Advances in parallelizing compilers to abstract parallelism from FORTRAN programs has been one way to achieve this end. Languages such as FORTRAN 8X have added operations on arrays as a whole at least for 1 and 2 dimensions(vectors and matricies). Although recently referred to as monolithic arrays[8] or functional arrays[21], the concept of performing operations on arrays as a whole is not new to programming languages. APL[11] was the first programming language to have monolithic arrays with an associated algebra. APL's algebra derived from work which was referred to as a Universal Algebra on Arrays originating in the 19th century by Joseph Sylvester[19] [20] and Arthur Cayley[6][5]. APL, until very recently, was an interpretive language also oriented toward von Neumann machines. In fact, originally, APL\360 was more than just a programming language, it was an environment, an operating system, a prototype for a machine[1]. Furthermore, APL's symbol set required special terminal and printer support which often necessitated extra equipment.

Due to FORTRAN's popularity, an abundance of research to parallelize FORTRAN and make FORTRAN more amenable to the scientific community flourished. APL and FORTRAN lacked a precise mathematical formalism for reasoning about arrays[9]. Reynolds[17] introduced preliminary axioms for reasoning about programs with arrays in an Algol-like language. All of his axioms evolve from assertions about subscripts. His elegant introduction of interval and partition diagrams sets the stage for indexing and its use in the definition of operations which partition, and permute an index set as well as concatenate index sets.

The seminal work by Backus[2] questions if programming languages could ever break away from a classical von Neumann view. He notes that we need to be able to verify the correctness of programs and construct programs with mathematical rigor. He advocated not only functional programming(FP) but formal functional programming(FFP) which would be based on precise mathematical rules leading to a formal progam verification of design. These rules/operations would be high-level constructs close to the mathematics used to define various scientific problems. Backus, as well as others[3] [17][18], commended APL for its contribution to higher-order constructs on arrays(i.e. massively parallel operations).

With all this in mind we develop an indexing function which will be used to operate on n-dimensional arrays over any axis given the size of each dimension. The operations will be a subgroup of permutation and transformation groups. MOA will evolve to include other transformations and permutations which consistently appear throughout nature, i.e. in scientific applications.

In this paper we introduce the Psi function and its algebraic properties. Using the Psi function, we give a few elementary operations on 1-dimensional arrays. In particular, we give the definition of Blelloch's scan operation[3] noting that scan is defined in MOA for n-dimensional arrays over any axis. [13]. We note that all operations are, by default, over the primary axis of an array. This includes scalars(0-dimensional arrays) and vectors(1-dimensional arrays) where the primary axis is the only axis. In this introductory paper we omit the higher order operation Omega which extends operations over all dimensions. Details on Omega as well as other operations may be referenced[13].

MOA: a historical perspective

As previously mentioned, arrays with an associated algebra have been around for over 100 years. It was not until 1970 when Philip Abrams[1] investigated the mathematical properties of certain APL operations with the idea of developing an APL Machine. He recognized that certain operations could be defined using the structural information of an n-dimensional array, A^n, i.e. the size of each of A^n's dimensions. He developed a meta-language as a preliminary to a full mathematical theory based on the definition of array operations with structural information and indexing as the building blocks. He described elementary properties of indexing with scalar operations and concatenation. He used these properties in what he refereed to as the *simplification of array expressions* which would be used in his D-Machine(or Deferred execution unit). The D-Machine parsed, simplified array expressions, and passed addresses of arguments to unary and binary operations in a stack oriented architecture called the E-Machine(or Execution unit). In this context he was the first to coin the word *deferred execution* of an array expression. We can now see that Abram's D-Machine is the basis for an intelligent compiler(i.e. a compiler than can simplify and derive optimal code) for a functional language with arrays. He left as open questions the need to develop a full mathematical theory on arrays using structure and indexing with the application of these ideas to parallel processing. Work by Perlis[16], Miller[12], Budd[4] and others furthered this development. MOA achieves closure on the class of operations introduced by Abrams and formally unifies the inner and outerproduct as he conjectured in his thesis.

Notation

Arrays are denoted by the letters A^n to Z^n where n is a non-negative integer representing dimensionality. All objects in MOA are arrays. For notational simplicity, a scalar, or 0-dimensional array, will be denoted by the letters a to z and a a vector, or 1-dimensional array, will be denoted by the letters $\vec{a}$ to $\vec{z}$.

To differentiate visually between a scalar and a vector or a vector and a higher order array we use angle brackets to denote vectors while square brackets are used to denote higher order arrays. For example, 3 is a scalar while $< 3 >$ is a one component vector. Similarly, $< 3 4 5 >$ is a 3 component vector and $[3\,4\,5]$ is a 1 by 3, 2-d array. $<>$ and Θ denote the empty vector.

Unary prefix as well as binary infix operations are used with no operator precedence. We explicitly parenthesize expressions to show order of execution. Whenever it makes sense, we use standard mathematical notation to facilitate our discussion.

All arrays A^n have structural information which describes the size of each of A^n's dimensions. This structural information is denoted by a vector with n components, $< s_0 \cdots s_{n-1} >$ where s_i, $0 \leq i \leq n$ represents the size of the ith dimension of A^n.

Def. 1 *Any array, A^n has a shape denoted by, ρA^n, a vector, whose entries are the lengths of each of A^n's dimensions.*

$$\rho A^n \equiv < s_0 \cdots s_{n-1} >$$

where $s_0 \cdots s_{n-1}$ are non-negative integers.

For example,

$$\rho 3 \equiv <> \equiv \Theta$$

$$\rho < 2\,3\,4 > \equiv < 3 >$$

$$\rho[2\,3\,4] \equiv <1\,3>$$

$$\rho\Theta^1 \equiv \rho\Theta \equiv <0>$$

Def. 2 *An array Θ^n is empty if at least one component of its shape vector contains a* 0.

The Psi Function: obtaining a scalar component

We typically write $A^n[i_0; \cdots; i_{n-1}]$ for $n \geq 1$, to denote the element of A^n selected by subscripts $i_0 \cdots i_{n-1}$. The subscripts must be within the bounds determined by an array's shape. For now, to be within bounds *(valid indices)* means that each subscript, i_j, satisfies $0 \leq i_j < (\rho A^n)[j]$. This customary notation for array elements suffers from a substantial defect. Although we can use informal constructions containing ellipses, as above, any well-formed expression of this sort already specifies the dimensionality of the array in question. We consequently introduce an *element-selection* operator which allows us to write expressions which are independent of dimensionality.

Def. 3 *Given A^n, with $n \geq 1$, let $\vec{i}$ be a vector(of subscripts) satisfying $\rho\vec{i} \equiv <n>$, and for $0 \leq j < n$, $0 \leq \vec{i}[j] < (\rho A^n)[j]$, we define Ψ to be the binary operation which access the element selected by $\vec{i}$ from A^n.*

$$\vec{i}\Psi A^n \equiv A^n[\vec{i}[0]; \cdots ; \vec{i}[n-1]]$$

For example, $<0> \Psi <2\,3\,4> \equiv <2\,3\,4> [0] \equiv 2$. We will frequently interchange this notation for 1-dimensional arrays to facilitate the readers understanding.

Def. 4 *Given A^n, with $n = 0$,*

$$\Theta\Psi a \equiv a$$

Def. 5 *Let R be any binary scalar relation. We write*

$$A^n R^* B^n$$

to say that $(\rho A^n) \equiv (\rho B^n)$, *and for any valid* $\vec{i}$,

$$\vec{i}\Psi(A^n R^* B^n) \equiv (\vec{i}\Psi A^n) R (\vec{i}\Psi B^n).$$

If a is a scalar, we write

$$a R^* B^n$$

to mean $(\rho(aR^*B^n)) \equiv (\rho B^n)$ *and for valid* $\vec{i}$, $\vec{i}\Psi(aR^*B^n) \equiv aR^*(\vec{i}\Psi B^n)$. *Similarly,* $A^n R^* b$ *means* $(\rho(A^n R^* b)) \equiv (\rho A^n)$ *and for valid* $\vec{i}$, $(\vec{i}\Psi A^n)Rb$.

We can now express the condition that $\vec{i}$ is a valid subscript vector for A^n for $n \geq 0$ by

$$0 \leq^* \vec{i} <^* (\rho A^n)$$

Def. 6 τ *is defined as a unary prefix operation where* τA^n *is the total number of components in* A^n, *namely*

$$\tau A^n \equiv \prod_{i=0}^{n-1} (\rho A^n)[i]$$

Note that $\tau a \equiv 1$ and $\tau \Theta \equiv 0$.

We defined point-wise and scalar extension for relations, let us now define this for unary and binary scalar operations.

Def. 7 *The point-wise extension of binary scalar operations* $\oplus$, *between non-empty arrays* A^n *and* B^n *such that* $(\rho A^n) \equiv (\rho B^n)$ *is defined by*

$$\rho(A^n \oplus B^n) \equiv (\rho A^n)$$

and for valid indices $\vec{i}$,

$$\vec{i}\Psi(A^n \oplus B^n) \equiv (\vec{i}\Psi A^n) \oplus (\vec{i}\Psi B^n)$$

Def. 8 *The point-wise extension of a unary scalar operation* $\ominus$ *on a non-empty array* A^n *is defined by*

$$\rho(\ominus A^n) \equiv (\rho A^n)$$

and for valid indices $\vec{i}$,

$$\vec{i}\Psi(\ominus A^n) \equiv \ominus(\vec{i}\Psi A^n)$$

We have described how to perform operations between arrays using the Ψ function. We now illustrate how to construct a new array via the concatenation of index sets.

Def. 9 *The binary infix operation concatenate, denoted by ; is defined whenever*

$$\rho(\vec{x};\vec{y}) \equiv (\rho\vec{x}) + (\rho\vec{y}) \equiv < (\tau\vec{x}) + (\tau\vec{y}) >$$

and for valid indices i, $0 \leq i < ((\tau\vec{x}) + (\tau\vec{y}))$

$$< i > \Psi(\vec{x};\vec{y}) \equiv \begin{cases} < i > \Psi\vec{x} & \text{if } 0 \leq i < \tau\vec{x} \\ < i - (\tau\vec{x}) > \Psi\vec{y} & \text{if } (\tau\vec{x}) \leq i < ((\tau\vec{x}) + (\tau\vec{y})) \end{cases}$$

Def. 10 *When scalars are concatenated they behave like their corresponding one-component vectors:*

$$a;\vec{b} \equiv < a >;\vec{b}$$

$$\vec{a};b \equiv \vec{a};< b >$$

$$a;b \equiv < a >;< b >$$

We note the following properties:

$$a \oplus (\vec{x};\vec{y}) \equiv ((a \oplus \vec{x});(a \oplus \vec{y}))$$

$$(\vec{x};\vec{y}) \oplus b \equiv ((\vec{x} \oplus b);(\vec{y} \oplus b))$$

The Psi Function: index generation and subarrays

We've discussed how to obtain a single component from an array using Ψ. We now want to describe how to obtain multiple components from an array given a shape vector. Let us begin with a 1-d array using our familiar bracket notation.

Def. 11 *For* $n \geq 0$ *we define the unary prefix operation* ιn *to be the vector whose entries are the integers* 0 *to* $n-1$. *More precisely* ιn *is defined whenever*

$$\rho(\iota n) \equiv < n >$$

and for valid indices $0 \leq i < n$

$$< i > \Psi(\iota n) \equiv (\iota n)[i] \equiv i$$

noting that $\iota 0 \equiv \Theta$.

The above definition is sufficient if all we care about is bracket notation and 1-d arrays. We need now to extend the definition of ι for vector arguments, i.e. arguments that are shape vectors, with a desire to generate all valid indices of an array. But before we do, we need to extend the definition for Ψ to allow for an array left argument. In extending the definition we will be able to obtain not just a scalar component but an entire subarray from an array. We introduce a few partitioning operations on vectors to facilitate our descussion. The $\triangle$ ($\bigtriangledown$) operation selects contiguous intervals from the beginning(end) or end(beginning) of a vector if the amount selected is positive or negative respectively.

Recall again that for a vector $\vec{v}$ with valid indices i, $< i > \Psi\vec{v} \equiv \vec{v}[i]$.

Def. 12 *$\vec{v}[\vec{x}]$ is defined whenever $0 \leq^* \vec{x} <^* (\tau\vec{v})$ and*

$$\rho(\vec{v}[\vec{x}]) \equiv (\rho\vec{x})$$

and for $0 \leq i < (\tau\vec{x})$

$$(\vec{v}[\vec{x}])[i] \equiv \vec{v}[\vec{x}[i]]$$

Def. 13 *$a \triangle \vec{v}$ is defined whenever $(-(\tau\vec{v})) \leq a \leq (\tau\vec{v})$ and*

$$\rho(a \triangle \vec{v}) \equiv < |a| >$$

and for valid i, $0 \leq i < |a|$

$$(a \triangle \vec{v})[i] \equiv \begin{cases} \vec{v}[i] & \textit{if } 0 \leq a \leq (\tau\vec{v}) \\ \vec{v}[(\tau\vec{v}) + a + i] & \textit{if } (-(\tau\vec{v})) \leq a < 0 \end{cases}$$

Def. 14 *$a \bigtriangledown \vec{v}$ is defined whenever $(-(\tau\vec{v})) \leq a \leq (\tau\vec{v})$ and*

$$\rho(a \bigtriangledown \vec{v}) \equiv < (\tau\vec{v}) - |a| >$$

and for valid i, $0 \leq i < ((\tau\vec{v}) - |a|)$

$$(a \bigtriangledown \vec{v})[i] \equiv \begin{cases} \vec{v}[a + i] & \textit{if } 0 \leq a \leq (\tau\vec{v}) \\ \vec{v}[i] & \textit{if } (-(\tau\vec{v})) \leq a < 0 \end{cases}$$

We now introduce extensions to Ψ which permit elementary forms of partitioning. These extensions represent some of the basic operations from which higher order partitioning and structuring operations are built in MOA.

Previously, *a valid index vector*, $\vec{i}$ for an array A^n was defined such that $\tau\vec{i} \equiv n$.

Def. 15 *We now extend the definition of* valid index vector *to allow* $0 \leq \tau\vec{i} \leq n$ *provided* $0 \leq^* \vec{i} <^* ((\tau\vec{i}) \Delta (\rho A^n))$ *and require*

$$\rho(\vec{i}\Psi A^n) \equiv ((\tau\vec{i}) \nabla (\rho A^n))$$

providing $0 \leq^* \vec{j} <^* ((\tau\vec{i}) \nabla (\rho A^n))$

$$\vec{j}\Psi(\vec{i}\Psi A^n) \equiv (\vec{i};\vec{j})\Psi A^n$$

noting that $(\vec{i};\vec{j})$ *is valid in the initial sense, i.e. when* $\tau(\vec{i};\vec{j}) \equiv n$.

As an example, if $n > 1$ and $0 \leq a < (\rho A^n)[0]$, $< a > \Psi A^n$ accesses the entire ath component from the 0th dimension of A^n. Substituting in our definition above we see that $\rho(< a > \Psi A^n) \equiv (1 \nabla (\rho A^n))$ and for $0 \leq^* \vec{i} <^* (1 \nabla (\rho A^n))$

$$\vec{i}\Psi(< a > \Psi A^n) \equiv (a;\vec{i})\Psi A^n.$$

Observe that this extension is consistent with previous definitions when $n \equiv 1$ and when $\tau\vec{i} \equiv n$. Notice also that $\Theta\Psi a \equiv a$ and $\Theta\Psi A^n \equiv A^n$. We can see that that the extended definition for Ψ with short index vectors has the property mentioned in the previous definition, i.e.

Lemma 1 $(\vec{i};\vec{j})$ *is a valid index vector for* A^n *iff* $\vec{i}$ *is valid for* A^n *and* $\vec{j}$ *is valid for* $\vec{i}\Psi A^n$, *in which case*

$$(\vec{i};\vec{j})\Psi A^n \equiv \vec{j}\Psi(\vec{i}\Psi A^n)$$

Proof
Recall that $\tau(\vec{i};\vec{j}) \equiv (\tau\vec{i}) + (\tau\vec{j})$ *by Definition 9.* $0 \leq \tau(\vec{i};\vec{j}) \leq n$ *iff* $0 \leq \tau\vec{i} \leq n$ *and* $0 \leq \tau\vec{j} \leq (n - (\tau\vec{i}))$. $0 \leq^* (\vec{i};\vec{j}) <^* (((\tau\vec{i}) + (\tau\vec{j})) \Delta (\rho A^n))$ *iff* $0 \leq^* \vec{i} <^* ((\tau\vec{i}) \Delta (\rho A^n))$ *and* $0 \leq^* \vec{j} <^* ((\tau\vec{j}) \Delta ((\tau\vec{i}) \nabla (\rho A^n)))$. *Therefore,* $(\vec{i};\vec{j})$ *is valid for* A^n *iff* $\vec{i}$ *is valid for* A^n *and* $\vec{j}$ *is valid for* $\vec{i}\Psi A^n$.

$$\rho(\vec{i};\vec{j})\Psi A^n \equiv ((\tau\vec{i}) + (\tau\vec{j})) \nabla (\rho A^n)$$

by Definition 9.

$$\rho(\vec{j}\Psi(\vec{i}\Psi A^n)) \equiv (\tau\vec{j}) \nabla ((\tau\vec{i}) \nabla (\rho A^n)) \equiv ((\tau\vec{i}) + (\tau\vec{j})) \nabla (\rho A^n)$$

by Definitions 15 Ψ *and 14.* $0 \leq^* \vec{k} <^* \rho((\vec{i};\vec{j})\Psi A^n)$ *implies* $\vec{k}\Psi((\vec{i};\vec{j})\Psi A^n) \equiv ((\vec{i};\vec{j});\vec{k})\Psi A^n \equiv (\vec{i};\vec{j};\vec{k})\Psi A^n$. *So with* $\vec{k}$ *as above we see that*

$$\begin{array}{lll} \vec{k}\Psi\vec{j}\Psi\vec{i}\Psi A^n & \equiv (\vec{j};\vec{k})\Psi(\vec{i}\Psi A^n) & \textit{Definition 15 } \Psi \\ & \equiv (\vec{i};(\vec{j};\vec{k}))\Psi A^n & \textit{Definition 15 } \Psi \\ & \equiv (\vec{i};\vec{j};\vec{k})\Psi A^n & \textit{associativity of concatenation} \end{array}$$

□

We can see at once that if $\vec{i}$ is valid for A^n
$(\Theta;\vec{i})\Psi A^n \equiv (\vec{i};\Theta)\Psi A^n \equiv \vec{i}\Psi A^n$

The Psi Function: enlarging and restructuring an array

We've seen how Ψ uses an index vector to obtain a scalar component of an array. The extended definition of Ψ allowed us to obtain a subarray. We now complete the definition of Ψ which allows us to obtain arbitrary components of an array. This process could get a subarray, the array itself, or enlarge an array. We extend the definition for Ψ to allow an array of valid index vectors, i.e. for expressions $A^n\Psi A^m$, in which certain subarrays of A^n are valid index vectors for A^m.

Def. 16 *Providing $n \geq 1$. Let $a \equiv ((-1) \bigtriangleup (\rho A^n))[0]$, $\vec{a} \equiv ((-1) \bigtriangledown (\rho A^n))$ and writing $\rho A^n \equiv (\vec{a}; a)$, $0 \leq a \leq m$, and for all $\vec{i}$, such that $0 \leq^* \vec{i} <^* \vec{a}$, $0 \leq^* (\vec{i}\Psi A^n) <^* (a \bigtriangleup (\rho A^m))$, i.e. $\vec{i}\Psi A^n$ is valid for A^m In brief, each 1-d subarray $\vec{i}\Psi A^n$ is a valid index vector for A^m. In such a case we define $A^n\Psi A^m$ by*

$$\rho(A^n\Psi A^m) \equiv (\vec{a};(a \bigtriangledown (\rho A^m)))$$

and for $\vec{i}$ such that $0 \leq^* \vec{i} <^* \vec{a}$,

$$\vec{i}\Psi(A^n\Psi A^m) \equiv (\vec{i}\Psi A^n)\Psi A^m$$

Lemma 2 *For vectors $\vec{i}$ and $\vec{j}$, $0 \leq^* \vec{i} <^* ((-1)\bigtriangledown(\rho A^n))$ and for $(\vec{i};\vec{j})$ valid for $A^n\Psi A^m$*

$$(\vec{i};\vec{j})\Psi(A^n\Psi A^m) \equiv ((\vec{i}\Psi A^n);\vec{j})\Psi A^m$$

Proof

$$\begin{array}{lll} (\vec{i};\vec{j})\Psi(A^n\Psi A^m) & \equiv \vec{j}\Psi(\vec{i}\Psi(A^n\Psi A^m)) & \textit{Lemma 1} \\ & \equiv \vec{j}\Psi((\vec{i}\Psi A^n)\Psi A^m) & \textit{Definition 16 } \Psi \\ & \equiv ((\vec{i}\Psi A^n);\vec{j})\Psi A^m & \textit{Lemma 1} \end{array}$$

□

From definition 12 we can see that $\vec{v} \equiv \vec{v}[\iota(\tau\vec{v})]$. We now extend the definition for ι to show how this identity holds for n-d arrays in general.

Def. 17 *$\iota\vec{n}$ is defined whenever $0 \leq^* \vec{n}$ and*

$$\rho(\iota\vec{n}) \equiv (\vec{n}; (\rho\vec{n}))$$

and for $0 \leq^* \vec{i} <^* \vec{n}$

$$\vec{i}\Psi(\iota\vec{n}) \equiv \vec{i}$$

noting that if any entry of $\vec{n}$ is 0, then $\iota\vec{n}$ is empty, and that $\iota\Theta \equiv \Theta$.

Lemma 3 *For a 1-d array $\vec{v}$*

$$(\iota(\rho\vec{v}))\Psi\vec{v} \equiv \vec{v}[\iota(\tau\vec{v})] \equiv \vec{v}$$

Proof

Recall that for valid indices i, $< i > \Psi\vec{x} \equiv \vec{x}[i]$ implies $\vec{v}[< i > \Psi\vec{x}] \equiv \vec{v}[\vec{x}[i]]$ which implies that $<< i >> \Psi\vec{x} > \Psi\vec{v} \equiv \vec{v}[\vec{x}[i]]$. We first show that the shapes of the expressions are equivalent. By the definition of ι, observe that

$$\rho(\iota(\rho\vec{v})) \equiv ((\rho\vec{v}); \rho(\rho\vec{v})) \equiv ((\rho\vec{v}); < 1 >).$$

Substituting in the above equation using Definitions 16 Ψ and 17

$$\begin{aligned}\rho(\iota(\rho\vec{v}))\Psi\vec{v} &\equiv (((-1) \bigtriangledown ((\rho\vec{v}); < 1 >)); ((-1) \bigtriangleup ((\rho\vec{v}); < 1 >)))[0] \bigtriangledown (\rho\vec{v})\\ &\equiv (\rho\vec{v}); ((< 1 > [0]) \bigtriangledown (\rho\vec{v})) \textit{Definitions 14 and 13}\\ &\equiv (\rho\vec{v}); (1 \bigtriangledown (\rho\vec{v}))\ \textit{Definition 3}\Psi\\ &\equiv (\rho\vec{v}); \Theta \equiv \rho\vec{v}\ \textit{Definition 14}\end{aligned}$$

$$\rho(\vec{v}[\iota(\tau\vec{v})]) \equiv \rho(\iota(\tau\vec{v})) \equiv < \tau\vec{v} > \equiv \rho\vec{v}$$

by Definitions 12, 11, 6, and 1. $< i >$ is valid for both expressions above if $0 \leq i < (\tau\vec{v})$ and

$$\begin{aligned}< i > \Psi(\iota(\rho\vec{v}))\Psi\vec{v} &\equiv (< i > \Psi(\iota(\rho\vec{v}))\Psi\vec{v} && \textit{Definition 16 }\Psi\\ &\equiv < i > \Psi\vec{v} && \textit{Definition 17}\end{aligned}$$

$$\begin{aligned}< i > \Psi(\vec{v}[\iota(\tau\vec{v})]) &\equiv \vec{v}[(\iota(\tau\vec{v}))][i] && \textit{Definition 3 }\Psi\\ &\equiv \vec{v}[i] \equiv < i > \Psi\vec{v} && \textit{Definition 3 }\Psi\textit{ and 11}\end{aligned}$$

□

In fact, we can now say in general that

$$(\iota(\rho A^n))\Psi A^n \equiv A^n$$

because for $0 \leq^* \vec{i} <^* \rho A^n$

$$\vec{i}\Psi(\iota(\rho A^n))\Psi A^n \equiv (\vec{i}\Psi(\iota(\rho A^n)))\Psi A^n \equiv \vec{i}\Psi A^n$$

by Definitions 16Ψ and 17.

The Psi Function and Blelloch's Scan

Blelloch[3] discusses how *scan operations* are *unit time* primitives in the PRAM model. He considers two primitive scan operators, integer addition and integer maximum and describes how they can be used to simplify the description of many algorithms. Blelloch gives the following definition for scan:
"...The scan operation takes a binary operator $\oplus$ with identity i, and an ordered set $< a_0; ...a_{n-1} >$ of n components and returns the ordered set $< i; a_0; (a_0 \oplus a_1); ...; (a_0 \oplus ... \oplus a_{n-2}) >$. ..."

In MOA, prefix scan is defined for binary scalar operations that have right identities and binary scalar operations that have both left and right identities. The general definition includes both types of operations in the basic definition. If we separate the definitions we can describe Blelloch's Parallel Scan by simply stating that the operation must have a right and left identity. This then allows us to exploit the associativity of the operation. It is because the operation is fully associative that we can feed the operations into a binary tree of adders which give us the $O(\log_2 n)$ complexity stated by Blelloch for a vector with n components.

There is a small difference between the MOA definition of scan and Blelloch's. MOA defines scan in terms of reduction. Hence, the identity is known at the time the binary operation is defined. In MOA the empty vector is returned if the scanned vector is empty and the last component of the vector is included in the operation. Blelloch puts the identity for the operation in the first component of the array and ignores the last component. What is returned in the empty case for Blelloch and why does he ignore the last component?

Let us now describe three classes of scan, (1) operations that are right associative(i.e. have a right identity), (2) operations that are fully associative (i.e. have a left and right identity and can be associated from the left and the right), and (3) operations that are left associative(i.e. have a left identity). We will in the appendix show how certain left and right associative(and seemingly sequential) operations fit the parallel scan model. It is important to discuss left associativity when we know classical expressions in mathematics require it, e.g. Let f denote a binary operation defined by:

$$xfy \equiv \frac{y}{1+x}$$

If we, for example, want to apply this function to a four component vector $< a_0; a_1; a_2; a_3 >$ which requires a left associative reduction, we get the familiar expression

$$a_0 f a_1 f a_2 f a_3 \equiv \frac{a_3}{1+\frac{a_2}{1+\frac{a_1}{1+a_0}}}$$

For now, let us give definitions for vectors and note that MOA scales these operations to n-dimensional arrays. Note in the above how scan saves partial results.

Def. 18 *For a binary operation $\oplus_{lr}$ that is both right and left associative with left and right identity $i_{\oplus_{lr}}$*

$$\oplus_{lr}\, red\ \Theta \equiv i_{\oplus_{lr}}$$

If the binary operation is right associative only, then denoting the operation by $\oplus_r$ we say

$$\oplus_r\, red\ \Theta \equiv i_{\oplus_r}.$$

Similarly, for left associative operations, $\oplus_l$,

$$\oplus_l red\ \Theta \equiv i_{\oplus_l}.$$

Def. 19 *For non-empty $\vec{v}$, when we substitute $\oplus_{lr}$ below we exploit the associativity of the following sequential recursive definitions to get $O(\log_2 n)$ complexity*

$$\oplus_r red\ \vec{v} \equiv \vec{v}[0] \oplus_r (\oplus_r\ red\ (1 \bigtriangledown \vec{v}))$$

$$\oplus_l red\ \vec{v} \equiv (\oplus_l\ red\ ((-1) \bigtriangledown \vec{v}) \oplus_l \vec{v}[(\tau\vec{v}) - 1]$$

Def. 20

$$\oplus_{lr} scan\ \Theta \equiv \Theta$$

$$\oplus_r scan\ \Theta \equiv \Theta$$

$$\oplus_l scan\ \Theta \equiv \Theta$$

Def. 21 *For non-empty $\vec{v}$, when we substitute $\oplus_{lr}$ below we exploit the associativity of the following sequential definitions*

$$\oplus_r scan\ \vec{v} \equiv (\oplus_r\ scan\ (-1) \bigtriangledown \vec{v}); \oplus_r\ red\ \vec{v}$$

$$\oplus_l scan\ \vec{v} \equiv (\oplus_l\ scan\ (-1) \bigtriangledown \vec{v}); \oplus_l\ red\ \vec{v}$$

Conclusion

The Psi function was introduced and its mathematical properties have been explored. We've seen how we can use MOA to describe primitive parallel unit time algorithms. No matter what language is chosen for an implementation of an algorithm, the prerequesite is a powerful mathematics governing expression simplification and formal derivation. The Psi function defines all operations in MOA. We are using MOA for the formal deriviation of scientific problems[15] and as the basis of a functional language[8]. We plan to address simplifications of array expressions in an intelligent compiler. The Psi function and MOA are hence the basis for an FFP.

Acknowledgements

I thank Martin Santavy for suggesting the left recursive example. I also thank Gaetan Hains for his Appendix discussion of how to make left and right associative operations fit the Parallel prefix model.

Appendix

Scan reduction of associative operations is a well-known generic parallelisable problem with many applications[3]. Its parallel solution is the Fisher-Ladner parallel prefix algorithm which can be simulated on a variety of architectures.

The following is a simple but potentially useful extension to the algorithm's applicability. Suppose $(*, i_*)$ is a monoid so that $*red$ is parallelisable. Then any instance of the following definition scheme:

$$a \circ b \equiv a * b^{-1} \text{where } (*, i_*, -1) \text{is an abelian group}$$

gives rise to a parallel algorithm for $\circ red$ as follows:

$$\circ red < x_0; x_1; ...; x_{n-1} > \equiv x_0 * x_1^{-1} * ... * x_{n-1}^{(-1)^{n-1}}$$

which only requires precomputation (in parallel) of each x_i's rank followed by the parity of that rank. The result may then be fed to a pyramid scan algorithm or more generally to a parallel prefix algorithm.

Example: If we associate our expression from the right for subtraction as follows

$$-red < 4\,3\,2\,1 >$$

we get

$$(4-(3-(2-1))) \equiv (4-(3-1)) \equiv (4-2) \equiv 2$$

which seems sequential. If we now apply the above concept to this expression noting that $i_- \equiv 0$ is the right identity for $-$ we get

$$(4-(3-(2-1))) \equiv (4(1)+3(-1)+2(1)+1(-1)) \equiv ((4+(-3))+(2+(-1)) \equiv 2$$

which is a fully associative and redfined in terms of parallel prefix +red.

References

[1] P. Abrams, An APL Machine, PhD Thesis, Stanford University, 1970.

[2] J. Backus, Can Programming be liberated from the von Neumann style: A functional style and its algebra of programs, Communications of the ACM 22, no. 8, pp. 613-641, Aug. 1978.

[3] G.E. Blelloch, Scans as Primitive Parallel Operations, IEEE Transactions on Computers, vol.38, no. 11, pp. 1526-1538, Nov. 1989.

[4] T.A. Budd, An APL Compiler, Springer-Verlag, 1988.

[5] A. Cayley, The Theory of Linear Transformations, Cambridge, 1876.

[6] A. Cayley, A Memoir on the Theory of Matrices, *Philosophical Transactions of the Royal Society of London*, vol. 148, 1858.

[7] A. N. S. I., FORTRAN 8X Draft, FORTRAN Forum, vol. 8, no. 4, Dec. 1989.

[8] G. Gao, L.R.Mullin & R. Yates, An Efficient Monolithic Array Constructor for Scientific Computation, McGill University, ACAPS TM no. 19, May 1990.

[9] S.L. Gerhart, Verification of APL Programs, PhD Thesis, Carnegie Melon University, 1972.

[10] C.A.R. Hoare, An Axiomatic Basis for Computer Programming, Communications of the ACM, vol.12, no. 10, 1969.

[11] K.E. Iverson, A Programming Language, John Wiley and Sons, 1962.

[12] T. Miller, Tentative Compilation: A Design for an APL Compiler, Yale University, TR no. 133, May 1978.

[13] L.M.R. Mullin, *A Mathematics of Arrays*, PhD thesis, Syracuse University, 1988.

[14] L.M.R. Mullin & G.Hains, Formal Program Derivation for a Shared-Memory Architecture: Gauss Jordan Pivoting, McGill University, TR in progress, Feb. 1990.

[15] L.M.R. Mullin, G. Gao, M. Santavy, & B. Tiffou, Formal Program Derivation for a Shared-Memory Architecture: LU-Decomposition, McGill University, TR in progress, May 1990.

[16] A.J. Perlis, Steps Toward an APL Compiler, Yale University, TR no. 24, Mar. 1975.

[17] J.C. Reynolds, Reasoning About Arrays, Communications of the ACM 22, no. 5, pp. 290-299, May 1979.

[18] D.B. Skillicorn, Architecture-Independent Parallel Computation, Queen's University, TR no. ISSN-0836-0227-90-268, Mar. 1990.

[19] J.J. Sylvester, Lectures on the Principles of Universal Algebra, American Journal of Mathematics, VI, 1884.

[20] J.J. Sylvester, A Constructive Theory of Partitions, American Journal of Mathematics, V, 1884.

[21] H. Tu & A.J. Perlis, FAC: A Functional APL Language, IEEE Software, Jan. 1986.

[22] A. N. Whitehead, A Treatise on Universal Algebra with Applications, Hafner Publishing, 1960.

13

GENOTYPE—A PURE FUNCTIONAL ARRAY LANGUAGE

Sebastian Shaumyan
Yale University
119 Whittier Road
New Haven, CT 06515

Abstract

Genotype is a universal programming language that has two primitive objects: arrays and functions. Two types of functions are distinguished: univalent and multivalent. They correspond to univalent (one-dimensional) and multivalent (many-dimensional) arrays. Arrays are viewed as invariants of transformations of data. Genotype is universal, being a language that describes invariants of transformations of data. Genotype is a pure functional language as it has no imperative features and side effects. Genotype is an intrinsically parallel language: arrays permit the manipulation of multiple large groups of data as a single unit.

Keywords: arrays, functions, valence, combinators, types, polymorphism, first-class objects, lazy evaluation, applicative universal grammar, reduction, parallel.

INTRODUCTION

The purpose of this paper is to give an overview of Genotype, a system that is intended to be a pure functional array programming language.

Genotype was not initially meant to be a programming language. I started my research in theoretical linguistics and semiotics and devised a mathematical model of natural languages—Genotype—in quest of the essence of natural languages. Genotype was conceived of as a metalanguage, that is, a language in which other languages are discussed and analyzed. And the grammar of Genotype I called *applicative universal grammar*. *Applicative* because this grammar used the calculus of combinatory logic in which the sole operation was application. *Universal* because this grammar was a theory of linguistic invariants.

Genotype and applicative universal grammar were introduced into linguistics in the early 1960's to define the universal concepts and laws underlying natural languages. This task was a challenge to linguistics. The popular generative grammar of Noam Chomsky could not cope with the task because it was based on sequential linear structures which cannot capture internal syntactic and semantic invariants of language which are nonlinear, non-sequential by their nature. By contrast, applicative universal grammar was based on functional relations, which, being nonlinear, non-sequential, were appropriate for the expression of the linguistic invariants of natural languages.

Later, I extended my studies to include artificial languages, such as languages of mathematics, chemistry, and genetics. So Genotype was expanded into a universal mathematical model of languages of any type.[1]

The idea of the implementation of Genotype as a programming language was an afterthought. It occurred to me that a universal mathematical model of languages might be useful as a programming language.[2]

There are amazing correspondences between the internal structure of natural languages, as modelled by Genotype, and the structure of functional programming languages. These correspondences result from the fact that the internal structure of natural languages is a network of functional relations. This is why the theory of Genotype and the theory of the design of functional computer languages independently have come up with the use of the same mathematical apparatus—combinatory logic and λ-calculus.

---

[1] A complete description of Genotype and applicative grammar as a semiotic theory of linguistic invariants of natural languages is given in my books: 1) Shaumyan, Sebastian. 1977. *Applicative Grammar as a Semantic Theory of Natural Language.* Chicago: University of Chicago Press; 2) Shaumyan, Sebastian. 1987. A *Semiotic Theory of Language.* Bloomington and Indianapolis: Indiana University Press.

[2] The possibility of implementing Genotype as a programming language was first discussed in: 1) Šaumjan, Sebastian. 1970. *Applikativnaja grammatika i perspektivy razvitija informacionnyx jazykov* (Applicative Grammar and an Outlook for the Development of Computer Languages for Representing and Processing Information). [In Russian]. Soviet Association of Sociology. Moscow; 2) Šaumjan, Sebastian; Movšon, L.M. 1970. Applikativnaja grammatika i informacionnye jazyki (Applicative Grammar and Computer Languages for Representing and Processing Information). [In Russian]. In *Naučno-texničeskaja informacija, serija 2, No. 2.* [Science and Technology Information]—a journal of the Information Institute, Academy of Sciences, USSR, Moscow.

It is interesting to observe a parallelism in the development of the theoretical thought in computer science and in linguistics. Just as functional programming languages are destined to replace imperative programming languages, so in linguistics functional mathematical models of natural languages are destined to replace generative models, which have a nonfunctional structure.

I had the good fortune of friendship with Professor Haskell B. Curry, who used to discuss with me my applicative universal grammar and Genotype at different stages of their development since the early 60's. I am happy to see now that his work has become influential in computer science.

I have learnt a lot from the study of the theory of programming languages. The theory of programming languages is useful for linguistics. And I feel linguistics is also useful for the theory of programming languages, which may be called *programming linguistics*. Both programming linguistics and traditional linguistics have common ground—semiotics, the general theory of sign-systems (sign-system is a generic term for languages of any type). It is in this spirit that I have decided to experiment with Genotype as a possible programming language.

The conceptual framework of Genotype shares many common concepts with the existing functional programming languages, which is natural because of the common mathematical heritage of Genotype and these languages.[3] Here I wish to express my indebtedness to the array theory of Dr. Trenchard More. Array theory, which explores intrinsic properties of data by means of identities for operations on arrays, is seminal. The central concept of this theory—the array—has a great unifying power. Arrays may be viewed as invariants of transformations on data.[4] Nial, the language based on array theory, designed in collaboration with Professor Michael A. Jenkins, is remarkable for its generality, simplicity, and expressiveness. It has a strong potential for new fruitful developments. In view of the utmost

---

[3] I wish to mention especially Turner's Miranda: 1) Turner, D.A. 1985. "Miranda: a Non-Strict Functional Language with Polymorphic Types." *Proceedings IFIP International Conference on Functional Programming Languages and Computer Architecture*, Nancy France, September 1985 (*Springer Lecture Notes in Computer Science*, vol. 201); 2) Turner, D.A. 1986. "An Overview of Miranda." *Sigplan Notices*, December 1986.

[4] The description of array theory is given by More and his associates in a series of publications. I wish to mention especially: More, T. 1981. "Notes on the Diagrams, Logic, and Operations of Array Theory," in *Structures and Operations in Engineering and Management Systems*. Bjorke and Franksen, eds., Tapir Publishers, Tronheim, Norway.

importance of the array concept I made the array part of the basic conceptual framework of Genotype, which is a system of semiotic invariants. Genotype also shares many other ideas and notation devices with array theory and Nial.[5]

THE HIGHLIGHTS OF GENOTYPE

Here are some of the highlights of Genotype.

Genotype is a functional language without imperative features and side effects.

Genotype has two kinds of primitive objects: *arrays* and *functions*. Functions are first-class objects: they may be passed as arguments and returned as results.

A program is a collection of recursive equations defining various functions and data structures.

Functions include a system of combinators.

Genotype is strongly typed. Every admissible expression has a type which is determined by the compiler. Strong typing guarantees the absence of a type error at run time, a common source of bugs. Although Genotype is strongly typed, declarations of types are not necessary: assignments of types are taken care of by the internal mechanism of Genotype.

Genotype has a polymorphic type system. Every function can have many types.

Genotype has a calculus that defines a hierarchy of types. Types are interrelated by levels of abstraction.

Genotype is statically scoped.

---

[5] We must distinguish two closely related but different concepts: Nial and Q'Nial. Nial—the Nested Interactive Array Language—is a generic term. Q'Nial is an excellent language interpreter developed by Jenkins at Queen's University, Kingston, Canada, to implement Nial. The basic description of Q'Nial is given in: Jenkins, M.A. 1985. *The Q'Nial Reference Manual.* Nial Systems Ltd., Kingston, Ontario.

Genotype has a "lazy" evaluation mechanism: no subexpression is evaluated until its value is required.

Let us turn to the discussion of the basic ideas and features of Genotype.

The topics I will discuss in order are:

Two concepts of function.

Functions in Genotype (currying, the application operation, reification, functions as first class objects, modelling functional processes in natural languages).

Arrays in Genotype.

Combinators.

Calculus of types.

Structure of programs.

Evaluation as a reduction process.

Forms of definition.

The Church-Rosser theorem and its implications.

Referential transparency.

Lazy evaluation.

TWO CONCEPTS OF FUNCTION

It is important to distinguish two meanings of the term "function": 1) a function as a process that may be applied to certain objects to produce other objects and 2) a function as a set of ordered pairs—the set-theoretic concept of function. These meanings are often confused in the current literature on functional programming but are strictly distinguished in logic. The set-theoretic concept of function is alien to combinatory logic and λ-calculus. They conceive of function as a process. Hindley and Seldin characterize this notion as follows:

> In the 1920's when λ and CL began, logicians did not automatically think of functions as sets of ordered pairs, with domain and range given, as they are trained to do today. Throughout mathematical history, right through to modern computer science, there has run another concept of function, less precise but strongly influential; that of a function as an operation-process (in some sense) which may be applied to certain objects to produce other objects. Such a process can be defined by giving a set of rules describing how it acts on an arbitrary input-object. (The rules need not produce an output for every input.) A simple example is the permutation-operation ϕ defined by
>
> $$\phi(\langle x,y,z \rangle) = \langle z,y,x \rangle$$
>
> Nowadays one would think of a computer program, though the 'operation-process' concept was not intended to have finiteness and effectiveness limitations that are involved with computation.[6]

In Genotype and applicative universal grammar the term "function" is used in the sense of operation-process. Let me now explain some terms and notions relating to this concept. A *function* is an operation that combines objects to form other objects. The objects combined by a function we shall call its *arguments*; the result of the combination we shall call its *value* or *closure*. We can classify functions by the number and kind of arguments and the nature of the value. The number of arguments of a function will be called its *degree*. Functions of degree *n* will be called *n*-place or *n*-ary. For example, a function of degree 2 will be called a two-place or a binary function.

The most important difference between a function as an operation and a function as a set of ordered pairs is that we may define an operation by describing its action without defining the set of inputs for which this action gets results, that is, without defining its domain. For example, the operation *divide*, applied to zero, does not get a result in ordinary mathematics.

Another important difference between the two concepts of functions is that operations have no restriction on their domain. They may accept any

[6]Hindley, J.R. and Seldin, J.P. 1986. *Introduction to Combinators and λ-Calculus*. Cambridge: Cambridge University Press.

input, including themselves. For example, a function called the combinator K, if applied to itself, may produce the equation:

$$KKxyz = y$$

Combinatory logic, λ-calculus, and theories of constructive mathematics treat functions (understood as operations) as a primitive concept (that is, a concept that cannot be defined in terms of other concepts) just as the set theory treats sets as a primitive concept.

FUNCTIONS IN GENOTYPE

As was said above, in Genotype and applicative universal grammar the term "function" is used in the sense of operation-process. A *function* is an operation that combines objects to form other objects. The objects combined by a function are its *arguments*; the result of the combination is its *value* or *closure*. By the number of arguments of a function we distinguish one-place and many-place functions. These are general concepts. But in Genotype we find special concepts relating to the function as operation-process. They will be described below.

Currying

Genotype has one-place functions and many-place functions. But every *n*-place function is defined in terms of one-place functions. For example, let $f(x,y)$ be a two-place function. Then we define it as a sequence of two one-place functions:

$$f(x,y) \equiv ((Fx)y)$$

Let $g(x,y,z)$ be a three-place function. Then we define it as a sequence of three one-place functions:

$$g(x,y,z) \equiv (((Gx)y)z)$$

The symbol ≡ is read: "*is defined as*"

The right part of the first expression is a sequence consisting of the one-place function F, whose argument is x, and the one-place function (Fx), whose argument is y.

The right part of the second expression is a sequence consisting of the one-place function *G*, whose argument is *x*, the one-place function *(Gx)*, whose argument is *y*, and the one-place function *((Gx)y)*, whose argument is *z*.

Defining an *n*-place function as a sequence of *n* one-place functions was introduced by M. Schönfinkel[7] and extensively used by Curry.[8] Hence it is known as *currying*. Notation representing currying is called *curried notation*.

Currying has a few advantages over the conventional treatment of *n*-place functions.

First, currying reduces the number of parentheses that have to be written in expressions. For currying to work properly in a consistent way we require that the application operation associate to the left, so *max x y* means *(max x) y* and not *max (x y)*. This requirement is called the *rule of association to the left*. Under this rule many parentheses can be omitted in Genotype. Thus we get *a b c d e* by omitting parentheses in *((((a b) c) d) e)*.

Second, currying enables us to keep one argument of a function fixed while the other varies. For example, applying function *ADD* to *1*, we get the new function *(ADD 1)*, meaning 'add *1* to any number *x*'. In particular, *(ADD 1)* is the successor function, which increments its argument by 1, and *(ADD 0)* is the identity function on numbers.

Third, currying enables us to attain an ultimate generality in characterizing *n*-place functions: any *n*-place function can by definition be reduced to a sequence of one-place functions.

Finally, currying enables us to model correctly functional processes in natural languages: these processes are curried by nature. This point will be discussed below.

The Application Operation

Currying involves the *application operation. Application* is a binary operation indicated by juxtaposition and parentheses, such that if *X* and *Y*

---

[7] Schönfinkel, M. 1924. "Über die Bausteine der mathematischen Logik." *Math. Annalen* 92, pp. 305-16. (Engl. trans. in *From Frege to Gödel*, ed. J. van Heijenoort, Cambridge, Mass.: Harvard University Press 1967, pp. 355-66).

[8] Curry, Haskell B. and Feys, Robert. 1958. *Combinatory Logic*. Vol. I. Amsterdam: North-Holland Publishing Company.

are expressions, then *(XY)* is an expression (where *X* is its first argument and *Y* is its second argument).

Application reduces an *n*-place function to a combination of a series of one-place functions. Consider the above examples of currying. Let us take again the two-place function *f(x,y)*. If we think of *f* as an object *F* used as an argument of application, then we can replace *f(x,y)* by a new expression in two steps: first, apply *F* to *x* and get *(Fx)*, then apply *(Fx)* to *y* and get *((Fx)y)*. By the same token, using application, we can replace the two-place function *f(x,y,z)* by a new expression in three steps: first, apply *F* to *x* and get *(Fx)*, then apply *(Fx)* to *y* and get *((Fx)y)*, finally apply *((Fx)y)* to *z* and get *(((Fx)y)z)*.

All function symbols are prefixes and application is represented by the juxtaposition of symbols designating one-place functions and symbols designating the arguments of one-place functions. So in the expression *((ADD 1)a)* application is used twice. The first instance of its use is the juxtaposition of *ADD* and *1* in *(ADD 1)*. The second instance of its use is the juxtaposition of *(ADD 1)* and *a* in *((ADD 1)a)*.

Reification

Notice the difference between *f* and *F*. The first expression designates a function viewed as a simple relation, while the second designates a function as a relation conceived of as an object. The difference between *f* and *F* is similar to the difference between a verb and a noun, say, between add and addition or between multiply and multiplication. If we interpret *f(x,y)*, say, as *x* plus *y*, then we should interpret *Fxy* as the sum of *x* and *y*. Application involves a phenomenon called reification in epistemology. Reification refers to the ability of man in the process of the cognition of the world to view properties of and relations between things also as things. The linguistic counterpart of reification is nominalization. Man reifies properties and relations through nominalizing adjectives and verbs. In linguistic terms, *F* can be characterized as the nominalized *f*.

Functions as First-Class Objects

An object is said to be a first-class object if it can be passed as an argument to functions and can be returned by functions. For example, numbers are first-class objects: any number, say, 5, can be passed as an argument to the function *square* and returned by this function as a number, in this case as 25.

Functions are also treated as first-class objects in Genotype. As an example, let us discuss the composition of two functions. Assume that f and g are functions that take one argument and that each value of the function g is a valid argument of the function f. We can then speak of the composition h of the two functions f and g as the function of one argument defined by $h(x) = f(g(x))$. That is, to get the value of h at x, we first evaluate g at x, and then invoke f on the value $g(x)$. The composition of functions is defined as follows:

$$compose\ (f(gx)) = (compose\ fg)x$$

(*compose fg*) is a one-place function. As an example of composition, let us take *double* for g and *square* for f. Then we can define the composition h by writing

$$h = (compose\ square\ double)$$

The new function h is the function that doubles x and then takes the square of the value. If we invoke h with the argument 3, we get $(h\ 3) \Rightarrow (2 * 3)^2 = 36$. This illustrates first that we can pass functions, such as *double* and *square*, as arguments to a function, and second that we can have the value of a function be a function.

If we reverse the order of the functions *double* and *square* as arguments of *compose*, we get the function

$$k = (compose\ double\ square)$$

The function k so defined first takes *square* of its argument and then doubles the value. For example, $(k\ 3) \Rightarrow 2 * 3^2 = 18$. So k is quite a different function from h.

Modelling Functional Processes in Natural Languages

In natural languages, for example, in English, all verbs are considered to be functions, so in applicative notation they are treated as prefixes. That is to say that in applicative notation verbs precede nouns. So in applicative notation *Mike slept* is represented as *slept Mike*, which is the same as *(slept Mike)*. And *Peter loves Mary* is represented as *loves Mary Peter*, which is the same as *((loves Mary) Peter)*. Note that in application notation object precedes subject; in our example object *Mary* precedes subject *Mike*.

One may wonder why in representing *Peter loves Mary* I write *loves Mary Peter* rather than *loves Peter Mary*, that is, why I prefer *((loves Mary) Peter)* to *((loves Peter) Mary)*.

The answer is that in studying natural languages of various types we discover an interesting phenomenon: in any complete sentence of a language, no matter to which type the language belongs, the verb is connected more closely with object than with subject. This phenomenon can be illustrated by two complementary processes: verbal split and verbal compression. Verbal split is a process of splitting a verb into a verbal phrase consisting of a transitive linking verb (so-called transitive copula) plus a noun. Examples from English: *he works* splits into *he does work*; *participate* splits into *take part*; *argue* splits into *have an argument*. Verbal compression is a process transforming verb + object into a single expression in which at least one of its components has lost its original meaning. English examples: *kill the bottle* (that is, empty it); *kill an audience* (that is, wow them); *kick the bucket* (that is, die).

This phenomenon is called an asymmetry of subject and object. In view of the asymmetry a complete sentence has a hierarchical binary structure: it consists of two parts—a noun phrase and a verb phrase. Verb phrase, in its turn, also has a binary structure: it consists of two parts—a verb and a noun as its object. To represent the hierarchy, we apply first a verb to its object, and the result of this application we apply to the subject of the verb.

ARRAYS IN GENOTYPE

Genotype has two kinds of primitive objects: *arrays* and *functions*. I have discussed functions above. Now let us turn to arrays.

An array is a rectangular arrangement of data. Each item of an array is also an array. An *atomic array* or *atom* is an array that contains itself as the only item. Atomic arrays are items such as symbolic expressions, characters, integers, booleans. Non-atomic arrays are constructed from atomic arrays. The basic properties of an array are: valence (number of dimensions, or axis), shape (extent of each dimension), tally (number of items on each dimension).

A univalent (one-dimensional) array is a *list*. A list is a collection of data objects of the same type ordered along one axis. For example, the list

[3 5 7 9 6 7]

is a collection of data objects of the same type—integers—ordered along one axis. The items of a list are separated by spaces. A list can consist of other lists. For example

[3 [5 7] [9 6 7]]

is a list consisting of three lists: *[3]*, *[5 7]*, *[9 6 7]*. The non-atomic items of a list are surrounded by square brackets.

The concept of list in Genotype is different from the concept of list in Lisp. First, in the Lisp list the first item must be a function while in the Genotype list the first item is not necessarily a function, it may be a simple item. Second, the Lisp list is rigidly ordered by the following binary pattern:

$$(\text{cons } exp_1 \ (\text{cons } exp_2 \ \ldots \ (\text{cons } exp_n \text{ nil}) \ \ldots \ ))$$

The expression "cons" is a binary function combining the items of a Lisp list into nested pairs. The parentheses in a Lisp list may be omitted under a rule of association to the right. Using a special function "list", we may get an equivalent presentation of the Lisp list without parentheses:

$$(\text{list } exp_1 \ exp_2 \ \ldots \ exp_n)$$

By contrast, the Genotype list has a free structure: it may have a binary nesting like a Lisp list, but it may also have a non-binary nesting or no nesting at all—it may be just a sequence of non-nested atoms.

Third, all the items of a Genotype list must belong to the same type while the items of a Lisp list may belong to different types.

So Genotype lists cannot be considered to be lists in Lisp.

The items of an array need not be all of the same type. They may belong to different types. So we must distinguish monotype and polytype arrays. A list is a univalent monotype array. A univalent polytype array is called a *tuple*. Examples of tuples: (*7 false*); (*John 35 true*). In the first tuple the first item belongs to the type "number" and the second item to the type "boolean." In the second tuple the first item belongs to the type "symbol", the second item to the type "number", and the third item to the type "boolean."

In representing non-atomic items square brackets are used for lists and round brackets for tuples.

A function is an object which can be applied to an array or to a function, including itself. When applied to an array, a function produces another array. When applied to a function, a function produces another function.

Given a function X applied to an object Y that can be an array or another function, the object Y is called an *argument* of the function X.

Given an object Z produced by the application of a function X to its argument Y, the object Z is called the *value* or *result* of the function X for its argument Y.

These definitions show that Genotype treats arrays, which are data, and functions, which are operations, the same way: both an array and a function can be arguments of a certain function. From this point of view both arrays and functions belong in the same class called *first-class objects*.

Genotype is an intrinsically parallel language: arrays permit the manipulation of multiple large groups of data as a single unit.

The system of functions and arrays in Genotype shares many common features with the system of operations, transformers and arrays in Nial. One difference is that Genotype does not need to distinguish between operations and transformers because every Genotype function is a first-class object and therefore can act both as an operation and as a transformer in Nial. It should be also noted that Genotype and Nial belong to different levels of abstraction. Nial is an object language—a language describing non-linguistic data directly; Genotype is primarily a metalanguage: it was designed for describing other languages, in the first place, although, of course, it may be applied to the direct description of non-linguistic data, as well.

COMBINATORS

A combinator is a function that satisfies the following requirements: 1) it can only take another function as its argument, 2) it can take another combinator (including itself) as its argument. Combinators are first-order objects, that is, they can be passed as arguments to combinators and returned by combinators.

The combinator system in Genotype has the following 24 combinators (in alphabetical order): **B, C, D, E, F, G, H, I, J, K, L, M, O, Q, Q1, Q2, R, S, T, U, V, W, W1, Y**. These combinators are useful for natural language processing.

Symbols designating combinators are bold sans serif capital letters to distinguish combinators from other functions.

As an example of a combinator, let us consider the combinator **B** called the *compositor*. Its fundamental property is:

$$\mathbf{B}fgx \rightarrow f(gx)$$

This expression is read as "**B***fgx reduces to f(gx)*".

The converse of it is the expression

$$f(gx) \leftarrow \mathbf{B}fgx$$

Which is read as "*f(gx) expands to* **B***fgx*".

These equations show that the combinator **B** performs the operation of combining two separate simple functions f and g into a single composite function **B***fg*. We may also think of the action of the combinator **B** as a compression: two different functions f and g are compressed into a single complex function **B***fg*.

As an example of the action of the combinator **B**, this combinator may be thought of as a two-place function which operates on a pair of transformations or on a pair of functions to give the *composition* of those two transformations or functions. By the composition we mean the single transformation (or single function) which gives the same value as the successive application of the two transformations (or functions). For instance, if f is a transformation representing a clockwise rotation of 45 degrees, and if g is a transformation representing a counterclockwise rotation of 15 degrees, then $\mathsf{B}fg$ would represent a clockwise rotation of 30 degrees. This is because $\mathsf{B}fgx = f(gx)$, so that if gx is the result of rotating x counterclockwise 15 degrees, and if $f(gx)$ is the result of rotating gx clockwise 45 degrees, then $f(gx)$ is the result of rotating x clockwise 30 degrees, and therefore so is $\mathsf{B}fgx$.

Here is another example of the action of the combinator **B**. The combinator **B** can be thought of as a function that combines two simple predicates into a single complex predicate. For instance, if f is a function representing the predicate *cause*, and if g is a function representing the predicate *sit down*, then $\mathsf{B}fg$ would represent the predicate *seat*. If gx represents *sit_down children*, and if $f(gx)$ represents *cause (sit_down children)*, then $\mathsf{B}fgx$ must represent *seat children*. It is reasonable to assume that *cause* and *sit* are discrete components of a complex predicate *seat*. If f and g are interpreted as simple predicates, then $\mathsf{B}fg$ must be interpreted as the corresponding complex predicate.

Let us turn to the combinator **W** called the *duplicator*. Its fundamental property is

$$\mathsf{W}fx \rightarrow fxx$$

This expression is read as "W*fx reduces to fxx*".

The reverse of it is the expression

$$fxx \leftarrow \mathsf{W}fx$$

This expression is read as "*fxx expands to* **W***fx*".

One possible use of the duplicator **W** is in conjunction with the coreferentiality relation. Let us substitute the predicate *shaves* for f and the noun *Peter* for x. Then the expression fxx must be interpreted as *Peter shaves Peter* (that is, as *Peter shaves himself*); and the expression $\mathsf{W}fx$ must be interpreted as *Peter shaves*. As a part of the expression $\mathsf{W}fx$ the expression x must be interpreted as a combination of subject and object: in *Peter shaves, Peter* is both the agent and the patient of the predicate *shaves*. We may think of the action of the combinator **W** as the generation of the function $\mathsf{W}f$, which compresses two coreferential arguments (that is, arguments that refer to the same thing) into a single dual argument.[9]

The action of a combinator may have different interpretations depending on the function to which the combinator is applied. For example, to find another interpretation for the function **W***f*, let us consider the connection between the multiplication function M and the square function Q. They are related as follows:

$$Qa = Maa$$

Now we can interpret **W** as the function that makes Q out of M. So we get the equation

$$\mathbf{W}Ma \rightarrow Maa$$

The combinator system deals only with one-place functions. All many-place functions are reduced by currying to sequences of one-place functions.

Combinators are defined by the so-called *reduction rules*, which have the form

$$X \rightarrow Y$$

The infix $\rightarrow$ designates the reduction relation. This reads: "*X reduces to Y.*"

The left part of it is called the *redex*, and the right part of it is called the *normal form*. A normal form is an expression of the combinator system that contains no combinators.

The converse of the reduction rule is the *expansion rule*, which has the form

$$Y \leftarrow X$$

The infix $\leftarrow$ designates the expansion relation. This expression reads "*Y expands to X.*"

Below I present reduction and expansion rules for 24 combinators of the

[9] Curry told me that he chose the symbol **W** to denote the duplicator because this symbol duplicates the letter V.

combinator system. Since expansion rules are the converse of reduction rules, both type of rules are integrated in a common form

$$X = Y$$

In this expression X is the redex, and Y is the normal form. Infix = is a combination of → and ←, so that this expression can be interpreted both as a reduction rule and as an expansion rule. It is a reduction rule if it reads from left to right: "*X reduces to Y.*" It is an expansion rule if it reads from right to left: "*Y expands to X.*"

Let us now turn to reduction and expansion rules for 24 combinators (rules are given in the alphabetic order of the symbols for the combinators).

Compositor	$\mathbf{B}xyz = x(yz)$
Permutator	$\mathbf{C}xyz = xzy$
Double Compositor	$\mathbf{D}xyzw = xy(zw)$
Stratified Compositor	$\mathbf{E}xyzwv = xy(zwv)$
Reverser	$\mathbf{F}xyz = zyx$
Incorporator	$\mathbf{G}xyzw = xw(yz)$
Symmetry Combinator	$\mathbf{H}xyz = xyzy$
Identificator	$\mathbf{I}x = x$
Rosser Combinator	$\mathbf{J}xyzw = xy(xwz)$
Cancellator	$\mathbf{K}xy = x$
Separating Duplicator	$\mathbf{L}xy = x(yy)$
Mimer	$\mathbf{M}x = xx$
Echo Combinator	$\mathbf{O}xy = y(xy)$
Permuting Compositor	$\mathbf{Q}xyz = y(xz)$

Weak Permuting Compositor	$\mathbf{Q1}xyz = x(zy)$
Strong Permuting Compositor	$\mathbf{Q2}xyz = z(xy)$
Shifter	$\mathbf{R}xyz = yzx$
Confluentor	$\mathbf{S}xyz = xz(yz)$
Strong Permutator	$\mathbf{T}xy = yx$
Turing Combinator	$\mathbf{U}xy = y(xxy)$
Reverse Shifter	$\mathbf{V}xyz = zxy$
Duplicator	$\mathbf{W}xy = xyy$
Converse Duplicator	$\mathbf{W1}xy = yxx$
Fixed-Point Combinator	$\mathbf{Y}x = x(\mathbf{Y})x$

In speaking about combinators I mean the use of combinators as part of Genotype. Combinators are useful in many respects. They are especially useful for description of natural languages and natural language processing.[10]

[10] The main works illustrating the use of combinators for description of natural languages are: 1) Shaumyan, Sebastian. 1977. *Applicative Grammar as a Semantic Theory of Natural Language.* Chicago: University of Chicago Press; 2) Shaumyan, Sebastian. 1985. "Constituency, Dependency, and Applicative Structure." In Adam Makkai & Alan K. Melby (eds.) *Linguistics and Philosophy. Essays in Honor of Rulon Wells.* Amsterdam/Philadelphia: John Benjamins Publishing Co.; 3) Shaumyan, Sebastian. 1987. *A Semiotic Theory of Language.* Bloomington and Indianapolis: Indiana University Press; 4) Desclés, Jean-Pierre. 1985. "Predication and Topicalization: A Formal Study in the Framework of Applicative Languages." *Second Conference of the European Chapter of the Association for Computational Linguistics*, Geneva, March 28 and 29; 5) Desclés, Jean-Pierre; Guentchéva, Zlatka; Shaumyan, Sebastian. 1985. *Theoretical Aspects of Passivization in the Framework of Applicative Grammar.* Amsterdam/Philadelphia: John Benjamins Publishing Company; 6) Desclés, Jean-Pierre; Guentchéva, Zlatka; Shaumyan, Sebastian. 1986. "Reflexive Constructions: Towards a Universal Definition in the Framework of Applicative Grammar." *Linguisticae Investigationes*, 2.

In his influential work Turner suggested the use of combinators as a tool for the implementation of functional languages.[11] A lot of research has been done along this line. And an analysis of its results shows there are problems here. One may wonder whether a modified λ-calculus of Klaus J. Berkling based on his theory of head order reduction is a more promising alternative method of the implementation of functional languages.[12]

I view the combinatory calculus and λ-calculus as two important theories of recursive functions that represent complementary principles: the combinatory calculus has no variables while the very essence of λ-calculus is the correct treatment of bound variables. The two calculi can be integrated smoothly if we conceive of them as belonging to different levels of abstraction. We have to find the right place for each of them.

CALCULUS OF TYPES

In Genotype the universe of functions and arrays is partitioned into collections called *types*. The concept of the type is taken as primitive. It corresponds to the concept of the class in set theory, where it is not primitive but is defined through the concept of the set. So, in terms of set theory 'type' is synonymous with 'class'.

Types are divided into two kinds. First, there are *primitive types* given as initial. Second there are *defined types* that are constructed from other types. For example, numbers constitute a primitive type (the type *num*), and function *add* belongs to a defined type of functions that take numbers as their arguments and return numbers as their values, such as *sub* (minus), *mult* (multiply), *div* (divide), *square*, *double*, etc.

The most important kind of type in Genotype is the function. In terms of types, a function is a rule of change of each element of a given type A into a unique element of a second type B. The type A is called the *source type* and B the *target type* of the function. I will express this information by writing

[11] Turner, D.A., 1979. "A New Implementation Technique for Applicative Languages." *Software—Practice and Experience*, **9**, 31—49.

[12] See Klaus J. Berkling's paper "Arrays and the Lambda Calculus" in this volume. Also various publications of Berkling and his associates as technical reports of the Case Center of Syracuse University, for example Klaus J. Berkling "The Pragmatics of Combinators" (Technical Report No.8803, February 1988), Michael Lee Hilton "Implementation of Declarative Languages" (Technical Report No. 9008, June 1990.)

$$f :: \mathbf{O}AB$$

where symbol **O** means a function changing each element of *A* into a unique element of *B*. This formula asserts that the type of the function *f* is **O***AB*. That is, the type-formula *f* :: **O***AB* denotes a type whenever *A* and *B* do, and describes the type of functions from *A* to *B*.

Initially, types were introduced into Genotype as part of the description of the universals of natural languages. Here is the linguistic motivation for the introduction of types into Genotype.

Genotype is based on a semiotic principle I call the Principle of Representational Relevance. This principle states:

> If we abstract from everything in the language used that is irrelevant to the representational function of the communication we have to recognize as essential only three classes of expressions: 1) the names of objects, 2) the names of messages, 3) the means for constructing the names of objects and messages.

Names of objects are called terms. The concept "term" covers nouns and noun-phrases: a term is either a noun or a noun-phrase. Examples of terms: *a dog* (a noun), *a black dog, a large black dog, the man I saw yesterday* (noun-phrases).

The names of messages are sentences in natural languages or statements in logic or computer languages.

The means for constructing the names of objects and the names of messages are expressions that serve as functions.

The above primitive concepts determine the simplest possible sign-system for a natural language. This simplest system is called the minimal sign-system. A language having the minimal sign-system does not distinguish so-called parts of speech. It has neither nouns nor verbs, neither adjectives nor adverbs. It has only terms—names for objects. The minimal sign-system is an object-system. An object-system represents anything in the real world only as an object. Not only things are objects but properties of things, processes, states, actions, messages, as well. It is difficult to find a natural language with a minimal sign-system. But such languages exist, for example, Yurak Samoyed.

Having defined the simplest possible sign-system, we turn to deriving from it all possible complex sign-systems. To this end we use the mathematical calculus of types of combinatory logic. Combinatory logic is a functional object-system. It has nothing but objects and the application operation for combining primitive objects to produce complex objects.

The machinery of the calculus of types of combinatory logic has the following four primitive notions:

1) Certain primitive types.
2) Means for constructing composite types from the primitives.
3) Axioms assigning primitive expressions, called atoms, to certain types.
4) Rules for inferring the type of a composite expression when the types of its components are known.

The concepts in 1) and 3) may vary considerably from one sort of sign-system to another. The concepts in 2) and 3), on the other hand, have a combinatory character, and therefore must be the same in a broad class of sign-systems.

We postulate a primitive function O, called the *operationality primitive*.[13] We postulate certain primitive types v_1, v_2,... concerning which nothing more is postulated; we do not even specify whether there is a finite or an infinite number of them. And we postulate an inductive class of *O-types*.

We define inductively the formal concept of *O-type* as follows:

1) The primitive types v_1, v_2,... are O-types.
2) If x and y are O-types, then Oxy is an O-type.

Using the definition of the formal concept of the O-type, we can devise a calculus of O-types based on the primitive types *t*, denoting terms, and *s*, denoting sentences or statements. This calculus is defined as follows:

---

[13] The terms *operationality* and *operationality primitive* correspond to Curry's terms *functionality* and *functionality primitive* (Curry and Feys: 262-266). Within the conceptual system based on the non-set-theoretical concept of function as operation-process, or operator, I prefer the terms *operationality* and *operationality primitive* since the term *functionality* involves associations with the function conceived of as a set-theoretical concept.

1) The primitive types t, s, are O-types.
2) If x and y are O-types, then Oxy is an O-type.

For the sake of brevity, below we will use the term "type" in the sense of the "O-type."

Taking *t* and *s* as primitives, we may generate an inductive class of types as follows: t, s, Ott, Oss, Ots, Ost, OtOts, OOtsOts, and so on.

In representing types I use Polish notation, which is completely free of parentheses. I find Polish notation more convenient for representing types than Curry's notation, which involves internal parentheses.

It should be noted that all the types, except for t and s, classify functions. The formula "Oxy" reads: "The type Oxy of functions that change functions of the type x into functions of the type y." The component *x* of the type *Oxy* is called the *source type* of *Oxy* and the component *y* is called the *target type* of *Oxy*. For example, the formula *Ots* reads: "The type Ots of functions that change functions of the type t into functions of the type s." The component *t* of the type *Ots* is its source type, and the component *s* is its target type.

By using the concept of the type we classify functions into two main classes: primary and secondary. Primary functions are those all of whose arguments are closed, that is, all of whose arguments cannot be used as functions of other arguments. There are only two types of closed expressions: *t* and *s*. Secondary functions are those of which at least one argument can be used as another function.

In what follows I will give examples of expressions belonging to various types. I will start with examples from ordinary English, and then will turn to examples from the language of mathematics.

A. Types of English Expressions

Closed Expressions

t: proper nouns, common nouns, pronouns.

s: sentences.

Primary Functions

Ott: modifiers of terms (adjectives, nouns with various prepositions).

OtOtt: functions transforming terms into modifiers of other terms such as suffixes like " -ly" in "friendly", "-ish" in "childish", or the preposition "of" in "the cost of living."

Ots: a one-place predicate or the combination of a two-place predicate with a term.

OtOts: a two-place predicate or the combination of a three-place predicate with a term.

OtOtOts: a three-place predicate such as "send", "lend", "give."

Ost: functions transforming a sentence into a term such as the conjunction "that."

Oss: a one-place function transforming a sentence into another sentence such as negation or adverbs "probably", "unlikely", "certainly", etc.

OsOss: a two-place function transforming two given sentences into one sentence such as "and", "or", "but", etc.

Secondary Functions

OOttOtt: modifiers of modifiers of terms such as "very" in "very good."

OOttOOttOtt: functions transforming modifiers of terms into modifiers of modifiers of terms such as "-ly" in "extremely fast."

OOtst: functions transforming one-place predicates into terms, for example "-ing" in "walking."

OOtsOts: modifiers of one-place predicates.

OtOOtsOts: functions transforming terms into modifiers of one-place predicates.

B. Types of Mathematical and Logical Expressions

Closed Expressions

t: natural numbers 1, 2,...; individuals.

s: statements such as $x = y$; $8 < 9$; $7 > 6$.

Primary Functions

Ott: one-place operations such as "the square of", "the factorial of."

OtOtt: two-place operations such as "sum of", "product of."

Ots: one-place predicate such as "is even", "is prime", "is boolean."

OtOts: two-place predicates such as "equals", "is the same (by definition) as", "precedes", "is included in."

OtOtOts: three-place predicates such as "is between" in "New Haven is between New York and Boston."

Oss: negation operation, refutation operation, assertion operation, necessity operation.

OsOss: a two-place function transforming two simple statements into one compound statement such as conjunction, disjunction, or implication.

Secondary Functions

OOttOtt: operations on operations such as iteration of an operation or square of a function.

OOttOOttOtt: composition of operations.

OOtst: a class of individuals with a given property such as "odd numbers."

OOtsOOtst: relation between properties such as inclusion.

OOttOOtts: relations between operations such as ordering.

OOtOtss: properties of relations such as monotony.

OOtOOtsOOtOtss: relations between relations such as "the converse of."

Let us turn to rules for inferring the type of a composite expression when the types of its components are known.

We interpret the expression

```
x E
```

as a statement that the expression E belongs to type *x*.

Then we adopt a rule called O-rule:

If Opq A and p B then q (AB).

The O-rule reads: "If the expression A belongs to the type Opq and the expression B belongs to the type p, the expression (AB) belongs to the type q."

The O-rule can be represented by the tree diagram:

```
Opq A        p B
  |____________|
        |
     q (AB)
```

Here are some examples of the use of the O-rule:

```
OOtsOts soundly     Ots slept
   |____________________|
             |
 Ots (soundly slept)            t Dan
             |____________________|
                       |
          s ((soundly slept) Dan)
```

This tree diagram is an abstract representation of the expression "Dan slept soundly."

```
Ott add          t 9
   |______________|
          |
     t (add 9)          t 5
        |________________|
                |
          t ((add 9) 5)
```

This tree diagram is a curried representation of an addition: 9 + 5.

Let us introduce the concept of the *type variable*.

Consider the word "hard." This word has the type *Ott* in the expression "hard work", the type *OOtsOts* in "to work hard", the type *OOtOtsOtOts* in the expression "to take it hard."

We assign the type *Ouu* to the word "hard" in the above expressions, where *u* is a type variable. We adopt the convention that any of the types *Ott*, *OOtsOts*, *OOtOtsOtOts*, can be substituted for the type variable *u* in *Ouu*, depending on the context.

If a function is assigned a type expression with one or more type variables, it is said to be *polymorphic*, which means that it can have several different types. A polymorphic function is said to have a *polytype*.

The types *t* and *s* and the types derived from them are abstract types. No matter which concrete type occurs in Genotype, it is always an instance of an abstract type. For example, the types *num* (number) and *char* (character) are instances of *t*; the type *O num num*, which includes the functions *square*, *add*, *div*, is an instance of the type *Ott*; the types *string* and *seq* (sequence) are instances of the type *s;* the type *O num O num s,* which includes the function *min*, is an instance of the type *OtOts*.

STRUCTURE OF PROGRAMS

A *program* is a collection of definitions provided by a programmer. Here is an example of a simple program:

```
square x = x * x
min x y  = x,    if x ≤ y
         = y,    if x > y
```

In this program two functions, *square* and *min*, have been defined.

Submitting a program to a computer is called a *session*. Here is an example, using our program:

square (2 + 4)
36
min 2 4
2
square (*min* 2 4)
4

Definitions are expressed as equations between certain kinds of expressions. There are two kinds of definitions: 1) definitions describing functions, O-definitions, and 2) definitions binding symbols to objects, S-definitions.

O-definitions have the form of recursive equations. S-definitions describe a symbol as the name of an object; a symbol described as the name of a certain object is said to be bound to that object.

Definitions in the above program describe functions *square* and *min*. They are O-definitions. And here is an example of a definition binding a symbol to an object, that is, of an S-definition:

$$a = 14$$

One may be misled to believe that S-definitions are a form of assignment statements used in imperative languages. This is not the case. S-definitions conform to one of the most important features of mathematical notation requiring that once a variable is bound to a certain object it always denotes the same object within the context of the definition associated with it. This feature of mathematical notation is called *referential transparency*. As to assignment statements, they treat a variable as a place holder for a value which can be periodically updated by assigning different values to that variable. This treatment of variables is quite different from the treatment of variables in mathematics.

EVALUATION AS A REDUCTION PROCESS

The meaning of an expression is called its *value*, and the process of describing the meaning of an expression is called its *evaluation*.

The computer evaluates an expression by a process called *reduction*. The computer reduces an expression to its simplest equivalent form called its *normal form.*

Here is an example of reduction.

```
square (2 + 3)      redex
square 5            (+)
5 * 5               (square)
25                  (*)
```

This reduction consists of a sequence of expressions in the left column. The right column presents labels referring to the use of the rules used in the reduction. The label *redex* (an acronym for "reducible expression") refers to the initial expression to be evaluated. The labels (+) and (*) refer to the use of built-in rules for addition and multiplication. The label (*square*) refers to the rule associated with the definition of the function *square*.

The evaluation of an expression can be represented by different reductions. Thus we can use the following reduction as an alternative to the above:

```
square (2 + 3)          redex
(2 + 3) * (2 + 3)       (square)
5 * (2 + 3)             (+)
5 * 5                   (+)
25                      (*)
```

FORMS OF DEFINITION

Genotype is a functional language, not an imperative language like Fortran, Pascal, or C. In C, Pascal, or Fortran the question is: "In order to do something what operations must be carried out and in what order?" In Genotype the question is: "How can be this function defined?"

The Genotype formal system consists of a handful of primitive functions and certain rules for defining more complex functions from the primitive ones. So, there are two kinds of functions: *primitive functions* and *defined functions*. Primitive functions are such as *add*, *sub*, =, <, >. Defined functions are, for example, *square, double*.

The definition has the following form:

<function> <arguments> = <body>

Often we define the value of a function by case analysis, for example:

```
min x y = x, if x ≤ y
        = y, otherwise
```

Other examples:

```
abs x = -x, if x < 0
      = x, otherwise

factorial n =  1,    if n = 1
            =  n * (factorial n - 1),
               otherwise

fib n  =  0,    if n = 0
       =  1,    if n = 1
       =  (fib n - 1) + (fib n - 2),
          otherwise

length seq  =  0,     if seq = null
            = add1 (length (rest seq)),
              otherwise
```

Definitions with logical functions and, or, not: &, ∨, ~.

These definitions can be illustrated by an abstract analysis of the shape of a triangle. The function *triangle_shape* is applied to three positive numbers a, b, c, representing the length of the sides of a possible triangle. Depending on these numbers, the value of the function may be: 1) no_triangle, 2) equilateral_triangle, 3) isosceles_triangle, 4) scalene_triangle. Here is the definition:

```
trg_shape = no_trg, if a + b ≥ c
          = equilat_trg, if a = b & b = c
          = iso_trg, if ~ (a = b) & (a = b or b = c)
          = scalene_trg, if a < b & b < c
```

Curried addition

```
add x y = add',
          where add' = (add x)
          (add x) y = x + y
```

Curried multiplication

```
mult x y =  mult'
            where mult' = (mult x)
            (mult x) y = x * y
```

It is important to distinguish between the *intension* and the *extension* of a function. The intension of a function is its definition. The extension of a function is the class of its values.

Two functions are different if they have different intensions and different extensions, that is, if they have different definitions and return different classes of values. Two functions are identical if they have different intensions, but return identical classes of values. Let us take, for example,

```
double  x = x + x
double' x = 2 * x
```

Although *double* and *double'* have different intensions they are identical functions because they return identical classes of values. Therefore we can assert that the equality

```
double = double'
```

is true.

THE CHURCH-ROSSER THEOREM AND ITS IMPLICATIONS

Genotype is a system of reduction processes that are independent from one another. This system is characterized by a very important mathematical law called *the Church-Rosser theorem.* The Church-Rosser theorem is stated as follows:

> If U $\geq$ X and U $\geq$ Y then there exists a Z such that
> X $\geq$ Z and Y $\geq$ Z.

The symbol $\geq$ in the theorem means "reduces."

We can state the following corollary from the Church-Rosser theorem:

Corollary :

> If a sentence X is reducible to normal form Y, then
> the normal form Y is unique; that is, if X is reducible to Y
> and X is reducible to Z, then Y and X are identical.

The Church-Rosser theorem has important implications.

First, the Church-Rosser theorem implies evaluation order independence.

Expressions can be evaluated independently of each other. Consider the following arithmetic expression:

$$(2 * a * b) * (2 + a + c)$$

where a = 2, b = 3, c = 1.

No matter in which order we evaluate the subexpressions of this arithmetic expression, we get the answer 60. We can work from left to right or from right to left, or choose any other order of evaluation—the result will always be the same: the number 60.

The arithmetic expression illustrates the important property of any functional expression—evaluation order independence. This property is called the *Church-Rosser property*. The Church-Rosser property allows the designing of compilers that choose the evaluation order making the best use of machine resources.

Second, the Church-Rosser theorem implies that functional expressions can be implemented in parallel.

The important thing to notice in the above arithmetical expression is that we can evaluate its several subexpressions simultaneously, that is we can do *parallel evaluation*. Depending on the various orders of the evaluation of its subexpressions, we can choose various parallel evaluations of it. One choice is shown in the following tree diagram:

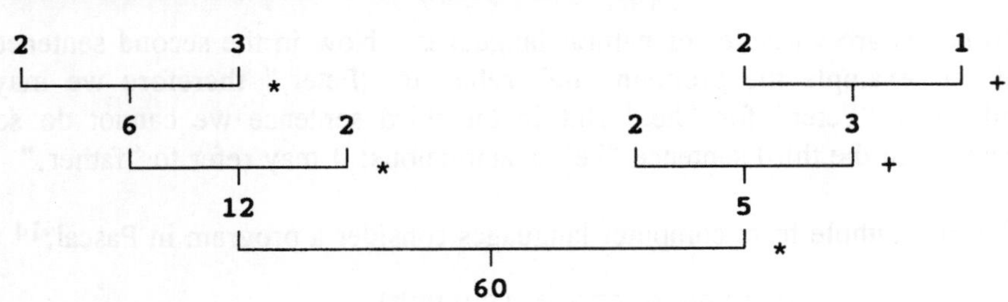

The symbols * and + on the right of the lines in the tree diagram denote the operations of multiplication and addition applied to numbers. It is obvious that we can evaluate the expressions represented by the left and right branches of the tree diagram in parallel.

The ability to use parallel evaluation suggests one way of using multiprocessor computers. Genotype provides an environment in which to devise and embed a language for parallel processing and experiment with it.

REFERENTIAL TRANSPARENCY

Referential transparency is the ability of the program to substitute equals for equals without change of meaning. For example, given the expression *f (16)* in a context in which *x* is 4, we may reasonably substitute for the argument any expression that is equal to 16 such as

f (6 + (2 * 5)), **f (square** (x)), **f** (x + x + x + x).

The imperative programming languages such as Pascal or C are not referentially transparent, they are referentially opaque. In Pascal or C it is not always the case that $f(16) + f(16) = 2 * f(16)$. This occurs because of so-called side effects, which are discussed below.

Imperative programming languages have side effects, that is, they can alter global variables. Side effects result from referential opacity—from inability of the programming language to substitute equals for equals without change of meaning. Referential opacity occurs in natural languages, too. Here is an example of referential opacity in natural languages:

> Peter went to the book store. He bought a detective novel for his father. He enjoyed reading detective novels.

Pronouns are variables of natural languages. Now in the second sentence of our example the pronoun "he" refers to "Peter," therefore we may substitute "Peter" for "he." But in the third sentence we cannot do so because in the third sentence "he" is ambiguous: it may refer to "father."

For an example from computer languages consider a program in Pascal:[14]

```
program example (output);
var flag: boolean;

function f (n: integer): integer;
begin
 if flag then f := n
        else f := 2 * n;
 flag := not flag
```

[14] Field, Anthony J. and Harrison, Peter G. 1988. *Functional Programming*. Wokingham, England: Addison-Wesley Publishing Company, Inc.

```
end;

begin
  flag := true;
  writeln(f(1) + f(2));
  writeln(f(2) + f(1))
end.
```

The executed program prints the numbers 5 and 4 at the terminal. This conflicts with the law of commutativity of addition in mathematics, which allows us to replace $x + y$ with $y + x$ for any x and y. In violation of this law, the Pascal expression f(1) + f(2) yields an answer which is different from f(2) + f(1).

The source of the problem in the Pascal program is the destructive assignment statement:

flag := not flag

which changes the value of flag.

Functional programs do not have destructive assignment statements. Imperative languages view a variable as a place holder for a value which can be periodically updated by assigning different values to that variable. By contrast, the variables in a functional program are like mathematical variables: the values bound to them do not change. In functional languages the statement

i := i + 1

is impossible.

In imperative languages a program is a sequence of imperatives describing *how* the computer must solve the problems in terms of state changes (updates to assignable variables). By contrast, a functional program describes *what* is to be computed: the program just contains expressions defined in terms of predefined and user-defined functions whose values do *not* change.

Referential transparency is important: it allows deducing new equations from given expressions, constructing proofs, and transforming expressions into more useful form. In addition, referential transparency is crucial for parallel programming because it means that the programmer is no longer concerned about synchronization errors caused by updating the values in the wrong order. Assignment is a constant source of synchronization errors, which poses a serious problem in the implementation of programs on multiprocessing systems.

One result of referential transparency is the absence of side effects. Imperative programming languages have side effects, that is, they can alter global variables—variables that are not local to them. Side effects result from referential opacity—from inability of the programming language to substitute equals for equals without change of meaning.

Genotype is referentially transparent and is free from side effects.

LAZY EVALUATION

Genotype has a "lazy" evaluation mechanism. This concept may be explained in terms of reduction strategies. Consider the expression *first (x,y).* We may reduce this expression to its simplest form in two ways: either we first reduce x and y to their simplest form and then apply *first* or we apply *first* immediately. The first reduction strategy is called *eager evaluation* and the second is called *lazy evaluation.*

One consequence of lazy evaluation is that it allows defining functions which are non-strict, that is, are capable of returning an answer no matter whether their arguments are defined or undefined.
Let us start with the meaning of a special symbol $\perp$, called *bottom.* This stands for the undefined value. For example, the value of 1/0 is $\perp$, and we may state: $1/0 = \perp$. The symbol $\perp$ is introduced for the sake of generality. We have to use $\perp$ or a similar symbol in order to be able to say that every well-formed expression denotes a value, without exception.

Every function *op* can be applied to $\perp$. If $op\ \perp = \perp$, then *op* is said to be a *strict* function; otherwise it is *non-strict.*

Consider, for example, the following definition:

$$five\ x = 5$$

Suppose we substitute (1/0) for x. The evaluator will return 5. So we get at the prompt:

five (1/0)
5

The evaluator does not require the value of the argument to *five* to determine the result. Therefore it is not evaluated. The function *five* is non-strict because the value of (1/0) is ⊥, so *five* ⊥ is not equal to ⊥.

There are a number of reasons why a non-strict semantics is preferable to a strict one. First, non-strict semantics leads to a simple and uniform treatment of substitution, providing a simpler logical basis for reasoning about functional programs. Second, non-strict semantics allows writing down definitions of infinite data structures. Infinite sequences enable us to write functional programs representing networks of communicating processes and have a number of other advantages.

All these points have been discussed in detail in current literature on functional programming, and I will not discuss them here.[15]

I will say a few words about the importance of lazy evaluation for modelling changes of states without the use of the notion of assignment.

Changes of states are dynamic while functions are inherently static. This poses a problem for functional programming: a description of changes of states requires the use of assignment in order to update values. However, one need not present a dynamic picture of changes of states. One may present a static picture of changes of states, which is the preferred method in modern linguistics. If we present a static picture of changes of states, then a functional description of these changes is appropriate.

Here is an example. A description of the changes of a bank account requires the use of assignment. But lazy evaluation allows an alternative description of these changes in functional terms. If we treat the functions *first*, *rest*, and *cons* as non-strict functions, then we can write a functional program modelling the changes of a bank account:

```
withdraw amounts-sequence balance = cons balance
                                    (withdraw (rest amounts-sequence)
                                    (balance — (first amounts-sequence)))
```

[15] One can find a very detailed discussions of these topics in: 1) MacLannon, Bruce J. 1990. *Functional Programming.* Wokingham, England: Addison-Wesley Publishing Company; 2) Reade, Chris. 1989. *Elements of Functional*

The evaluator does not require the value of the expression *rest amounts-sequence* to determine the result. But *withdraw* is a well-defined mathematical function whose output is completely determined by its output. With the lazy-evaluation version of the program there is no assignment and no local state variables.[16]

ACKNOWLEDGEMENTS

I would like to thank Trenchard More for his encouragement and incisive discussion and Rufus S. Hendon of Yale University for his meticulous comments. And I am indebted to Rufus S. Hendon for developing a marvelous multiple font system (MFS) and constant advice and assistance in my work with computers.

Programming. Wokingham, England: Addison-Wesley Publishing Company.

16 A penetrating discussion of the use of lazy evaluation for the functional description of changes of states in terms of Scheme, a dialect of Lisp, is presented in Abelson, Harold and Sussman, Gerald Jay. 1985. *Structure and Interpretation of Computer Programs*. Cambridge, Mass.: MIT Press.

14

A Comparison of Array Theory and a Mathematics of Arrays

Michael A. Jenkins
Queen's University
Kingston, Ontario, Canada

Lenore R. Mullin
Centre de recherche informatique de Montreal
Montreal, Quebec, Canada

Abstract

Array-based programming began with APL. Two mathematical treatments of array computations have evolved from the data concepts of APL. The first, More's array theory, extends APL concepts to include nested arrays and systematic treatment of second order functions. More recently, Mullin has developed a mathematical treatment of flat arrays that is much closer to the original APL concepts. The two approaches are compared and evaluated.

1. Introduction

The modern concept of an array as a multidimensional data structure has evolved from its use in early programming languages. The original motivation of arrays was to find a counterpart to subscript notation used for sequences, vectors, matrices and higher dimensional objects. The array concept was introduced in Fortran with static arrays of a fixed type and with a limited number of dimensions. It was extended in Algol 60 by allowing an arbitrary (≥1) number of dimensions and by having the size of the array determined dynamically at block entry.

This research was supported in part by the Ontario Information Technology Research Centre, the Centre de Reserche infomatique de Montreal, and the Natural Sciences and Engineering Research Council of Canada.

In Algol 60 and Fortran, arrays are treated as data containers for scalar values. The array is viewed as a collection of variables each capable of holding a scalar value. Arrays can be passed as parameters to procedures, but cannot be returned as results from value returning functions. Similar restrictions have been passed on in most subsequent procedural languages such as Pascal and Turing.

APL extended the array concept by treating it as a value at the same level as a single number or character, thus permitting expressions with array values to be used. One of the original contributions of APL was to give a consistent treatment of scalar values as arrays, thus allowing the universe of data objects in the language to be entirely arrays. This brought to the notation a mathematical uniformity that has much appeal. In APL as originally developed, an array was either an array of characters or an array of numbers. A formal description of APL arrays and the operations of APL was developed as part of the APL standard[ISO82].

This paper examines two mathematical treatments of arrays that have followed from APL concepts. The first was motivated by a desire to extend APL to permit arrays of arrays in a way consistent with the nesting concepts of set theory. The treatment, called *array theory* (AT) [More 73], has gone through several versions and has been the basis for the data structures in the programming language Nial [Jenkins 85]. An earlier version motivated the extension of APL arrays to nested arrays in APL2[Brown 84]. Based on experience gained using Nial, efforts are underway to refine array theory and to publish a definitive account [More 90, Franksen 90].

The second mathematical treatment was developed to provide a firm mathematical reasoning system for algorithms involving flat arrays of numbers. This treatment, called *a Mathematics of Arrays* (MOA) [Mullin 88], has been used to prove theorems about register transfer operations in hardware design, and to describe the partitioning of linear algebra operations for parallel architectures [Mullin 89]. MOA follows APL more closely than AT and is largely concerned with having a succinct notation in which definitions can be stated and theorems on array transformations can be proved. This work has attracted the attention of researchers attempting to extend functional languages to include array objects.

Both AT and MOA have their roots in APL and it is not surprising that they are consistent with each other as theories of arrays. The purpose of this paper is twofold: first, to explain the correspondence between concepts in the two notations in order to assist users of the two notations to communicate, and second, to compare the effectiveness of the two approaches for their purposes.

2. The Universe of Arrays

The fundamental concepts of arrays in the two systems are identical. In both, an array is a multidimensional rectangular object with items placed at locations described by a 0-origin addressing scheme. An array can have an arbitrary number of dimensions, including zero. The object is viewed as being laid out along orthogonal axes, one for each dimension. The length of the object along each *axis* is called the *extent* of the corresponding dimension. The vector formed from the extents is called the *shape* of the array.

In MOA, the items of arrays are numbers. The formal development involves arrays of integers, but it is clear that the theory is applicable to arrays of numbers in general, and can easily be extended to arrays of any homogeneous scalar type. A scalar in this treatment is an array with no dimensions and with shape the empty vector. There is no concept of an item of a scalar.

In AT, the items of arrays are themselves arrays; thus, AT arrays are inherently nested. They can be vectors of matrices of integers, or matrices of 3-dimensional arrays of real numbers. The nesting recursion is terminated by postulating that the scalar arrays, of which there are seven types, are self-nesting. AT arrays are inherently heterogeneous since there are no constraints on the types of items of an individual array. Thus, the universe of arrays described by AT is much richer than that described by MOA.

The two approaches have a consistent interpretation of flat arrays. In [Gull 79], it is shown that the flat arrays of APL can be viewed in two ways. One is to view a flat array as hiding *atomic* data that is never directly accessible. The standard indexing function that corresponds to subscript notation, A[I], selects a hidden item and then containerizes it as a 0-dimensional array. The other view is that flat arrays simply contain scalar arrays as their items and the standard indexing function selects the item.

The two views are termed the *grounded* and *floating* views respectively. The difference between them is only clear when one wants to extend the universe to include nested arrays using an operation that *scalarizes* an arbitrary array. The two different views of arrays has led to two different extensions of APL systems. In [Jenkins 80], it is shown that the floating system of arrays is implied if the nesting concept in APL is the same as that used in Lisp.

In this terminology, MOA can be interpreted as either floating or grounded, whereas AT is a floating system of arrays. For the purposes of the comparison we will interpret the universe of arrays in MOA as a depth-limited floating system.

Different terminology is used in AT and MOA for the same concepts. Table 1 gives the correspondences.

concept	array theory	mathematics of arrays
a scalar object	atom	scalar
component of an array	item	element
subscript	address	index
vector of extents	shape	shape
number of dimensions	valence	dimensionality, rank
1-dimensional array	list	vector
2-dimensional array	table	matrix
vector of length 0	void	the empty vector, Θ
vector of length 1	singleton	-
vector of length 2	pair	-

Table 1. Comparison of Terminology

The two systems also use different conventions for writing and displaying arrays. In AT, 1-dimensional arrays (lists) may be denoted by either strand notation: 34 56 35 27, or by bracket-comma notation: [34,56,35,27]. In MOA the notation for a vector is <34 56 35 27>. For both systems, the denotation of an array of dimensionality ≥2 is achieved using an operation that reshapes a list to have a given shape.

In this paper we display pictures of arrays using the output diagrams of Nial. A scalar array is displayed directly. A 1 or 2-dimensional array is displayed in a grid of lines with each cell holding the diagram of the corresponding item. The diagram of a higher dimensional array is displayed in 2 dimensions by displaying two dimensional subarrays in alternating directions, with increasing spacing between higher dimensions. For example, the array 2 3 3 2 *reshape count* 48 is displayed as

1	2	7	8	13	14
3	4	9	10	15	16
5	6	11	12	17	18

19	20	25	26	31	32
21	22	27	28	33	34
23	24	29	30	35	36

3. Operations on Arrays

The choice of operations on arrays in the two systems is affected by the limitations of the respective universe of arrays. In MOA, the result of every operation must be a flat array; whereas in AT, if it is more convenient to store the result of an operation as an array of arrays, this possibility exists. Similarly, the encoding of data as an argument to an operation must be as either one or two flat arrays in MOA, whereas in AT, the argument is a single array, but which may have any number of arrays as items.

In MOA, all operations are either unary or binary. Following APL, the same symbol can be used for both a unary or a binary operation. For example, the symbol ρ is used both for *shape* and *reshape*. Expressions consisting of a number of binary operations are associated right to left with no precedence.

In AT, each operation is unary, although it may be used in infix notation with the interpretation that its argument is formed by the list of length two of the values on each side. In an expression with a sequence of infix uses of operations, the association is left to right with no precedence.

In AT, one of the design goals was to develop a set of operations that are defined for all arrays and return an array value. Such operations are called *total* operations. In addition, the operations are constrained to obey certain *universal* laws or equations.

For example, the operation *rows* converts a matrix to a list of the list of items in each row, and the operation *mix* converts an array of equishaped arrays to an array with one less level of depth and with shape the concatenation of the shape of the original array and the shape of the items. On a table T, *mix* is the left inverse of *rows* and hence the equation

mix rows T = T

holds for all nonempty tables. In AT, the operations *mix* and *rows* have been extended to all arrays so that the above equation holds universally [Jenkins 84].

The search for total operations that satisfy universal equations has driven much of the development of array theory. This has led to an elegant mathematical system, but one which has placed constraints on some operations that may not be practical for computational use. Nial implements AT in its full generality and provides an experimental test bed for AT concepts.

Like APL, MOA has not attempted to achieve total operations. Instead the operations are defined over their natural domains and then extended to the extent that seems practical and/or elegant. There are some universal laws, but to a large extent they are those inherented from APL.

The set of operations in AT is very large and cannot be described in full detail here. A complete description of the operations, with many of the universal equations stated, can be found in [Jenkins 85]. Here we focus on a comparison of similar operations in AT and MOA, presenting all the central operations of MOA in terms of their counterparts in AT.

Both AT and MOA also have second order functions, that is functions whose arguments are operations. In AT, second order functions are called *transformers* and may take one or more operations as their argument. The transformers are general and may take any operation for their argument. Transformers can be constructed by a number of mechanisms in AT and give Nial much of its functional language flavour.

In MOA, the corresponding concept is a small number of second order functions, called *second order operations*, which evolved from similar ones in APL. They are restricted by the requirement that the operation resulting from an application of a second order operation to an operation must be guaranteed to always produce a flat array.

4. The Operations of MOA

The operations are discussed in roughly the same order in which they are presented in [Mullin 88], although in some cases the description is deferred until a complete description can be made. The Appendix to this paper is a Nial model for the MOA operations.

4.1. Array Measurement Operations

One feature that distinguished APL from earlier programming languages was its use of functions that provided information on the size and dimensionality of arrays. This is a necessity in APL since arrays can be formed dynamically and passed to functions that do not know how they were formed. Both MOA and AT provide such functions.

There are three such operations in both MOA and AT:

measurement	AT	MOA
number of dimensions	valence	δ
vector of extents	shape	unary ρ
number of items	tally	τ

The operations *valence* and *tally* behave the same as their MOA counterparts, but *shape* in AT is a little unusual. Because it is convenient to deal with the shape of lists as a single integer, the *shape* operation in AT returns either an integer or a list of integers depending on whether the argument has one dimension or not.

4.2. Indexing

In MOA, limited use is made of a notation based on subscript selection as done in Fortran, Algol 60 and APL. For the array *A* of shape [2,3,4]

5	6	7	8
9	10	11	12
13	14	15	16

17	18	19	20
21	22	23	24
25	26	27	28

the notation $A[1;0;2]$ denotes the element in the second plane in the first row and third column, namely, 19. MOA, like APL, extends this notation to select slices along each axis.

This bracket notation for indexing is not functional in that no single symbol is used to denote the function, and the address must be given component by component. Hence, it cannot be used in conjunction with second order operations or to express indexing of an arbitrary n-dimensional array. For these reasons, both MOA and AT (and extended APLs) introduce an operation that does the equivalent of subscript selection.

In AT, the operation *pick* is used to select one item from an array. For example, for the above array *A*, the corresponding selection is done with the expression [1,0,2] *pick A*.

In general, *I pick A* denotes the item of array *A* at the address given by array *I*. In MOA, the corresponding operation is *index*, denoted by ψ.

The notion of a valid address in AT and of a valid index in MOA are identical. For an array of *n* dimensions with shape $[s_0, \cdots, s_{n-1}]$, an index $[i_0, \cdots, i_{n-1}]$ is valid if $0 \le i_k < s_k$, $k=0,1,...,n-1$. For arrays with precisely one dimension, it is convenient to use an integer to denote an index rather than insisting that it must be a list of length one (a solitary). AT treats an integer as a valid index of a list. Both AT and MOA treat the empty numeric vector (*Null* in AT and Θ in MOA) to be the valid index for a scalar.

Both systems have an operation to generate the valid indices for a shape. In AT, the operation is called *tell*; in MOA, it is denoted by unary ι. In AT, *tell* generates an array of the given shape with items the corresponding addresses. In MOA, ι generates an array of one dimension higher with the items corresponding to the rows of the array. For example, *tell* [2,3] is

0 0	0 1	0 2
1 0	1 1	1 2

while ι<2 3> is

0	0		1	0
0	1		1	1
0	2		1	2

Both of these operations are defined for an integer argument and in this case generate the list of integers of the length of the argument starting at zero. For example, *tell* 10

0	1	2	3	4	5	6	7	8	9

In MOA, the operation ψ is extended to do multiple selections, whereas in AT there is a separate operation *choose* to do this. These are designed around the identities

$$\textit{tell shape } A \textit{ choose } A = A$$

in AT, and

$$(\iota\rho A)\psi A = A$$

in MOA. This multiple selection is associative in both systems, that is,

$$(A \textit{ choose } B) \textit{ choose } C = A \textit{ choose } (B \textit{ choose } C)$$

and

$$(A\psi B)\psi C = A\psi(B\psi C)$$

provided *A* is an array of valid full indices for *B* and *B* is likewise an array of valid full indices for *C*.

MOA also extends ψ to do a subarray selection with a partial index. For example, if *A* is

6	7	8	9
10	11	12	13
14	15	16	17

18	19	20	21
22	23	24	25
26	27	28	29

the <1> ψA is

18	19	20	21
22	23	24	25
26	27	28	29

and <0 2> ψA is

14	15	16	17

AT does not have an operation to do this directly, but it can easily be accomplished using the length of the partial index vector to partition the array using *raise* and then selecting the partition with *pick*. For example, [0,2] *pick* (2 *raise* *A*) is

14	15	16	17

4.3. Array Construction

Both MOA and AT have adopted APL's approach to constructing arrays of higher dimension. The operation *reshape* in AT has identical semantics to the binary operation ρ in MOA for the arrays for which the MOA version is defined. If *A* is a shape vector and *B* is a nonempty list, then *A reshape B* is the array of shape given by *A* with items chosen from *B* in a row major order. If *B* does not have enough items, its items are used cyclically until the result is filled. For example, [2,3,4] *reshape tell* 5 is

0	1	2	3
4	0	1	2
3	4	0	1

2	3	4	0
1	2	3	4
0	1	2	3

In MOA, the left argument of reshape must be a vector, whereas in AT it can be an integer to generate a list.

There is also an operation in both systems that transforms an array of n dimensions into an array with 1 dimension. In AT this is called *list* while in MOA it is *rav*. Both systems satisfy a structuring identity. In AT it is

$$\textit{shape } A \textit{ reshape list } A = A$$

whereas in MOA it is

$$(\rho A)\rho \textit{ rav } A = A$$

The extent of the list of items of an array is the number of items in the array. This is expressed in AT by

$$\textit{tally } A = \textit{shape list } A$$

and in MOA by

$$\textit{rav } \tau A = \rho \textit{ rav } A$$

4.4. Scalar Operations

Both AT and MOA follow APL and use pointwise extension of scalar operations to entire arrays. Examples are

[2,3,4] + [7,8,9]

9	11	13

abs [3,–5,–9]

3	5	9

[3,4,5] + 5

8	9	10

AT extends this idea by applying it recursively at each level of a nested array as described in section 5.1 below.

4.5. Operations on Lists

There are many operations that are naturally defined for lists. For example, given two lists A and B, the list made up of the items of A followed by the items of B is a convenient list to be able to build. In AT this is done by the operation *link*, whereas in MOA it is done by the operation *catenate*, which is denoted by the symbol ,.

The operations *take* and *drop* are used to select a contiguous part of a list. In AT the left argument must be positive and indicates how many items to take or drop from the front of the list. There are operations *takeright* and *dropright* that operate from the end of the list. MOA follows APL's lead by permitting the left argument to be a negative integer to indicate that the operation should be done at the end of the list. MOA uses ↑ to denote *take* and ↓ for *drop*.

The operations *reverse* and *rotate* in both MOA and AT behave like their APL counterparts on lists: *reverse* returns the list that has the items of the argument in reverse order, and *rotate* uses the left argument to determine how much to shift the items of the right argument to the left in a cyclical fashion. MOA uses the symbol ϕ for *reverse* and θ for *rotate*.

The operation *sublist* in AT uses a left argument consisting of a boolean list to select the items of the right argument in the corresponding positions where a *true* value is found. MOA has a similar operation *compress*, denoted by ⌿, which has the same effect. Following APL, MOA also has an operation *expand*, denoted by ⍀ , which uses a boolean list to expand a list of numbers placing items of the given list or zeros depending on whether the boolean entry is true or not.

4.6. Extension of List Operations to Arrays

The operations described in the previous section are extended to higher dimensional arrays and to scalars in different ways in AT and MOA. In AT, the operations are carried out on the list of items of the array. Depending on the operation, the result may be a list or a higher dimensional array. For example, if *A* is

1	2	3	4
5	6	7	8
9	10	11	12

then *reverse A* is

12	11	10	9
8	7	6	5
4	3	2	1

2 *rotate A* is

3	4	5	6
7	8	9	10
11	12	1	2

A > 5 *sublist A* is

6	7	8	9	10	11	12

and *A mod* 2 *match* 0 *sublist A* is

2	4	6	8	10	12

In MOA, the operations are carried out on the lists selected along the first dimension of an array. For example, with the same *A*,

1	2	3	4
5	6	7	8
9	10	11	12

ϕA is

9	10	11	12
5	6	7	8
1	2	3	4

$2\theta A$ is

9	10	11	12
1	2	3	4
5	6	7	8

and 1 0 1 / A is

1	2	3	4
9	10	11	12

4.7. Axis Transposition and Partitions

The concept of axis transposition is familiar from the matrix transpose operation in linear algebra. If A is the matrix

45	39	21
14	256	-5

then its transpose is

45	14
39	256
21	-5

In AT, the operation *transpose* has this functionality, while in MOA the corresponding operation is denoted by unary ⍉. For a general array of $n \geq 2$ dimensions, both AT and MOA provide a generalized version of this operation that can be used to do an arbitrary remapping of the axes, including the combining of two axes resulting in a diagonalization.

In AT, the operation is called *fuse* and its left argument indicates the mapping of the axes of the right argument. The left argument is encoded so that the value of the ith item of the left argument indicates which axis (or axes) of the right argument are mapped to the ith axis of the result. Thus, the tally of the left argument indicates the valence of the result. Let *A* be the 3 dimensional array

1	2	3	4
5	6	7	8
9	10	11	12

13	14	15	16
17	18	19	20
21	22	23	24

Then [2,0,1] *fuse A* is

1	5	9
13	17	21

2	6	10
14	18	22

3	7	11
15	19	23

4	8	12
16	20	24

and [[0,2],1] *fuse A* is

1	5	9
14	18	22

In MOA, following APL, the operation is called *generalized transpose* and is denoted by binary ⍉. In this version the left argument is encoded by having the value of the ith item in the left argument indicate where th i^{th} axis of the argument is to be mapped. Thus, <1 2 0> ⍉ *A* is

1	5	9
13	17	21

2	6	10
14	18	22

3	7	11
15	19	23

4	8	12
16	20	24

and <0 1 0> ⍉ *A* is

1	5	9
14	18	22

The use of the direct mapping of the axes in the AT version rather than the inverse mapping used in MOA is permitted because the left argument can be a nested array.

A closely related idea to axis transposition is that of partitioning an array along one or more axes. There are four primitive operations in AT that do this: *rows*, *cols*, *raise* and *split*. The first three are special cases of the last one which does a general partitioning. The expression *A split B* partitions *B* such that the axes mentioned in *A* becomes axes of the items of the result and the remaining axes are the axes of the result. For example, if *B* is

1	2	3	4
5	6	7	8
9	10	11	12

13	14	15	16
17	18	19	20
21	22	23	24

then [0,2] *split B* is

1	2	3	4
13	14	15	16

5	6	7	8
17	18	19	20

9	10	11	12
21	22	23	24

By reordering the axis numbers in the left argument an axis transposition in the items can also be achieved. For example, [2,0] *split B* is

1	13
2	14
3	15
4	16

5	17
6	18
7	19
8	20

9	21
10	22
11	23
12	24

The operation *raise* is defined in terms of split by

$$A \; raise \; B = (A \; drop \; tell \; valence \; B) \; split \; B$$

The AT operations *mix* and *blend* undo a partitioning. With *mix*, the axes of the items are added to the right end of the axes of the argument; with *blend*, its left argument specifies where the axes of the items are to be put. These operations satisfy the identities

$$mix \; (A \; raise \; B) = B$$

and

$$A \; blend \; (A \; split \; B) = B$$

There are no corresponding operations in MOA that build and undo partitions since the AT operations assume the existence of nested arrays. However, in section 5.1 we discuss a second order function in MOA that operates on partitions.

5. Second Order Functions

Both AT and MOA have inherited the concept of second order functions from APL, where they are called *operators*. In this section the principal second order functions of AT (called *transformers*) and MOA (called *second order operations*) are described. In AT, a transformer T is applied to a single operation f by the expression $T\ f$. If T_1 takes two operations then the form is $T_1\ [f, g]$. In both cases the result is an operation which can be applied to an array by juxtaposition. A given transformer has a fixed number of operations to which it applies.

In MOA, the application notation is similar in spirit to APL, but uses subscripting to make the resulting operation easier to distinguish visually. A second order operation can take one or two arguments. If it takes one it is a subscript on either side. If it takes two arguments they are placed as subscripts on either side, but only one of the arguments needs to be a function.

5.1. Positional Transforms and Axis

The most fundamental transformer in AT is *EACH*, which behaves as a mapping function over arrays. Given an arbitrary operation f and an array A, then $EACH\ f\ A$ results in an array of the same shape as A with each of the items being the result of applying f to the corresponding item of A. For example, given the table A,

3	2
1	4

then *EACH tell A* is

[0 | 1 | 2]	[0 | 1]
[0]	[0 | 1 | 2 | 3]

The *unary pervasive* operations of AT, such as *abs*, sin, etc., satisfy the equation

$$f\,A = EACH\ f\ A$$

which implies that the result has the same nesting structure as *A* with the atoms at the leaves of the array replaced by the result of applying *f* to the corresponding leaves of *A*.

The *binary pervasive* operations of AT, such as *plus*, *minus*, etc., satisfy the equation

$$A\ f\ B = EACH\ f\ (A\ pack\ B)$$

where *pack* is an operation that produces an array of pairs of items from *A* and *B* in corresponding positions. If one of *A* or *B* is an atom then it is replicated to the shape of the other. If they are not of the same shape then they are *trimmed* to have the same shape before doing the pairing. There is a related operation *flip* that assumes that *A* and *B* are of the same shape and has the effect of interchanging the top two levels.

The effect of this identity is that the result of such an operation between two nested arrays of the same structure is an array of the same structure with leaves formed by applying the operation on the corresponding leaves of the arguments.

Since MOA has only flat arrays, it has a more elaborate second order operation, denoted by Ω, which applies an operation across partitions of an array, provided the results can be glued together into a flat array again. The second order operation has two arguments, a left argument that is an array operation and a right argument that is a vector of one or two integers. The result of Ω differs depending on whether the left argument is a unary or binary operation.

In the case that the left argument f is unary, the definition of ${}_f\Omega_{<C>}A$ can be expressed in AT as *mix EACH f (C takeright axes A split A)*, where *axes* is *tell valence*. In words, the result is obtained by partitioning A so that the last *C* axes are placed in the partitions, apply *f* to each partition, and mix the resulting arrays to a flat one. This is well defined only if all the results of applying *f* to the partitions of *A* are of the same shape. For example using *reverse*, if *A* is

1	2	3	4
5	6	7	8
9	10	11	12

13	14	15	16
17	18	19	20
21	22	23	24

then ${}_{\phi}\Omega_{<2>} A$ is

9	10	11	12
5	6	7	8
1	2	3	4

21	22	23	24
17	18	19	20
13	14	15	16

In the case of the left argument g being binary, then the definition of $A\ {}_{g}\Omega_{<C,D>} B$ can be expressed in AT as
mix EACH g ((*C takeright axes A split A*) *pack* (*D takeright axes B split B*)).
In words, the result is obtained by partitioning both A and B as above, applying g to the pairs formed from the partitions, and mixing the result into a flat array. An example using *rotate* with the same A as above is $<1\ 2>{}_{\theta}\Omega_{<1\ 2>} A$

5	6	7	8
9	10	11	12
1	2	3	4

21	22	23	24
13	14	15	16
17	18	19	20

which rotates the first plane of A by one and the second plane by two.

The *rank* operation in MOA can only partition along the last axes of an argument. To partition along others, a *generalized transpose* must be applied first. In AT, the generality of split allows direct partitioning along a chosen set of axes. The restriction in MOA is imposed by the constraints on the number of arguments and on the fact that all arrays are flat.

5.2. Reduction and Scan

There is a natural extension of any binary operation to a list by applying the operation between each pair of items in the array. This process is called *reduction*. The terminology comes from APL, where the corresponding second order function can only be applied to a binary scalar operation and reduces a list of scalars to a single one. MOA follows APL's lead and introduces a second order function *red*. It is restricted to be used on the binary scalar operations. Thus, if A is a list of numbers then ${}_{+}red\ A$ gives the sum of the numbers. The introduction of a reduction operation raises a number of difficult questions. What should its effect be when the resulting operation is applied to a list with fewer than two items? What is its meaning on binary operations that are not scalar ones? What should be assumed about the order in which the operations are applied? How should the operation be generalized to higher dimensional arrays? Some of these issues are examined in depth in a theory of lists developed by Bird [Bird 87] and in a paper proposing an approach for APL2 [Brown 81].

In MOA, as in APL, the solution to the first problem is to introduce identity scalars for each of the operations to which *red* can be applied. MOA defines reduction for the arithmetic operations and for *max*, *min* and *mod*. For example, the identity element of + is 0, while that of × is 1. Thus, ${}_{+}red\Theta$ is 0 . Initially, MOA addresses right associative binary operations and later left associative ones [Mullin 90]. For higher dimensional arrays the reduction is done along the first axis.

AT has taken a different approach. It has defined the reductive process directly into the primitive operations where it appropriate, and has provided transformers *REDUCE* and *LEFTREDUCE* that do not assume the existence of an identity for an operation. The approach in AT is to define the reductive process directly in the unary operations *sum*, *prod*, *max*, *min*, *and* and *or*. These operations can also be used in infix notation and for convenience the binary operations *plus*, ×, etc., and the symbols + and * are provided as renamings of the unary operation.

AT also builds the reduction process into the operation *link* which joins lists into one large list, and into *cart*, which forms a generalized cartesian product of its items.

MOA also defines the second order operation *scan* which produces the list of partial results that are formed in doing a reduction. AT does not have an equivalent primitive, but it can easily be defined in Nial.

5.3. Inner and Outer Products

The concepts of inner product and outer product in array languages are generalizations of similar operations in linear algebra. Given two column vectors $\overline{x}$ and $\overline{y}$ of length n, then

$$\overline{x}^T \cdot \overline{y} = \sum_{i=0}^{n-1} x_i\, y_i$$

In MOA, this is denoted $\overline{x}\,{}_{+}\!\bullet_{\times}\,\overline{y}$. The inner product operation in MOA can be applied to any pair of arrays A and B such that the last dimension of A has the same length as the first dimension of B and results in the array formed from all the inner products of rows from A and columns from B.

In AT, the similar transformer is denoted by *A INNER* [+,*] *B*. For both systems the operations are parameterized because there are other combinations of operations for inner products that provide interesting results. For example, *A INNER* [*and,or*] *B* does a boolean matrix product and *A INNER [and,match] B* gives a boolean pattern where a vector matches a row of a table.

The outer product corresponds to the linear algebra expression $\bar{x} \cdot \bar{y}^T$ which produces the matrix of all products of items of the column vectors $\bar{x}$ and $\bar{y}$. This involves only one operation. In MOA, the *outer product* operation can be applied to any binary scalar operation to form a new operation. For example, $\bullet_{\times}$ denotes the conventional linear algebra outer product. The shape of the result is the catenation of the shapes of the arguments.

AT has a more general form of outer product in that it can apply to any operation and can combine any number of arrays. It is defined by the equation

$$OUTER\ f\ A = EACH\ f\ cart\ A$$

where *cart* is the generalized cartesian product operation. For a scalar binary operation *f*, *A OUTER f B* has the same meaning as the corresponding notation in MOA.

There are direct relationships between *inner product* and *outer product*. In a universe of flat arrays such as MOA, the inner product can be expressed in terms of an outer product, a diagonalizing generalized transpose, and a reduction. This result has been independently discovered by Abrams [Abrams 70] and in a much earlier treatment of array-like concepts by the American mathematician Peirce [Franksen 88]. In AT notation the relationship is

$$A\ INNER\ [f, g]\ B = EACH\ f\ rows\ (C\ fuse\ (A\ OUTER\ g\ B))$$

where $C = (front\ axes\ A)\ link\ (valence\ A + rest\ axes\ B)\ append\ [last\ axes\ A\ ,\ valence\ A + first\ axes\ B\ ]$.

In a universe of nested arrays, the relationship can also be expressed by partitioning the arrays into lists, applying the outer product of the partitions and then doing the reduction on each item. In AT, assuming that *f* is one of the reductive scalar operations, and *g* is a binary scalar operation, then

$$A\ INNER\ [f, g]\ B = EACH\ f\ (rows\ A\ OUTER\ g\ (0\ split\ B))$$

6. Strengths and Weaknesses of AT and MOA

The preceding sections have given an overview of two systems that provide a mathematical treatment for n-dimensional array data structures. Both systems have their roots in APL, but both have made significant contributions beyond APL.

MOA is essentially a mathematical notation intended for use at the blackboard or in doing proofs of theorems. The target has been mathematical areas where flat arrays are conventionally used, such as descriptions of registers and memories in computers, and in vectors and matrices used in scientific computation.

AT has been developed as an axiomatic theory intended to suit descriptions of broad areas of finite mathematics and also to serve as a computational notation for constructive solutions to problems. The concept of nesting is central to AT; flat arrays are simply those arrays all of whose items are scalars. It is pleasing that these two systems have turned out to be completely consistent with each other.

MOA and AT have taken different approaches in generalizing operations on lists to those on higher dimensional arrays as observed in section 4.6. In AT, the tendency is to define the operation on the list of items of the higher dimensional array. For example, if A is [3,4] *reshape count* 12

1	2	3	4
5	6	7	8
9	10	11	12

then *sum A* is 78, whereas $_+$ *red A* is

10	26	42

In essence, AT decided not to bias any of the operations to prefer a particular axis, whereas MOA extends most operations by assuming partitioning along one axis. Since such partitions are easily expressed in AT, the extended meanings of MOA are easily achieved in AT as we have seen above. As far as expressibility is concerned, then, it appears to be a matter of taste as to which system is preferred.

It is clear that AT is superior to MOA as a notation for expressing algorithms for general purpose problem solving. AT expressions can be directly executed in a Nial processor, whereas MOA must be translated to some implemented array language. Moreover, AT with its complete treatment of symbolic scalar data and its ability to handle heterogeneous and nested arrays, is much better suited for many problems of data representation than MOA. In particular, AT has proven to be a rich environment for doing applications in knowledge based systems [Jenkins 88].

However, MOA is well suited to problems within its target domain. The constraint to flat homogeneous arrays guarantees efficient space storage and efficient access to the items of arrays. Thus, for those problems in which MOA provides a succinct algorithm, the latter can be translated into effective programs on both conventional and parallel computers [Mullin 89]. The same effect could be obtained in AT by providing mechanisms for constraining the types of arrays, by providing more APL-like operations that utilize flat arrays [Jenkins 78], and by implementing AT expressions in Nial so that intermediate nested arrays are not explicitly constructed.

7. Conclusion

The advent of readily available parallel computers has focussed attention on the need for programming systems in which parallel algorithms can be easily expressed. Many researchers are looking to n-dimensional arrays as an underlying data structure that inherently supports parallel decomposition of some classes of engineering and scientific problems. The desire is to find an array system that fits well with a pure functional programming language and encourages parallel descriptions of algorithms for such problems. It is hoped that both AT and MOA will prove to be useful steps along the way to achieving this goal.

8. References

[Abrams 70]
P.S. Abrams, *An APL Machine*, PhD Thesis, Computer Science, Stanford University, STAN-CS-70-158, Palo Alto, California (1970).

[Bird 87]
R. S. Bird, *An Introduction to the Theory of Lists*, in Logic of Programming and Calculi of Discrete Design, ed. M. Broy, Springer-Verlag, Berlin (1987).

[Brown 81]
J.A. Brown, M.A. Jenkins, *The APL Identity Crisis*, APL81 Conference Proceedings, San Francisco, October 1981.

[Brown 84]
J.A. Brown, *The Principles of APL2*, Technical Report TR 03.247, IBM Santa Theresa Lab, San Jose, (1984).

[Franksen 88]
O.I. Franksen, *private communication*,(1989).

[Franksen 90]
O.I. Franksen, *DTH Notes 1- 3 on More's Proposal for Version VIII: revised operations "tell" and"size", and associated operations*, Electric Power Engineering, Technical University of Denmark, Lyngby, (1990).

[Gull 79]
W.E. Gull, M.A. Jenkins, *Recursive Data Structures in APL*, Comm. ACM. 22 Number 1, pp 79-96 (1979).

[ISO 82]
International Standard for the Programming Language APL, ISO TC97/SC5/WG6-N28, 1982.

[Jenkins 78]
M.A. Jenkins, J. Michel, *Operators in an APL Containing Nested Arrays*, APL Quote/Quad, Vol 10, No. 2, 8-20 (1978).

[Jenkins 80]
M.A. Jenkins, *On Combining the Data Structure Concepts of Lisp and APL,* Tech. Rep. 80-109, Dept. of Computing and Information Science, Queen's University, Kingston (1980).

[Jenkins 84]
M.A. Jenkins, *The Role of Equations in Nial,* Tech. Rept. 84-161, Queen's University, July 1984.

[Jenkins 85]
M.A. Jenkins and W.H. Jenkins, *The Q'Nial Reference Manual*, Nial Systems Ltd., Kingston, Canada, 461 pages (1985).

[Jenkins 88]
M.A. Jenkins, J.I. Glasgow, E. Blevis, E. Hache, D. Lawson, *The Nial AI Toolkit,* Proceedings of the Avignon 8th International Workshop on Expert Systems and their Applications, June 1988.

[More 73]
T. More, *Axioms and Theorems for a Theory of Arrays,* IBM J. Res. Development 17, number 2, pp. 135-175 (1973).

[More 90]
T. More, *private communication,*(1990).

[Mullin 88]
L. M. Mullin, *A Mathematics of Arrays,* PhD Thesis, Computer and Information Science, Syracuse University, CASE Centre T.R. 8814, Syracuse, 1988.

[Mullin 89]
L. Mullin, D. Iyengar, and A. Krishnamurthi, *The Dot Product: A New Definition,* CASE Centre T.R. 8901, Syracuse University, Syracuse, 1988.

[Mullin 90]
L. Mullin, *The Phi Function: a basis for FFD with arrays,* First International Workshop on Arrays, Functional Languages and Parallelism, Montreal, 1990.

Appendix

```
# MOA definitions in Nial

# support operations for the definitions below

axes IS tell valence

sortup IS SORT <=

gradeup IS GRADE <=

# the definitions of split1 and blend1 below reflect the correct
versions of split and blend that have been implemented in version 5.

split1 IS OPERATION A B {
 IF valence B = 0 THEN
   single B
 ELSEIF diverse A and . A allin tell valence B THEN
   Axesup := tell valence B except A ;
   tally Axesup raise ( gage ( Axesup link A ) fuse B )
 ELSE
   ??invalid_split
 ENDIF }

# mix1 restricts mix to only work on arrays whose items are of the same shape.

mix1 IS OPERATION A {
 IF equal EACH shape A THEN
  mix A
 ELSE
  ??unequal_shapes_in_items
 ENDIF }

blend1 IS OPERATION A B {
 Bb := mix B ;
 IF A allin axes Bb THEN
   Axesup := tell valence Bb except list A ;
   C := gage GRADE <= link Axesup A ;
   C fuse Bb
 ELSE
   ??invalid_blend
 ENDIF }
```

```
# some simple MOA definitions

moa_shape IS list shape

dimensionality IS valence

rav IS list

moa_pi IS prod

total IS tally

iota IS EXTERNAL OPERATION

moa_grid IS iota moa_shape

is_moa_shape IS OPERATION A {
  valence A = 1 and (and EACH isinteger A) and (and (A >= 0)) }

# I psi A implements the indexing operation of MOA denoted by psi.
  There are 3 cases:
    if I is a vector of length equal to the valence of A :
        return the element at address I if I is a valid index.
    if I is a higher dimensional array whose rows are indices :
        return the array of elements at the indices.
    if I is a vector of length less than the valence of A :
        return the partition of A selected by I

psi IS OPERATION I A {
     IF valence I = 1 and (tally I = valence A) and
          (I in rows moa_grid A) THEN
       I pick A
     ELSEIF valence I > 1  and and (rows I EACHLEFT in rows moa_grid A) THEN
       rows I choose A
     ELSEIF valence I = 1 and (tally I < valence A) and
            (I in tell (tally I take moa_shape A)) THEN
       I pick (tally I raise A)
     ELSE
       ??invalid_psi
     ENDIF }

# I gamma S converts an index I for shape S into the corresponding
position in the list of items of an array of shape S.
```

```
gamma IS OPERATION I S {
   IF shape I = shape S and (valence I = 1) THEN
     IF empty I THEN
       0
     ELSEIF tally I = 1 THEN
       first I
     ELSE
       last I + (last S * (front I gamma front S))
     ENDIF
   ELSE
     ??invalid_gamma
   ENDIF }
```

N inv_gamma S converts a position N in the list of items of an array of shape S to the corresponding index.

```
inv_gamma IS OPERATION N S {
   IF isinteger N and (N >=0) and (N < prod S) THEN
     IF tally S = 1 THEN
       [N]
     ELSE
       (N div last S inv_gamma front S) append (N mod last S)
     ENDIF
   ELSE
     ??invalid_inv_gamma
   ENDIF }
```

A catenate B implements the catentation operation in MOA. For scalars or vectors, it behaves the same as "link" in AT. For arrays of the same valence it permits the catenation if their shapes differ only in the first axis extent, in which case the arrays are joined along the first axis. Catenate is also extended to allow catenation of scalars to higher dimensional arrays by replication.

```
catenate IS OPERATION A B {
   IF valence A <= 1 and ( valence B <= 1 ) THEN
     A link B
   ELSEIF valence A = valence B and
       ( rest moa_shape A = rest moa_shape B ) THEN
     sum EACH ( first moa_shape ) A B hitch rest moa_shape A
       reshape link A B
   ELSEIF atomic A THEN
```

```
    (1 hitch rest moa_shape B reshape A) catenate B
  ELSEIF atomic B THEN
    A catenate (1 hitch rest moa_shape A reshape B)
  ELSE
    ??invalid_catenate
  ENDIF }
```

iota A generates a list of integers if A is an integer; otherwise if A is a shape, it generates an array of shape A catenate tally A with rows corresponding to the indices of A.

```
iota IS OPERATION A {
  IF isinteger A THEN
    tell A
  ELSEIF is_moa_shape A THEN
    mix tell A
  ELSE
    ??invalid_iota
  ENDIF }
```

A moa_take B selects a subarray from B with a shape that depends on the absolute values of integers in A. If an item of A is negative, the selection is taken from the end of the axis rather than the beginning. If A is shorter than the valence of B then the missing axes are taken in their entirety. If A is an integer it is treated as if it were the corresponding 1-vector.

```
moa_take IS OPERATION A B {
  IF and EACH isinteger A and and (abs A <= (tally A take moa_shape B)) THEN
    I gets tell abs list A EACHLEFT +
        (A < 0 * (tally A take moa_shape B + list A));
    I OUTER link tell (tally A drop moa_shape B) choose B
  ELSE
    ??invalid_take
  ENDIF }
```

A moa_drop B selects a subarray from B with a shape that depends on shortening the axes of B by the absolute values of the items of A. If an item of A is negative the dropping is done from the end of the axis. If A is shorter than the valence of B then the missing axes are not shortened. If A is an integer, it is treated as if it were the corresponding 1-vector.

```
moa_drop IS OPERATION A B {
  IF and EACH isinteger A and and (abs A <= (tally A take moa_shape B)) THEN
```

```
  I gets tell (tally A take moa_shape B - abs list A) EACHLEFT +
      (A > 0 * list A);
  I OUTER link tell (tally A drop moa_shape B) choose B
ELSE
  ??invalid_take
ENDIF }
```

MOA_REDUCE A does the right to left reduction of a vector using the binary operation f. It is assumed that f is "reductive" and has an identity element. The code below only works for the AT operations that have such an identity. For a higher dimensional array the reduction is done over the partitions along the first axis.

```
MOA_REDUCE IS TRANSFORMER f
  OPERATION A {
   IF valence A = 1 THEN
    IF empty A THEN
      f A
    ELSE
      first A f MOA_REDUCE f rest A
    ENDIF
   ELSE
    mix EACH MOA_REDUCE f (0 split1 A)
   ENDIF }
```

MOA_SCAN A does the right to left scan of a vector using the binary operation f. It is assumed that f is "reductive" and has an identity element. The code below only works for the AT operations that have such an identity. For a higher dimensional array the scan is done over the partitions along the first axis.

```
MOA_SCAN IS TRANSFORMER f
  OPERATION A {
   IF valence A = 1 THEN
    IF empty A THEN
      Null
    ELSE
      MOA_SCAN f front A append MOA_REDUCE f A
    ENDIF
   ELSE
    0 blend EACH MOA_SCAN f (0 split1 A)
   ENDIF }
```

x[y] is defined in MOA for a vector x and y an index or a vector of indices.

We denote this in this simulation by X index Y.

```
index IS OPERATION X Y {
 IF valence X = 1 THEN
   IF atomic Y THEN
     [Y] psi X
   ELSEIF valence Y = 1 and and (Y EACHLEFT in iota tally X) THEN
     Y EACHLEFT pick X
   ELSE
      ??invalid_index
   ENDIF
 ELSE
    ??invalid_index
 ENDIF }
```

A compress B uses a list of 0 and 1's to select items from the vector B.
For higher dimensional arrays, the selection is done over the first axis.
It uses blend1 to fix a minor problem in Nial's blend operation in version 4.1.

```
compress IS OPERATION A B {
  IF atomic B THEN
    B := list B;
  ENDIF;
  IF A allin [0,1] and (tally A = first moa_shape B) THEN
    0 blend1 EACH ( A match 1 sublist ) ( 0 split1 B )
  ELSE
    ??invalid_compress
  ENDIF}
```

A expand B uses a list of 0 and 1's to expand items from the vector B.
For higher dimensional arrays, the expansion is done over the first axis.
It uses blend1 to fix a minor problem in Nial's blend operation in version 4.1.

```
expand IS OPERATION A B {
  IF atomic B THEN
    B := list B;
  ENDIF;
  IF A allin [0,1] and (sum A = first moa_shape B) THEN
   IF valence B = 1 THEN
     Res := tally A reshape 0;
     J := 0;
     FOR I WITH grid Res DO
```

```
      IF A@I = 1 THEN
        Res@I := B@J;
        J := J + 1;
      ENDIF;
    ENDFOR;
    Res
  ELSE
    0 blend1 EACH ( A expand ) ( 0 split1 B )
  ENDIF
ELSE
  ??invalid_expand
ENDIF}
```

moa_reverse A reverses the items of a list. If A is higher dimensional the reversal is done along the first axis.

```
moa_reverse IS OPERATION A {
  0 blend1 EACH reverse ( 0 split1 A ) }
```

N moa_rotate A rotates along the first axis of A if N is a scalar. If N is an array of values of shape rest moa_shape A, then the individual rotation is done for each corresponding vector in 0 split A.

```
moa_rotate IS OPERATION N A {
  IF isinteger N THEN
    0 blend1 EACH ( N rotate ) ( 0 split1 A )
  ELSEIF moa_shape N = rest moa_shape A THEN
    0 blend1 (N EACHBOTH moa_rotate (0 split1 A))
  ELSE
    ??invalid_rotate
  ENDIF }
```

A moa_transpose B does a generalized transpose using the MOA encoding of the left argument.

```
moa_transpose IS OPERATION A B {
  IF tally A = valence B and (gradeup A choose A = axes B) THEN
    Aa := sortup cull A EACHLEFT findall A ;
    Aa fuse B
  ELSE
    ??invalid_transpose
  ENDIF }
```

V OMEGA f A implements the version of "omega" in MOA for

unary operations f. V indicates how many axes at the end of A are to be partitioned. The operation is applied to the partitions and the results gathered. The constraint on f is that the shape of its result depends only on the shape of its argument, and hence the result on each partition will be of the same size.

```
OMEGA IS TRANSFORMER f
    OPERATION V A {
      mix1 EACH f ( V takeright axes A split1 A ) }
```

[Va,Vb] BOMEGA f [A,B] implements the version of "omega" in MOA for binary operations f. Va indicates how many axes at the end of A are to be partitioned, and Vb does the same for B. The operation is applied to pairs of partitions from A and B and the results gathered. The constraint on f is that the shape of its result depends only on the shape of its arguments, and hence the result on each partition will be of the same size.

```
BOMEGA IS TRANSFORMER f
    OPERATION Vab AB {
      Va Vb := Vab ;
      A B := AB ;
      mix1 ( (Va takeright axes A split1 A) EACHBOTH f
        (Vb takeright axes B split1 B)) }
```

X MOA_OUTER f Y computes the outer product using a construction involving reshapes and a generalized transpose. All the f combinations are computed using scalar extension.

```
MOA_OUTER IS TRANSFORMER f
    OPERATION X Y {
      Newx := shape Y link shape X reshape X;
      Newy := shape X link shape Y reshape Y;
      (valence Y rotate tell (valence X + valence Y) fuse Newx) f Newy }
```

X MOA_INNER [f,g] Y computes the inner product using a construction involving reshapes and a generalized transpose. All the g combinations are computed in an array with one extra axis on the end, which is removed by an f reduction.

```
MOA_INNER IS TRANSFORMER f g
    OPERATION X Y {
     IF last shape X = first shape Y THEN
```

```
  Newx := rest shape Y link shape X reshape X;
  Newy := front shape X link shape Y reshape Y;
  Vals := (valence Y - 1 rotate tell (valence X + valence Y - 1)
         fuse Newx) g Newy;
  EACH REDUCE f cols Vals
ELSE
  ??invalid_inner_product
ENDIF }
```

a natural definition for the MOA equivalent of cart is formed by mixing the results of the AT cart.

```
moa_cart IS OPERATION A {
   mix cart A }
```

15

Alternative Evaluation of Array Expressions

Cory F. Skutt
IBM T. J. Watson Research Center
P. O. Box 704
Yorktown Heights, NY 10598

Abstract

Traditionally, languages that support array-style programming have evaluated array expressions by computing all the elements of an array before making it available for subsequent computation. This method is simple, easily implemented, but generally inefficient. Narrowly viewed as an optimization problem, recent work has focused on using lazy evaluation to improve the efficiency of various subsets of array expressions. This work describes advances in two important areas. First, alternative orders of evaluation are well defined and easily controllable. Language semantics are introduced that provide three forms of array element evaluation: eager, latched, and lazy. Second, a method is described for efficiently applying lazy evaluation to *all* array expressions, not just grid selections. A rule based system is used to transform symbolic representations of arrays that use functions of index vectors.

Keywords: arrays, expressions, evaluation, eager, latched, lazy, APL, LISP, rewriting, symbolic manipulation, optimization.

1 Introduction

Scalar programming languages and styles characteristically manipulate arrays through sets of loops and induction variables in combination with a scalar indexing primitive. Over twenty years ago, array programming languages and styles were introduced, in which arrays are characteristically manipulated with concise expressions written with a rich set of primitives that operate on arrays in their entirety. Since then, experience with APL and other languages has shown that array-style programming accrues several advantages over scalar-style programming:

- Array-style programming is very productive; programs can be written much more concisely.

- Array-style programs are easier for people to understand since they have fewer loops and induction variables.

- It is easier for a compiler or interpreter to recognize parallelism. Analysis of scalar-style programs proceeds pessimistically, presuming sequentiality, attempting to prove independence. Analysis of array-style programs proceeds optimistically, presuming independence unless dependencies are introduced via the conspicuous use of certain primitives.
- It is possible to employ high level idiom recognition, possibly resulting in better computational complexity.
- The need for subscript checking is significantly reduced.

Despite these advantages and a renewed interest in array programming in support of parallelism, it has generally been supported by new language designs in only a very limited form: array operations that apply a simple arithmetic primitive to similarly shaped arrays, element by element[1] .

1.1 Problem

To illustrate the problem addressed in this paper, consider the following computation. A variable, *Bals*, represents a vector of beginning account balances. A variable, *Trans*, represents a matrix of daily net transactions against the accounts, each row representing a day, each column representing an account and corresponding to a position in *Bals*. A variable, *Active*, contains a list of (column) indexes into *Bals* and *Trans* that describes active accounts. Now, derive a vector of ending balances for the active accounts. The solution expressed in APL might be:

```
(+⌿Bals⍪Trans)[Active]
```

Current practice in evaluating this expression is to fully compute all elements for each array subexpression. First, a new matrix is built (*Bals*⍪*Trans*) with the first row coming from *Bals* and subsequent rows from *Trans*. Second, a new vector is formed by summing the columns (+⌿) of the new matrix. Last, the sums for the active accounts will be extracted from the new vector.

Most programmers using traditional, scalar-style programming would write a program containing an outer loop with each iteration representing an active account, and an inner loop with each iteration representing one day's transactions. This later program would have allocated only the final vector of active balances and would not have performed any computations for inactive accounts.

[1]later referred to as an each operation.

In summary, array-style programming as occurring in current practice, has the following, sometimes profound, disadvantages:

- Array-style programs cannot minimize storage requirements by avoiding the formation of temporary arrays implied by the literal interpretation of array expressions. This may adversely affect the storage space *order of complexity* of an algorithm, e.g. changing it from linear in its amount of space to quadratic.
- Array-style programs generally do too much computation. Elements not used in a subsequent computation are unnecessarily computed.
- Reliably programming with side effects becomes difficult, if not impossible, if compilers or interpreters arbitrarily use lazy evaluation in an attempt to solve these problems.
- Purely lazy evaluation does not always result in an improvement; sometimes it makes things worse.

The problem addressed by this work is to effectively eliminate these disadvantages while effectively preserving the previously mentioned advantages of array-style programming.

1.2 Background

To date, several works have proceeded along these lines. Very nearly all the work done in this area involves attempts to improve the performance of APL interpreters and compilers by expanding the class of array expressions having their elements lazily evaluated. The first published work, by Abrams [3], presented methods he called drag-along and beating which together provided for the lazy evaluation of array elements. The subset of expressions he applied the technique to involved array primitives from three groups: (a) scalar functions, which are applied to an array element by element, (b) operators or functionals, which apply argument functions to arrays in ways that involve cumulations or cartesian products, and (c) grid selectors, which define one array as having fixed strides through the row major order of another. Abrams observed that a grid selection of a grid selection was also a grid selection. The primitives he treated as grid selectors were take, drop, reverse, transposes, and indexing with arithmetic progression vectors. The ranks of these expressions had to be known at compile time. Guibas and Wyatt[8] later added certain forms of conforming reshapes which replicated arrays along new dimensions. In addition, they were able to relax the fixed rank constraint. They also treated cases in which elements were used repeatedly and developed methods to avoid their recomputation. Several other works were based on these earlier techniques without significantly expanding the class of expressions amenable to lazy evaluation [11][19][5][6]. Driscoll and Orth[7] applied additional special case techniques capable of handling a larger, difficult to characterize, class of expressions. Tu[17] presents work in which he introduces arrays in which elements are always evaluated lazily. He also presents a simple method capable of handling all expressions, though not very efficiently. Work on lazily evaluating aggregate data structures other than arrays has been undertaken by the LISP community. Streams are lazily evaluated lists found in Scheme[1] and Waters[20] has developed a system for manipulating similar structures in Common LISP.

1.3 Overview

In the next section, we describe three forms of evaluation, suggesting that, collectively, they are necessary and sufficient to allow array-style programs to compete with scalar-style programs. In the third section, formal properties of these forms of evaluation are presented as a basis for making various optimizing transformations upon array-style code. In the last section, an implementation method, based upon an executable prototype, is presented. This method is shown to provide a basis for efficiently evaluating all array expressions using any of the three forms of evaluation.

From this point forward all programming notation will use LISP syntax. The operations used in this paper parallel those found in APL and are described in appendix A. Although most of the examples can be understood from their context and from explanations in the text, some exposure to both APL and LISP is presumed and is important to the comprehension of this paper.

2 Forms of Evaluation

This section presents the motivation for, and description of, three forms of array expression evaluation.

2.1 No Single "Best" Form of Evaluation

Before proceeding, consider the problem of minimizing the cost of computing the array represented by the expression:

```
(slice (each + a b) x)
```

where a, b, and x all represent vectors. The computation involves using indexes in x to select items from the vector produced by adding each of the elements in vector a to those of vector b. When attempting to find an optimal way to evaluate the expression, three obvious cases arise:

- If x refers to every element at least once, then forming the full intermediate array of sums should be optimal.
- If x refers to a small subset, and each sum is selected at most once, then computing the sums "on demand" for each element in x should be optimal.
- If x represents a small subset, but there are a significant number of duplications in it, then it might be optimal to compute the sum the first time a particular index is found, save it, and use it again if the same index is encountered again.

This example demonstrates that, since the salient characteristics of x cannot, in general, be known before run time, there is no single "best" method for evaluating elements of arrays. The approach we take is to provide multiple evaluation strategies, allowing the programmer to predict and control which one will be put to use.

2.2 General Characteristics

Each of the following three forms of evaluation share some general characteristics. First, these forms of evaluation properly apply to the order in which *elements* are evaluated, not arrays. The order in which *arrays* are evaluated is the same as the order in which expressions are evaluated. Expression order of evaluation is generally independent of element order of evaluation, but some interaction naturally occurs and is more fully described in section 2.7.2. From this point forward, unless otherwise noted, the term *evaluation* will refer to the method for evaluating array elements, not expressions. Second, there is an object type for each form of evaluation. In the subsections that follow, the characteristics of both the objects and their associated method of element evaluation are described. These characteristics are briefly summarized in Table 1.

2.3 Eager Evaluation, Eager Arrays

An *eager array* is one in which, conceptually, all of its elements have been computed and placed in storage. Referring to an element results only in a

	Contains Previously Computed Objects	Performs Computation Upon Element Access
Eager Array	always	never
Latched Array	sometimes	first time
Lazy Array	never	each time

Table 1: Array Characteristics

storage access. *Eager evaluation* refers to the technique of evaluating each element immediately after the array object is formed as a part of evaluating an array expression. Accessing an element in an eager array cannot cause a side effect. All side effects associated with the computation of an element occur when the array is created. The `eager` primitive causes eager evaluation of the elements in its argument. For example, the expression:

```
(slice (eager (each princ #(a b c d))) #(0 1 3 1))
```

prints:

```
ABCD
```

and produces for its result:[2]

```
#(A B D B)
```

Nearly all common programming languages include only this form of array evaluation.

2.4 Lazy Evaluation, Lazy Arrays

Conceptually, a *lazy array* is one in which none of its elements are maintained in storage. An element is computed every time it is accessed; if it is never accessed, it is never computed. *Lazy evaluation*[3] refers to the technique of computing each element as it is accessed and not beforehand. Since the

[2]These three variant expressions are assumed to occur in contexts in which the elements of the "`slice`" expression are eagerly evaluated.

[3]In this paper we use this term to denote a form of evaluation in which the computation is defined as being performed each time it is requested. In functional programming literature, this term is frequently applied to forms of evaluation which are designed to be performed only once, as in graph reduction (see [14]). We refer to this latter form of evaluation as memoized or "latched".

computation associated with an element may be arbitrary, with lazy arrays, a side effect may occur each time an element is accessed. The `lazy` primitive causes lazy evaluation of the elements in its argument. For example, the expression:

```
(slice (lazy (each princ #(a b c d))) #(0 1 3 1))
```

prints:

```
ABDB
```

and produces for its result:

```
#(A B D B)
```

The characteristics, advantages, and uses of lazy arrays are described by Tu[17], Tu and Perlis[18], (as array comprehensions) Hudak, Wadler, et. al.[9], and Anderson and Hudak [4]. The treatment of lazy arrays here differs only in that we permit and define behavior for side effects. Lazy evaluation makes it possible for arrays to have infinitely large (unbounded) dimensions. [10][15][17][18].

2.5 Latched Evaluation, Latched Arrays

A *latched array* combines desirable characteristics of both eager and lazy arrays, avoiding unnecessary or duplicate element computations. An element is computed and stored only when it is accessed for the first time. Subsequent accesses refer to the stored value. *Latched evaluation* refers to the associated evaluation technique. With latched arrays, a side effect may occur at most once per element. The `latched` primitive causes lazy evaluation of the elements in its argument. For example, the expression:

```
(slice (latched (each princ #(a b c d))) #(0 1 3 1))
```

prints:

```
ABD
```

and produces for its result:

```
#(A B D B)
```

Except that it refers to element evaluation instead of expression evaluation, this form of evaluation is very similar to memoized evaluation[1]. Latched arrays may also have infinitely large (unbounded) dimensions.

2.6 Default Form of Evaluation

Eager evaluation is not a suitable default; once a computation has been performed there is, in general, no way of undoing its side effects or otherwise affecting it. Both latched and lazy arrays can be created without computing their elements, so either could be a suitable default. In the embedded language and implementation described in section 4, latched evaluation serves as the default; it is the form that performs the least number of element evaluations.

Therefore, in this system:

- All array primitives except `eager` and `lazy` produce latched arrays.
- The only primitive that produces an eager array is `eager`.
- The only primitive that produces a lazy array is `lazy`.

2.7 Miscellaneous Characteristics

2.7.1 Array Nesting

All three kinds of arrays may be nested, and the types of arrays may vary among these three at any level. For example, it is possible to have an eager array of lazy arrays, etc. This may at first seem strange, but only the second level *arrays* need be computed as top level array elements – the second level *elements* do not. A lazy array of eager arrays might also seem strange, but one way of describing it is as an array with elements *that when evaluated* are eager arrays. Within the same array, elements may be mixed: some lazy arrays, some latched, some eager, and some not even arrays at all. With lazy and latched arrays, in some sense, elements do not exist until they are evaluated, making undefined elements possible.

2.7.2 Conditional Execution

When an argument expression serves directly as an element of a lazy or latched array, then it is lazily evaluated. For example, in the expression:

```
(pick
  (vec (eager (each foo x))
       (bar x)
       (eager (each baz x))
       (/ 1 0))
  n)
```

a single element is selected from a latched (by default) vector of length four. Only one element is selected and evaluated. If `n` is 0, `foo` will execute, but `bar` and `baz` will not. An error will occur only if `n` is 3. This effect makes it possible to achieve the semantics of conditional execution constructions like `cond, if, case`, etc.

3 Properties of Evaluation Order

In this section, properties of these three forms of arrays are presented. These are useful in delimiting when program transformations may be applied for the purposes of optimization. In the tables and sections that follow, the symbol $\Longleftrightarrow$ means that two expressions are equivalent. This equivalence means not only do the two expressions produce the same value, but they also produce the same side effects in the same order.

3.1 Double Application Transformations

When two evaluation ordering primitives are applied in immediate succession the following transformations may be applied in an attempt at optimization:[4]

```
(eager   (eager x))  <=>  (eager x)       (1)
(latched (eager x))  <=>  (eager x)       (2)
(lazy    (eager x))  <=>  (eager x)       (3)

(eager   (latched x))  <=>  (eager x)     (4)
(latched (latched x))  <=>  (latched x)   (5)
(lazy    (latched x))  <=>  (lazy x)      (6)

(eager   (lazy x))  <=>  (eager x)        (7)
(latched (lazy x))  <=>  (latched x)      (8)
(lazy    (lazy x))  <=>  (lazy x)         (9)
```

3.2 Preferred Orders of Evaluation

In cases where freedom exists to choose the order of evaluation for an element of an array expression, such a decision can best be made by considering the

[4]It is also possible to define a consistent system in which (2) and (3) have `(latched x)` and `(lazy x)` on the right, respectively.

access pattern for array elements. Two major aspects of this pattern are key: whether or not all the elements are accessed; and how many times elements are accessed. If all the elements in an array are accessed, the array is said to be *totally accessed*; if some are not, it is *partially* accessed. In some cases, another aspect matters: relative to one another, the order in which elements are accessed. This order within the array is only relevant to eager evaluation; lazy and latched evaluation do not involve sequencing the evaluation of different elements within the same array. This order, called *eager order*, is not defined by this paper, but usually corresponds to row major order for sequential implementations. Parallel implementations will conveniently leave this order undefined.[5]

Table 2 describes the preferred order of evaluation for an array, given characteristics of how its elements are accessed.

	Not All Elements Accessed	**All Elements Accessed**
Elements Multiply Fetched	latched	eager
Elements Singly Fetched	lazy	lazy

Table 2: Preferred Forms of Evaluation

3.3 Properties Related to Side Effects

In the sections that follow, the term *free array* will be used to denote an array in which it is not possible to generate a side effect from evaluating any of its elements. A *sensitive array* is one in which evaluation of an element may produce a side effect.

3.3.1 Properties of Free Arrays

Discounting memory requirements and performance and concerning ourselves only with program behavior, it does not matter how a free array is evaluated. Free arrays have the following important property:

$$\begin{aligned}\texttt{(eager x)} &\Longleftrightarrow \texttt{(latched x)} \qquad \texttt{x} \text{ a free array}\\ &\Longleftrightarrow \texttt{(lazy x)}\end{aligned} \qquad (10)$$

[5]In systems supporting parallel execution, it may be desirable to introduce two variants of `eager`, one which evaluates elements sequentially, the other in parallel.

3.3.2 Properties of Sensitive Arrays

Sensitive arrays, as the name implies, are sensitive to the order in which their elements are evaluated, and may produce different behavior depending upon which form of evaluation is used. It is still possible (and useful) to determine some equivalences for sensitive arrays, but in general, they must have more conditions met than their free array counterparts:

`(eager x)` $\Longleftrightarrow$ `(latched x)` $\Longleftrightarrow$ `(lazy x)`	x totally, singly accessed in eager order	(11)
`(eager x)` $\Longleftrightarrow$ `(latched x)`	x totally accessed in eager order the first time	(12)
`(latched x)` $\Longleftrightarrow$ `(lazy x)`	x singly accessed	(13)

3.4 Application of Optimizations

In general, these properties can be exploited in ways that may give better performance. Useful element access patterns can usually be inferred from analyzing array expressions. However, care must be taken to avoid making performance worse. In particular, whether or not a reordering optimization should be performed in a case where an evaluation order is explicitly coded[6] requires special consideration. Unless it can be inferred that the optimization will always (as opposed to probably) make performance better, it is best to avoid such an optimization on the grounds that what the programmer wanted and requested should be respected.

4 Implementation

In this section a method is described for efficiently evaluating array expressions. This method has been embodied in a prototype written in Common LISP. The array expression language, described in Appendix A, is embedded in LISP with semantics similar to APL. This approach offers the following advantages:

[6]Recall that latched evaluation is the default.

- Neither an entire language nor an entire language processor has to be written.
- LISP already has arrays, providing an obvious representation for what we describe as eager arrays.
- LISP supports strong data abstraction, making it possible to introduce new first class objects (latched and lazy arrays).
- LISP has macros, making it possible to employ sophisticated techniques for evaluation, analysis, and code generation without the necessity of producing an entire language processor.
- LISP is well suited for the symbolic manipulation used here to optimize code.
- LISP has function objects, closures, and lexical binding which work well in situations where code is executed far away from the environment in which it is defined.

There are some important things to note about the particular way arrays are processed in this language. First, since we have three kinds of arrays, two of which are different than the standard LISP array, we have introduced some primitives which appear to duplicate function currently found in LISP. For example, we introduce `vec` which does essentially the same thing as `vector`, the current LISP primitive. We have given different names to our primitives to avoid confusion and to preserve the distinction. In general, these primitives will work in the same situations LISP's will. However, only ours will work on our representations of latched or lazy arrays. Second, because none of the arithmetic primitives in LISP are defined for arrays, they cannot be presumed to be scalar functions, as in APL. As a consequence, many expressions that could be coded in APL with just a single scalar function need to be coded in our embedded language with surrounding `each` and `box` primitives. Third, because not all objects in LISP are arrays, the particular system of nested arrays used here is a grounded system, as opposed to a floating system. In grounded systems, encapsulation of an object into a scalar array (an operation called "box") always results in a new, distinct object. In floating systems, basic data are considered to be scalar arrays and the corresponding operation (called "enclose") does not produce a distinct object in those cases.

In the sections that follow, an implementation of this embedded language is described in which expressions are evaluated in two different modes: expression by expression, object by object, as is traditional; and across multiple expressions at once, as is necessary for lazy evaluation. Both modes may be freely interleaved and both work from a common symbolic representation of array expressions.

4.1 Symbolic Representation

The symbolic representation of an array expression used here is a LISP S-expression consisting of five parts:

order The kind of evaluation to be used when computing elements of the array. It is one of the following four symbols: `build-free`, `build-eager`, `build-latched`, or `build-lazy`.

lets A LISP `let` list of variable bindings that are established prior to building the array object. These are most commonly used to hold previously computed arrays, latch hit arrays, latch data arrays, etc.

rank A LISP expression that represents the rank of the array.

shape A LISP expression that represents a vector of dimensions for an array.

index function A LISP expression that represents a function. This function takes as its argument a vector of indexes. When evaluated, it returns the value of the element at those indexes.

Additional conventions govern these symbolic representations. For convenience, we introduce our own special form, distinct from a general `lambda` called `a-lam` which has the following meaning:

`(a-lam` *v body*`)` $\Longleftrightarrow$ `(lambda (`*v*`)` *body*`)`

In these forms *v* is a "gensym", that is, a generated symbol distinct from any normal symbol. The four `build-` symbols also designate names of LISP macros. In the sections that follow the symbol ⇓ will be used to mean "has a symbolic representation like".

As Examples:[7]

```
(iota n)
⇓
(BUILD-FREE NIL
            1
            (VECTOR N)
            (A-LAM V664 (AREF V664 0)))
```

[7] `iota` produces a vector of the first n integers, starting at zero. `outer` produces a cartesian product.

```
(outer f (iota m) (iota n))
⇓
(BUILD-LATCHED NIL
               2
               (VECTOR M N)
               (A-LAM V702 (F (AREF V702 0)
                              (AREF V702 1))))
```

```
(each iota (iota n))
⇓
(BUILD-FREE NIL
            1
            (VECTOR N)
            (A-LAM V691
                   (BUILD-FREE
                    NIL
                    1
                    (VECTOR (AREF V691 0))
                    (A-LAM V692 (AREF V692 0)))))
```

4.2 Array Object Representations

Under various circumstances it is necessary to create, or *form*, an array object. If the array to be formed is an eager array, then a normal LISP array may be used to represent the object. If it is a lazy array, then a suitable representation might be a structure with the following fields:

- Function object to compute the rank.
- Function object to compute the shape.
- Function object to compute the element at a given index.

If it is a latched array, then two additional fields might be added:

- Bit array indicating whether an element has been evaluated.
- Array containing elements that have been evaluated.

Hash tables might also be used for these fields of a latched array object.

4.3 Blind Representations

When nothing is known about an expression other than it presumably represents some type of array, it is given a "blind" representation as in the the following case:

```
b
⇓
(BUILD-LAZY NIL
            (A-RANK B)
            (A-SHAPE B)
            (A-LAM V707 (A-PICK B V707)))
```

The functions `A-RANK`, `A-SHAPE`, and `A-PICK` are all designed to produce the appropriate result at run time. They are designed to work with all objects that represent arrays. In cases where objects are latched, free, or lazy arrays, they may invoke lambda expressions (functional objects) contained in the array objects. As was shown by Tu[17], using blind representations, run-time functions, and array objects, *all* array computations can be lazily evaluated. However, this method is generally expensive; a stored function object must be called for each element in each array subexpression. Most of this overhead can be avoided through manipulation of the symbolic representations of the array expressions.

4.4 Manipulation of Symbolic Representations

The general representation[8] of the catenation of two free vectors `a` and `b` might be represented symbolically with the following template:

```
(BUILD-FREE
   NIL
   1
   (VECTOR (+ (AREF (shape of A) 0) (AREF (shape of B) 0)))
   (A-LAM
      v
      (IF (< (AREF v 0) (AREF (shape of A) 0))
          ((index function of A) v)
          ((index function of B) (VECTOR (- (AREF v 0)
                                            (AREF (shape of A) 0)))))))
```

Assuming that `a` is represented by:

---

[8]The template actually used is considerably more complex since it must treat arbitrary rank and evaluation order. For exposition purposes, we use this simpler rank 1, free array template.

```
(each + (box x) (iota m))
⇓
(BUILD-FREE NIL
            1
            (VECTOR M)
            (A-LAM V664 (+ X (AREF V664 0))))
```

and that b is similarly represented by (each + (box y) (iota n)), then by making the appropriate substitutions with the shape and index function expressions from the symbolic representations of a and b, the following results:

```
(cat (each + (box x) (iota m)) (each + (box y) (iota n)))
⇓
(BUILD-FREE NIL
            1
            (VECTOR (+ (AREF (VECTOR M) 0)
                       (AREF (VECTOR N) 0))
            (A-LAM
              V682
              (IF (< (AREF V682 0) (AREF (VECTOR M) 0))
                  ((A-LAM V664 (+ X (AREF V664 0))) V682)
                  ((A-LAM V679 (+ Y (AREF V679 0)))
                     (VECTOR (- (AREF V682 0)
                                (AREF (VECTOR M) 0)))))))
```

Performing beta-reductions and applying some rewriting rules that remove aref - vector combinations, yields:

```
(BUILD-FREE NIL
            1
            (VECTOR (+ M N))
            (A-LAM
              V682
              (IF (< (AREF V682 0) M)
                  (+ X (AREF V682 0))
                  (+ Y (- M) (AREF V682 0)))))
```

4.5 Rule Based Rewriting

It is absolutely essential to rewrite the expressions produced by performing these substitutions. Without the simplifications, even the most basic operations produce representations that grow out of control. In our prototype, there are about three hundred rules that govern how expressions should be rewritten in order to perform the necessary simplifications. The rewriting system is fairly simple and was originally based upon a system sketched out by Abelson and Sussman[2]. Later, the rules were changed in form and were compiled, resulting in an orders-of-magnitude performance improvement. Below is a typical cluster of rules that get applied to `if` forms:

```
(defun simplify-norm-if (form)
       (apply-rules
        ((  (if a b c)
                     c
            (and (sym-const 'a)
                 (null 'a))   )
         (  (if a b c)
                   b
            (and (sym-const 'a)
                 (not (null 'a)))  )
         (  (if a b c)
                   b
            (sym-equal? 'b 'c)  )
        )
       form))
```

The first two rules check for a constant predicate while the third checks for duplicate consequents.

Besides obvious characteristic like consistency and non-circularity of rules, the following characteristics were also introduced based on experience:

- Every attempt is made to reduce rank expressions to constants; when ranks are non-constant expressions, the shape and index function expressions are many times larger.
- Even though they exist only on paths that can never be taken, invalid expressions are produced. As a result, all rules involving constant propagation through functions must be guarded.
- Subtraction and division are normalized into their monadic or unary forms. This allows them, expressed as a sum or product with an inverted term, to be processed by rules designed for general series or products, reducing the number of rules significantly. (A second level of expression optimization occurs later that may change them back).

- To achieve better performance, common subexpressions share their representations, and rewriting is performed destructively. This avoids simplifying the same expression multiple times.

4.6 Index Function Representation

The current representation of index function is a curried variant of the ψ indexing function used by Mullin[12]. Two alternative representations for the index function were considered, one of which was implemented before being abandoned. The first to be considered was one in which the index function had multiple arguments, one for each dimension. This would have required all ranks to be known at analysis time, precluding variable rank expressions. The second representation was one in which the argument was a single scalar, representing the position of an element in row major order. This representation, used by Tu[17], is tempting because it makes it possible to design a system in which simplification need only consider scalar expressions instead of expressions involving small vectors, as with the shape and index expressions. However, this representation requires, in the general case, that each separate index be derived from the row-major-order index with an expression of the form:

```
(mod (floor index stride1) stride2)
```

In this system, writing rules to achieve such basic identities as:[9]

$$\texttt{(rev (rev x))} \iff \texttt{x} \tag{14}$$

$$\texttt{(pose (pose x))} \iff \texttt{x} \tag{15}$$

became intractibly complex. With our current representation separate indexes are derived with expressions of the form:

```
(aref index n)
```

These are usually reduced to single variables by the array formation optimizations described in section 4.8.2.

4.7 Implementation via Macro Expansion

In the prototype, symbolic manipulation is performed in conjunction with macro expansion to produce code that executes in the intended way. Each

[9] `rev` means "reverse"; `pose` means "transpose".

array-style primitive is implemented as an *array* macro described in appendix A. When the operation represented by the macro is defined to return an array, the macro expansion produced is an S-expression representation of the array result of the form previously described. This representation is used in two ways:

- It represents a call to a *build* macro designed to form the object. Such a macro is naturally invoked when no array macro surrounds it. It performs optimizations described later in section 4.8.2 before producing code that creates an array object. That array object is a first class object fully capable interacting with other LISP code, in addition to responding to the blind representation functions described in section 4.3.
- The representation produced by the macro is used by another, outer array macro. In the previous example the `cat` macro expands the `each` macro producing the `build-free` S-expression. The S-expression produced by expanding the `each` macro is not expanded further nor is it executed. Instead, it is used to derive the shape and index function expressions that are used to fill in the catenation template. In the process of expanding the `each` macro, the `iota` and `box` macros are expanded and used in the same way. Only the final `cat` macro produces an S-expression that is used as a subsequent build macro, actually constructing an array object.

4.8 Optimization

Optimizations are divided into two parts and described separately: those that manipulate the symbolic representations of arrays; and those that manipulate code that forms array objects.

4.8.1 Optimization of Symbolic Representations

Some optimizations are designed to reduce overhead in accessing and computing array elements. These were described in section 4.5 and are relatively independent of the order of evaluation. But other optimizations, those designed to select preferred orders of evaluation (see section 3.2), need additional information such as access characteristics not immediately available in the symbolic representations. Symbolic representations are processed inside out; that is, a symbolic representation produced by an inner macro is used to produce a new symbolic representation by an outer macro. Access attributes need to be processed "outside-in". The nature of an array operation determines whether elements of its *arguments* are multiply accessed, not its own elements. For example, in the absence of a surrounding context, the single element of the following scalar array may be presumed to be accessed only once (during the formation of the array):

```
(box (+ a b))
⇓
(BUILD-FREE NIL 0 #() (A-LAM V699 (+ A B)))
```

However, if that same expression is used as an argument to each, its element may be presumed to be multiply fetched. In such a case, it makes sense to evaluate the scalar array eagerly, thus performing the addition only once:

```
(each f (box (+ a b)) (iota n))
⇓
(BUILD-LATCHED ((A716 (BUILD-EAGER
                        NIL
                        0
                        #()
                        (A-LAM V709 (+ A B)))))
                1
                (VECTOR N)
                (A-LAM V718
                       (F (AREF A716)
                          (AREF V718 0))))
```

This type of optimization is most easily performed if, at the time the inner macro (box) produces its representation, it knows its element will be multiply fetched. Since access characteristics are determined by the outer macro (each), one way of doing this is for the outer macro to pass additional context information to the inner macro. In the prototype, a variation of this technique is implemented: there are two sets of inner macros that an outer macro can call depending upon whether elements will be singly or multiply fetched. In this example, a macro called box-m will be called instead of the macro box.

In those cases where a preferred order of evaluation cannot be obtained because of semantic constraints due to side effects, the programmer can explicitly code an order of evaluation:

```
(each - (box (g a b)) (iota n))
⇓
(BUILD-LATCHED
  ((H764 (MAKE-ARRAY '() :ELEMENT-TYPE BIT
                          :INITIAL-ELEMENT 0))
   (S765 (MAKE-ARRAY '())))
  1
  (VECTOR N)
  (A-LAM V767
         (- (IF (= 1 (AREF H764))
                (AREF S765)
                (PROGN (SETF (AREF H764) 1)
                       (SETF (AREF S765)
                             (G A B))))
            (AREF V767 0))))
```

```
(each - (eager (box (g a b))) (iota n))
⇓
(BUILD-LATCHED ((A827 (BUILD-EAGER
                        NIL
                        0
                        #()
                        (A-LAM V820 (G A B)))))
               1
               (VECTOR N)
               (A-LAM V829
                      (- (AREF A827)
                         (AREF V829 0))))
```

```
(each - (lazy (box (g a b))) (iota n))
⇓
(BUILD-LATCHED NIL
               1
               (VECTOR N)
               (A-LAM V853 (- (G A B)
                              (AREF V853 0))))
```

4.8.2 Optimization of Array Formation Code

A second level of optimization is performed when build macros are finally invoked. The primary responsibility of a build macro is to create an array object. Since no further use will be made of the symbolic representation, optimizations that would otherwise interfere with those described above can finally be made. These transformations may transform expressions out of any canonical form previously presumed, or they may introduce code that is not purely functional and uses state.

Of particular importance is the case where an eager array is formed. In the most general case (corresponding to a non-constant rank), a single loop is generated. During each iteration of the loop, an "odometer" vector is adjusted to refer to the next element of the array in row major order. In addition to other, more common loop optimizations, two specific optimizations have proven invaluable. In the first, if the rank is known to be constant, the single general loop with its odometer vector is replaced by a set of nested loops, each with a single induction variable representing an index along a given dimension. In the second, if a loop contains a predicate involving the induction variable and a loop invariant comparand, a "loop fission" optimization is performed, producing two new loops neither of which contains the predicate inside of it.

5 Future Work

The work described in this paper is actually work in progress; some of its finding are tentative. More importantly, there are several additional aspects to this line of research that are not addressed here, suggesting future work. These tasks are to:

- Implement infinite arrays[10][15][17][18]. Some additional work is necessary to support shape computations on infinities.
- Understand replacement (assignment) of elements in non-eager arrays, while attempting to retain notions of first-class places[16].
- Implement cached evaluation of free arrays. The difference between latched evaluation and cached evaluation is that, with cached evaluation, the cache may be purged. With the semantic constraints presented here, this can only be done with free arrays. Cached evaluation has been shown to be very effective in functional languages[13].
- Understand the relative order of evaluation for rank, shape, and data. In this paper no semantics have been presented that specify this relative order. The best relative order depends upon the primitive.

- Understand how to efficiently perform operations involving recurrences. There is a method for computing arbitrary reductions symbolically, without creating intermediate objects and invoking stored function objects. This method is intricate, would take up too much space to describe here, and will be the subject of another paper.

- Understand how to implement these concepts on parallel computers.

- Treat the symbolic representations as attributes that can be propagated throughout a program, providing further optimization.

- Extend these concepts to other aggregate data structures. This work has focused on arrays, but the concept of using expressions to denote aggregate data structures without forming intermediates, appears applicable to most other aggregates, e.g. lists, hash tables, structures, etc.

6 Summary

In general, experience with the prototype implementation has been good. It appears that the techniques presented here do remove most of the disadvantages traditionally associated with array-style programming. More specifically, the most important preliminary findings are:

- The order in which elements are evaluated between array expressions should be precisely predictable and controllable.

- One of three methods – eager, latched, or lazy – will generally produce optimal performance.

- Each method of evaluation has a language primitive which can invoke it.

- Each method of evaluation should be capable of being represented as a first class object, allowing the method to be applied later.

- Nested arrays are effectively handled by these methods. Each element of a nested array may be of any evaluation type.

- Latched evaluation makes the best default.

- *All* array expressions may be lazily evaluated through composition of their indexing functions or through blind calls to stored function objects.

- The efficiency of lazy evaluation is significantly enhanced through the use of a rule based rewriting system.

- Index functions that have vector index arguments are more effectively manipulated than those with a single, row-major-order index.
- Optimizations may be safely applied to many expressions in order to achieve a preferred order of evaluation.
- Array style programming is easily imbedded in an existing language (LISP) by exploiting macro expansion features.

7 Acknowledgement

The author would like to thank Cyril Alberga, Don Orth, Adin Falkoff, and Martin Mikelsons for their many helpful suggestions in producing this paper. Special thanks go to Martin Mikelsons, Daniel Sabbah, and the management of the IBM Research Division for making this work possible.

References

[1] Abelson, H., and Sussman, G. J. *Structure and Interpretation of Computer Programs*. McGraw Hill, New York, Nov. 1985.

[2] Abelson, H., and Sussman, G. J. Lisp: A language for stratified design. *BYTE 13*, 2 (Feb. 1988), 207–220.

[3] Abrams, P. S. *An APL Machine*. PhD thesis, Stanford University, Jan. 1970.

[4] Anderson, S., and Hudak, P. Compilation of Haskell array comprehensions for scientific computing. In *ACM SIGPLAN '90 Conference on Programming Language Design and Implementation* (June 1990), pp. 137–149.

[5] Budd, T. A. An APL compiler for the UNIX timesharing system. In *APL83 Conference Proceedings* (Apr. 1983), pp. 205–210.

[6] Ching, W.-M. Program analysis and code generation in an APL/370 compiler. *IBM Journal of Research and Development 30*, 6 (Nov. 1986), 594–602.

[7] Driscoll Jr., G. C., and Orth, D. L. Compiling APL: The Yorktown APL translator. *IBM Journal of Research and Development 30*, 6 (Nov. 1986), 583–593.

[8] Guibas, L. J., and Wyatt, D. K. Compilation and delayed evaluation in APL. In *Proceedings of the Fifth Annual ACM Symposium on Principles of Programming Languages* (Jan. 1978), pp. 1–81.

[9] Hudak, P., Wadler, P., et al. Report on the functional programming language Haskell. Research Report YALEU/DCS/RR-666, Yale University, Dec. 1988.

[10] McDonnell, E. E., and Shallit, J. O. Extending APL to infinity. In *APL80* (June 1980), pp. 123–132.

[11] Miller, T. C. *Tenative Compilation, A Design for an APL Compiler*. PhD thesis, Yale University, May 1978.

[12] Mullin, L. M. R. *A Mathematics of Arrays*. PhD thesis, Syracuse University, Aug. 1988.

[13] Pugh, W. An improved replacement strategy for function caching. In *1988 ACM Conference on LISP and Functional Programming* (July 1988), pp. 269–276.

[14] Revesz, G. *Lambda-Calculus, Combinators, and Functional Programming*. Cambridge Tracts in Theoretical Computer Science. Cambridge University Press, 1988.

[15] Shallit, J. O. Infinite arrays and diagonalization. In *APL81 Conference Proceedings* (Sept. 1981), pp. 281–285.

[16] Skutt, C. F. APL reference arrays, structure functions, and specification fucntions. Research Report RC14584, IBM, Nov. 1985.

[17] Tu, H.-C. *FAC: Functional Array Calculator and Its Application to APL and Functional Programming*. PhD thesis, Yale University, May 1986.

[18] Tu, H.-C., and Perlis, A. J. FAC: A functional APL language. *IEEE Software 3*, 1 (Jan. 1986), 36–45.

[19] Van Dyke, E. J. A dynamic incremental compiler for an interpretive language. *Hewlett-Packard Journal 28*, 7 (July 1977), 17–23.

[20] Waters, R. The series macro package. *LISP Pointers 3*, 1 (Mar. 1990), 7–11.

A Notation

Table 3 provides descriptions of the LISP notation used throughout this paper and the corresponding APL expression. The first three are proposed and described in this paper. In the LISP notation, upper case arguments must be array objects.

APL Expression	LISP Expression
⍁A	(EAGER A)
⌧A	(LATCHED A)
⍂A	(LAZY A)
⍳A	(IOTA a)
<A	(BOX a)
(F¨)A	(EACH f A)
A(F¨)B	(EACH f A B)
⊖A	(REV A)
⍉A	(POSE A)
A⍪B	(CAT A B)
A(∘.F)B	(OUTER f A B)
A⊃B	(PICK B a)
A[I;J;]	(SLICE A I J)
(A B C)	(VEC a b c)

Table 3: Summary of Notation Used in this Paper

16

MATRIX INVERSION IN 3 DIMENSIONS *

Gaétan Hains
Université de Montréal,
Informatique et Recherche Opérationnelle,
Montréal, Québec, Canada H3C 3J7,
hains@iro.umontreal.ca

Abstract. A three-dimensional mesh implementation of Csanky's method is shown to be asymptotically faster than systolic algorithms for $n \times n$ full matrix inversion. This requires the fastest known sequential matrix multiplication algorithms with large hidden constants. It nevertheless suggests the possibility of $o(n)$ matrix inversion on a scalable architecture with realistic communication costs. Three-dimensional fan-in requirements imply a lower bound of $\Omega(n^{\frac{1}{2}})$ or $\Omega(n^{\frac{2}{3}})$ depending on the input's spatial distribution. The example of inversion illustrates general methods for optimal mesh implementation of matrix algorithms.

Key Words. Mesh-connected computers, communication costs, matrix inversion.

1. Mesh-Connected Computer. We define an MCC3 or three-dimensional mesh-connected computer as consisting of P sequential random access machines (*processors*), each with unlimited local memory. A processor is labeled with a point $(x, y, z) \in \{1, \ldots, P_x\} \times \{1, \ldots, P_y\} \times \{1, \ldots, P_z\}$ where $P_x P_y P_z = P$ and is connected to processors (x', y', z') for which $|x - x'| + |y - y'| + |z - z'| = 1$. At each of T parallel steps, a processor can execute one unary or binary arithmetic operation, the associated local data movements and at most 12 communications: two

* Supported by an NSERC operating grant and FAS-CAFIR grants, Université de Montréal.

in each direction of its communication channels. The distance between two processors is $d_2((p_1, p_2, p_3), (q_1, q_2, q_3)) = \sum_{i=1}^{3} |p_i - q_i|$ so that after $k \geq 0$ time steps, a message originating at a processor can reach at most $\sigma(k)$ processors or vice-versa: $\sigma(k) = \frac{4}{3}k^3 + 2k^2 + \frac{8}{3}k + 1$ which is less than $2k^3$ for $k \geq 6$.

The MCC3 model is preferred for analysing massively parallel algorithms because of its realistic measure of communication time, as suggested by general lower bounds of Vitányi. Hypercubes and cube-connected cycles are known to require connections of average physical length $\Omega(P^{\frac{1}{3}} / \log P)$ [12]. It follows that most algorithms can only support execution times of the order of *diameter * edge length* or $\Omega(P^{\frac{1}{3}})$. On a MCC3, communication delays are within a constant factor of the graph distance d_2 (d_2 is within a constant factor of Euclidean distance when the mesh is built with constant length connections). Clearly this is also the case for the MCC2, and the main question raised here is whether three-dimensional algorithms can improve on systolic (or other planar) matrix algorithms.

We consider MCC3 algorithms for *direct* inversion of a nonsingular full matrix $A \in F^{n \times n}$ where F is a field of characteristic zero (more precisely one where Csanky's method [3] is applicable). A direct inversion algorithm computes the exact answer in a finite number of arithmetic operations, as opposed to a numerical approximation.

2. Lower Bounds. As expressed by Cramer's rule, any element of the output depends on every A_{ij}. An inversion algorithm must therefore perform enough arithmetic and communication operations to combine n^2 values into each output. The simplest way to quantify this constraint is to assume (as in [4] for two dimensions) that the initial distribution of elements A_{ij} is bijective.

PROPOSITION 2.1. *If the input matrix is placed in n^2 processors, one element in each, then $T > 0.79\, n^{2/3}$ for inversion.*

Proof. Each of the input processors must communicate with a processor which will eventually compute $(A^{-1})_{ij}$. Therefore $2T^3 > \sigma(T) \geq n^2$. □

Relaxing the hypothesis to allow an arbitrary input distribution brings the lower bound down to $\Omega(\sqrt{n})$.

PROPOSITION 2.2. *Any inversion algorithm requires time $T > 0.84\, n^{1/2}$.*

Proof. Consider the first arithmetic operation whose result is $(A^{-1})_{ij}$

in processor P_0. This operation is at the root of a binary tree with at least n^2 leaves (inputs) and at least $n^2 - 1$ inner nodes (operations). For the result to reach P_0 in time T, the tree must be evaluated by at most $\sigma(T)$ processors. Therefore $T\sigma(T) \geq n^2 - 1$ and $2T^4 \geq n^2$. □

The above bounds apply to any non-degenerate function of n^2 variables. Given that every processor may initially contain an arbitrary subset of the matrix elements, it remains sensible to require that the output's distribution be the same as the input. This ensures the algorithm leaves the machine in the same state it was initialised (as in the Shell parallel linear algebra library [13]).

PROPOSITION 2.3. *Under the above hypothesis, inversion in time T with P processors implies $T > 0.31\, P^{1/3}$.*

Proof. Let P_1 and P_5 be any two processors initially storing A_{ij} and A_{kl} respectively. Let also P_2 and P_4 be processors where $(A^{-1})_{ij}$ and $(A^{-1})_{kl}$ are respectively computed. By hypothesis, $(A^{-1})_{ij}$ must be transmitted back to P_1 so that $T \geq d_2(P_1, P_2)$ and similarly $T \geq d_2(P_4, P_5)$. Now because each output depends on every input, there must be a P_3 initially storing A_{ij} and within distance T of P_4 so $T \geq d_2(P_3, P_4)$. Because it initially contains A_{ij}, P_3 must also receive a copy of $(A^{-1})_{ij}$ from P_2 and so $T \geq d_2(P_2, P_3)$. By the triangle inequality it follows that $4T \geq d_2(P_1, P_5)$. Because this holds for any pair A_{ij}, A_{kl}, all processors holding inputs (and therefore outputs) must be within a d_2-ball of radius $2T$. These processors can also communicate with intermediate processors within distance $\frac{1}{2}T$, so messages may return within time T. Therefore all processors must be within a $2\frac{1}{2}T$ radius: $P < \sigma(\frac{5}{2}T) < 2(\frac{5}{2}T)^3$. □

The known methods for direct inversion can be classified as partitioning algorithms [10], and variants of Csanky's Method [3] which allow massive parallelism.

Bordering methods such as Gauss-Jordan and pivoting or systolic variants are essentially unbalanced binary partitioning algorithms based on the recursive scheme

$$(1)\quad \begin{pmatrix} A_{11} & A_{12} \\ A_{21} & A_{22} \end{pmatrix}^{-1} = \begin{pmatrix} A_{11}^{-1} + A_{11}^{-1}A_{12}\Delta^{-1}A_{21}A_{11}^{-1} & -A_{11}^{-1}A_{12}\Delta^{-1} \\ -\Delta^{-1}A_{21}A_{11}^{-1} & \Delta^{-1} \end{pmatrix}$$

where $\Delta = A_{22} - A_{21}A_{11}^{-1}A_{12}$, $A_{11} \in F^{a\times a}$, $\Delta \in F^{b\times b}$ and $a + b = n$. Any such algorithm must first invert A_{11}, possibly a scalar *and then* invert $\Delta(A_{11}^{-1})$. Total time must satisfy $T(n) > T(a) + T(b) + 1 \in \Omega(n)$.

Pease [10] described generalised partitioning methods where an $r \times r$ partition requires the sequential solution-substitution of r subproblems. The resulting algorithms are $\Omega(n)$ as for $r = 2$.

Csanky's method yields an $O(\log^2 n)$ PRAM algorithm on $\Theta(n^4)$ processors. Apart from its numerical instability, it is usually dismissed as impractical for its high processor requirement. In the context of a MCC3, this requirement would imply a computation time $\Omega(n^{4/3})$ (by proposition 2.3), worse than partitioning methods, even if partially serialised. We will see however that a more efficient version of Preparata and Sarwate brings the time exponent below one.

3. PRAM Solution. Parallelising the Coppersmith-Winograd [2] $O(n^{2.376})$ multiplication method yields a $O(\log n)$ PRAM algorithm on $O(n^{2.376}/logn)$ processors [8]. Substitution into Preparata and Sarwate's [11] improvement of Csanky's method gives an $O(\log^2 n)$ inversion algorithm on $O(n^{2.376+\frac{1}{2}}/\log^2 n) = O(n^{2.876}/\log^2 n)$ processors.

4. Mesh Implementation. A basic tool for constructing mesh algorithms is routing by sorting. Nassimi and Sahni [9] have shown how to implement a random access read and exclusive random access write in $O(n)$ steps of an $n \times n \times n$ MCC3, thus allowing the mesh to simulate PRAM steps (see also [6]). Brute force application of this method allows a mesh of $O(n^{2.876}/\log^2 n)$ processors to simulate the PRAM algorithm in time $O(P^{1/3}\log^2 n) = O(n^{0.959}\log^{4/3} n)$. A direct mesh implementation increases locality and avoids the logarithmic factor. In designing it, we generalise the recursive routing scheme of Gibbons and Srikant [5] to a superlinear number of processors.

4.1. Multiplication. The Coppersmith-Winograd multiplication algorithm is based on partitioning like Strassen's original method. Its detailed description is not relevant here. Without loss of generality, we may assume that it recursively performs a independent additions and m independent multiplications of $\frac{n}{r} \times \frac{n}{r}$ matrices. Its time complexity is bounded by

$$T_{seq}(n) \leq mT_{seq}(\frac{n}{r}) + O(an^2) = O(n^\alpha)$$

where $\alpha = \log_r m < 2.376$. Let T_M, T_A be the time complexity of a mesh multiplication or addition respectively, and unfold the recursion three times:

$$T_M(n) \leq aT_A(\frac{n}{r}) + maT_A(\frac{n}{r^2}) + m^2aT_A(\frac{n}{r^3}) + m^3T_M(\frac{n}{r_3}).$$

If we use a cubic (symmetric) mesh of $P(n) = m^3P(\frac{n}{r^3}) \in O(n^{\log_r m})$ processors then it can be recursively subdivided into m^3 cubic meshes, each one solving a multiplication subproblem.

1. Route the a pairs of $\frac{n}{r} \times \frac{n}{r}$ matrices to a regions of n^2/r^2 processors: $O(n^2)$ in all (time $O(P^{1/3})$).
2. Perform a additions in time $O(1)$.
3. Route ma pairs of matrices to ma regions of n^2/r^4 processors, $O(n^2)$ in all (time $O(P^{1/3})$).
4. Perform ma additions in time $O(1)$.
5. Route m^2a pairs of matrices to m^2a regions of n^2/r^6 processors, $O(n^2)$ in all (time $O(P^{1/3})$).
6. Perform m^2a additions in time $O(1)$.
7. Route m^3 pairs of matrices to m^3 square meshes of $P(n/r^3)$ processors.
8. Perform m^3 multiplications in parallel.

The total time $T_M(n)$ is then bounded above by

$$4O(P^{1/3}) + O(1) + T_M(n/r^3) \in O(\sum_{i=0}^{\log_{r^3} n} (nr^{-3i})^{\frac{1}{3}\log_r m}) \subseteq O(n^{\frac{1}{3}\log_r m}).$$

We have shown that,

LEMMA 4.1. *Matrix multiplication is computable on a MCC3 with $P \in O(n^{2.376})$ and $T \in O(P^{1/3})$.*

4.2. Triangular Inversion. Csanky's method depends on the solution of a triangular system to evaluate the coefficients of A's characteristic polynomial. In the case of a lower triangular matrix, equation 1 becomes:

$$\begin{pmatrix} A_{11} & O \\ A_{21} & A_{22} \end{pmatrix}^{-1} = \begin{pmatrix} A_{11}^{-1} & O \\ -A_{22}^{-1}A_{21}A_{11}^{-1} & A_{22}^{-1} \end{pmatrix} \tag{2}$$

where A_{11}, A_{22} are lower triangular. This simplification removes the need for sequential execution of subproblems and allows a fast parallel solution.

The obvious strategy is to invert $A_{11}, A_{22} \in F^{\frac{n}{2}\times\frac{n}{2}}$ in parallel and then compute A_{21}^{-1} in two successive multiplications. PRAM solutions based on this recursion are well-known; see for example [1]. Given enough processors for the multiplications $P(n) = O(2(\frac{n}{2})^{\alpha}) = O(n^{\alpha})$, the mesh only requires two routing phases, two multiplications and two parallel recursive calls ($P(n) \geq 2P(n/2)$):

$$T(n) \leq O(P(n)^{1/3}) + O((n/2)^{\alpha/3}) + T(\frac{n}{2}) \in O(n^{\alpha/3}).$$

LEMMA 4.2. *Triangular matrix inversion is computable on a MCC3 with $P \in O(n^{2.376})$ and $T \in O(P^{1/3})$.*

4.3. Inversion. The most costly step in Csanky's method is the computation of $A^2, A^3, \ldots, A^n$ i.e. a prefix calculation [7] with matrix multiplication as associative operator. The key improvement of Preparata-Sarwate is to compute only $A^2, \ldots, A^{\sqrt{n}}$ and only then to compute $A^{2\sqrt{n}}, A^{3\sqrt{n}}, \ldots, A^n$. Implementing this on the mesh can be done in a purely functional manner: design a MCC3 parallel prefix algorithm and then substitute a matrix multiplication algorithm for each processor.

An optimal mesh algorithm for parallel prefix is built as follows. Assume one processor holds the input value a and the m processors are required to compute successive powers $a, a^2, \ldots, a^m$ for a given associative product operation (computable in unit time and space). The input is first broadcast to all processors, then products are accumulated along each individual line of the mesh. In each plane, last processors of each line accumulate products along their common column to obtain $a^{m^{1/3}i}, i = 1, \ldots, m^{1/3}$. These results are individually broadcast back to their respective lines where, in parallel, each processor performs a single multiplication. At this point each plane holds a copy of $a, a^2, \ldots, a^{m^{2/3}}$. Then maximal powers are accumulated vertically through planes and redistributed in the same manner, completing the algorithm in optimal time $O(m^{1/3})$.

Setting $m = \sqrt{n}$ and substituting our mesh multiplication algorithm for each node processor simply inflates the prefix algorithm to a mesh of side $O(m^{1/3}n^{\alpha/3}) = O(n^{(1/2+\alpha)/3}) \in O(n^{0.959})$ and since matrix movements (loading) between adjacent blocks are faster than the products themselves, total time is also $O(m^{1/3}n^{\alpha/3})$.

THEOREM 4.3. *Matrix inversion is computable on a MCC3 in time $O(n^{0.959})$.*

5. Conclusion. Because of its constant and exponent, the above algorithm is only of theoretical interest. However the known lower bounds are weak and leave open the possibility of more efficient and perhaps practical parallel algorithms. Non-trivial lower bounds require a problem-specific analysis of locality if they are not to rely on a lower bound for the number of operations PT i.e. a breakthrough in sequential complexity. Accelerations may come through faster sequential multiplication or a new $O(\log n)$ PRAM algorithm which would, as suggested by Csanky [3], use a radically new direct method for parallel inversion. An open question specific to the MCC3 model but independent of matrix problems is the relationship between interleaved sequential procedures: what if anything can be gained from unbounded local memories when the communication network is a mesh.

Acknowledgements. Bill McColl directed me to Vitányi's work, Alan Gibbons introduced me to recursive mesh algorithms and David Skillicorn corrected some inconsistencies in the draft.

REFERENCES

[1] D. P. Bertsekas and J. N. Tsitsiklis, *Parallel and Distributed Computation. Numerical Methods*, Prentice-Hall International, 1989.

[2] D. Coppersmith and S. Winograd, *Matrix multiplication via arithmetic progressions*, in Proceedings 19th ACM STOC, New-York, 1987, pp. 1–6.

[3] L. Csanky, *Fast parallel matrix inversion algorithms*, SIAM Journal on Computing, 5 (1976), pp. 618–623.

[4] W. M. Gentleman, *Some complexity results for matrix computations on parallel processors*, Journal of the ACM, 25 (1978), pp. 112–115.

[5] A. M. Gibbons and Y. N. Srikant, *A class of problems efficiently solvable on mesh-connected computers including dynamic expression evaluation*, Information Processing Letters, (1989), pp. 305–311.

[6] M. Kunde and T. Tensi, *Multi-packet-routing on mesh connected arrays*, in ACM Symposium on Parallel Algorithms and Architectures, Santa Fe, New-Mexico, June 1989, pp. 336–343.

[7] R. E. Ladner and M. J. Fischer, *Parallel prefix computation*, Journal of the ACM, 27 (1980), pp. 831–838.

[8] S. Lakshmivarahan and S. K. Dhall, *Analysis and Design of Parallel Algorithms. Arithmetic and Matrix Problems*, McGraw-Hill, 1990.

[9] D. Nassimi and S. Sahni, *Data broadcasting in SIMD computers*, IEEE transactions on computers, c-30 (1981), pp. 101–107.

[10] M. C. Pease, *Inversion of matrices by partitioning*, Journal of the ACM, 16 (1969), pp. 302–314.

[11] F. P. PREPARATA AND D. V. SARWATE, *An improved parallel processor bound in fast matrix inversion*, Information Processing Letters, 7 (1978), pp. 148–150.

[12] P. M. B. VITÁNYI, *Locality, communication, and interconnect length in multicomputers*, SIAM Journal on Computing, 17 (1988), pp. 659–672.

[13] J. G. G. V. D. VORST, *Solving the least squares problem using a parallel linear algebra library*, Future Generation Computer Systems, 4 (1988–1989), pp. 293–297.

17

Fuzzy Inference using Array Theory and Nial

Jan Jantzen
Technical University of Denmark
Building 325, DK-2800 Lyngby
E-mail: STARDUST at NEUVM1

Abstract

To prevent sewage floods during rainstorms, a prototype of a fault diagnosis system has been built. The prototype is written in the Nested Interactive Array Language, Nial. A fuzzy inference method has been implemented by means of array theory. Thus, a rule like *Clog := Big if (Level is High)* is directly executable. As a result, a whole rule-base executes without overhead from parsing.

Keywords: production rules, simplification, applied array theory.

Introduction

Sewerage networks in Danish cities often carry both rain and waste water in shared pipes. A number of times during the past decade, bad rainstorms have caused flooded streets and basements. The pipes are not sized after worst case rainfalls, and many are old and in a poor condition. Unpurified waste water spills into the environment on these occasions.

To prevent the floods, an automatic control system is now being designed. The idea is simply to pump water into reservoirs and partly filled pipes, and keep it there until the rain is over. A diagnosis system that detects clogs, leakages and sensor defects is part of the project. A prototype in the Nested Interactive Array Language, Nial (Jenkins & Jenkins, 1985) runs on a two-tank water rig in the laboratory.

In order to deal with imprecise statements like *a high water level* or *a big clog*, the diagnosis system applies fuzzy sets (Zadeh, 1965; Zadeh, 1973). An example of a fuzzy inference is:

```
  if water level is high then clog is big
  water level is high'
  ---------------------------------------    (0)
  clog is big'
```

The inference can be stated as follows: If it is known, that a high water level always indicates a big clog, and also, that the measured level is high, or slightly different from high cf. the prime in high', then the clog is big or slightly different from big (big').

Zadeh (1973) has defined inference between two fuzzy variables, one input and one output. It is a combination of fuzzy implication and fuzzy composition ('compositional rule of inference'). In an automatic control application Mamdani (1977) defined inference with two non-fuzzy inputs and one fuzzy output. Holmblad & Østergaard (1982) use the same approach, but with a slight, empirical modification in computing the conclusion. Various other definitions of fuzzy implication and inference have been studied with respect to modus ponens etc. (e.g. Mizumoto et al., 1979; Yamazaki, 1982). The present study just considers the simplest one (Mamdani, 1977; Holmblad & Østergaard, 1982). The work that initiated the study was by Wenstøp (1975, 1980) in the language APL; he transformed a theoretical inference definition into a simple, operational APL description, and built a language around it for linguistic modelling.

The present study was carried out in Nial. The purpose was to implement statement (0) such that it would be as close as possible to natural language, directly executable, and in accordance with fuzzy set theory. Furthermore, the purpose was to try and apply array theory (More, 1981), in order to make generalisations. The result is the Nial expression

```
Clog := Big iff ( Level isf High )
```

where names beginning with upper-case letters are variables, and the other names are defined operations. This type of expression may include the connectives *and*, *or* and *not*.

Approach

Scenario: non-fuzzy singleton

Suppose a sensor measures 3 meters of water in a manhole. The measurement gets transmitted to a central computer. The computer has to decide whether 3 meters is 'high', in order to detect a clog. According to a local expert, the lowest possible level is 0 meters, the normal level is 2 meters, and everything on or above 4 meters is high.

Comparing the measurement against threshold values is a simple, but crude approach; transitions from 'low' to 'normal' to 'high' would be abrupt. To get a finer, gradual transition we use the fuzzy set on Fig. 1. The graph relates the range of possible measurement values (the universe) to a degree between 0 and 1 (membership grades). It is characteristic that the set has membership values between 0 and 1, opposed to a non-fuzzy set. Assume that a 'big clog' is defined by the right graph. Its universe is perhaps a psychologic continuum, or a range of pipe resistance values.

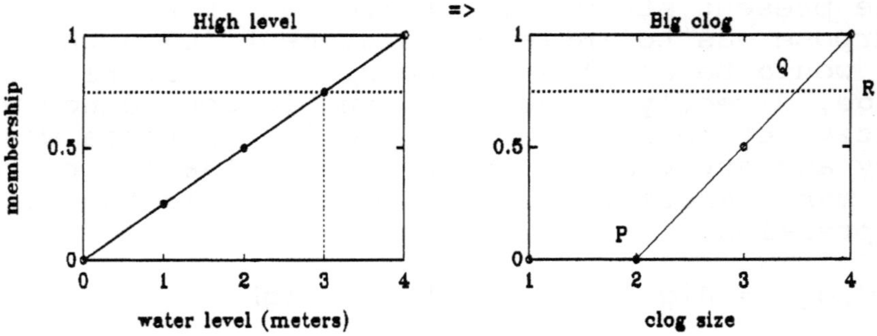

Figure 1. *Inference with non-fuzzy input.*

Referring to Fig. 1, the fuzzy inference proceeds as follows: Step 1, read the left graph, and find the water level is *High* in the degree 0.75 at 3 meters. Step 2, project the 0.75 onto the neighbouring graph by following the dotted line, in order to reduce its 'weight'. Final step, read the result, i.e. the graph P-Q-R. Had the measurement been 4 meters or above, the result would have been the full graph for BIG CLOG. Had the measurement been 0 meters, the result would have been undefined (all zeros, the empty set).

In Nial, it is convenient to represent the graphs by vectors (lists). Discretize the universes, and get

```
Level_universe := 0 1 2 3 4
High := 0 0.25 0.5 0.75 1
Level := 0 0 0 1 0
Big := 0 0 0.5 1.0
```

The ':=' is the Nial assignment operator. Each number in Level and High correspond to a point on the Level_universe axis. The *Level* variable has only one item of full membership. This is a 'non-fuzzy singleton'.

Scenario continued: fuzzy singleton
The sensor still measures 3 meters, but it behaves strangely. The operator only believes it to some degree, say 0.6. How does that compare with High ?

To represent the level measurement with its degree of belief, change the *Level* vector to

```
Level := 0 0 0 0.6 0
```

Clearly, the belief in the output of the inference *Clog* cannot be larger than the belief in the input *Level*. Zadeh (1973) proposes to choose the smallest membership value, when composing two fuzzy variables. We will call this operation 'single composition'. Referring to Fig. 1 again, the horizontal line that cuts the set Big should be lowered to 0.6 in this case.

Scenario continued: several fuzzy singletons
The sensor breaks and there is no measurement. The operator supplies the input *Medium*. In Nial,

```
Medium := 0 0.5 1 0.5 0
Level := Medium
```

The Level variable now has several fuzzy membership grades.

Regard it as a collection of fuzzy singletons. This is an important point to note, because the central argument is: Being a collection of singletons, we will treat each singleton separately, but in parallel with the others. So, each singleton in *Level* must be composed with the corresponding singleton in *High* (single composition in parallel),

```
Level min High
```

0.	0.25	0.5	0.5	0.

The Nial terminal drew the box diagram automatically to emphasize the array structure. The *min* is an item-by-item minimum operation on the two lists, *Level* and *High*. Each of the items in the result must then be projected onto the set *Big*

```
Level min High EACHLEFT min Big
```

0. 0. 0. 0.	0. 0. 0.25 0.25	0. 0. 0.5 0.5	0. 0. 0.5 0.5	0. 0. 0. 0.

EACHLEFT is a Nial 'transformer' which operates on *min* in order to apply it to each item on the left in turn. This is instead of item-by-item. There are five results now, that need to be reduced to one vector. The general rule is to pick the strongest evidence across the vectors for the result (Zadeh, 1973). Applying a *max* operation yields

```
Clog := max (Level min High EACHLEFT min Big)
```

0.	0.	0.5	0.5

(1)

This output could be interpreted 'maybe a rather big clog'.

Expression (1) can be simplified to get an expresssion closer to natural language, and array

Equivalences	Notes
Clog:=max (Medium min High EACHLEFT min Big)	equation (1)
== max (Medium min High) min Big	min distributes over max
== max (min (Medium High)) min Big	infix to prefix notation
== (max min) (Medium High) min Big	array theoretic composition
== Medium (max min) High min Big	prefix to infix
== Big min (Medium (max min) High)	min commutes

Figure 2. *Array theoretic proof of equivalence between (1) and (4).*

theory provides means of transforming the expression. Fig. 2 shows the steps in the transformation. Define

```
iff IS min                                   (2)
isf IS max min                               (3)
```

and the result is

```
Clog := Big iff ( Level isf High )           (4)
```

The IS is a Nial keyword, that serves to bind a name to an expression. The appended 'f' in the names stands for 'fuzzy' and serves to avoid naming conflicts. The equivalences in Fig. 2 are valid due to array theoretic rules (More 1981; Jenkins & Jenkins, 1985).

Expression (4) agrees in essence with Wenstøp's work (1975, 1980). It is straight forward to prove, that expressions (1) and (4) are also equivalent to

Clog := Medium INNER[max,min] (High OUTER min Big)

where *INNER* is the inner (matrix) product using *max* and *min* instead of addition and multiplication; *OUTER* is the outer product operator, which applies *min* to the cartesian product of *High* and *Big* in a matrix. The outer *min* product complies with one definition (Zadeh, 1973; Mamdani, 1977) out of at least ten suggestions for a fuzzy implication (in Yamazaki, 1982; Mizumoto et al., 1979). The whole expression complies with Zadeh's definition of the 'compositional rule of inference' (Zadeh, 1973).

The general case

The inferences so far have been single-input-single-output (SISO); one variable in the if-part and one variable in the then-part. For the sewage prototype, it was necessary to generalise to multiple-inputs-single-output inferences. A two-input inference is, symbolically

```
A and B implies Z
A'
B'
-----------------
Z'
```

This kind of inference was implemented by Holmblad & Østergaard (1982) to control rotating cement kilns. However, their inputs are non-fuzzy, so it was necessary to generalize to accomodate vector input.

For the connective 'and' we use *min*, in accordance with the definition of fuzzy set intersection (Zadeh, 1965). Following the principles of SISO inference, we must (fuzzy) compose A and A', and also B and B', <u>before</u> projecting onto the output Z. Since A and B are not necessarily from the same universe, and perhaps not even the same length, they should be intersected in a cartesian product,

```
andf IS min
(A min A') OUTER andf (B min B')
```

Combining each item with the vector *Z* produces many fuzzy vectors. Like previously, we apply a max operation to reduce the output to a vector:

```
   Z' := max ((A' min A) OUTER andf (B' min B)
EACHLEFT min Z)                                    (5)
```

Expression (5) is equivalent to

```
   Z' := Z iff (A' isf A andf (B' isf B))          (6)
```

Fig. 3 has a proof. For generality, the proof uses the symbolic operations *f* and *g* instead of the *min* operation. The reason is, that some authors (e.g. Holmblad & Østergaard, 1982) prefer multiplication (*prod* in Nial) for 'andf', instead of *min*.

The bottom line of the proof is definition (6) when *g* and *f* are both *min*. Also, *g* and *f* can independently be *min* or *prod* without violating the constraints in lines 3 and 9 of Fig. 3. The fuzzy

Equivalences	Notes
max ((A' g A) OUTER andf (B' g B) EACHLEFT f Z)	
== max ((A' g A) OUTER min (B' g B) EACHLEFT f Z)	def of andf
== max ((A' g A) OUTER min (B' g B)) EACHLEFT f Z	f must distribute over max
== max ((A' g A) OUTER min (B' g B)) f Z	f's left arg is a single
== max ((A' g A) EACHLEFT EACHRIGHT min (B' g B)) f Z	def of OUTER
== max ((max (A' g A) min (B' g B))) f Z	min distributes over max
== ((max (A' g A) min (max (B' g B)) f Z	same, and min associates
== A' (max g) A min (B' (max g) B) f Z	pre- to infix; composition
== Z f (A' (max g) A min (B' (max g) B))	f must commute

Figure 3. *Proof of equivalence between equations (5) and (6).*

'orf' connective is defined as a *max* operation, and the proof also holds for 'A orf B implies Z'.

Summary of findings

MISO fuzzy inference,

if A' is A and B' is B then Z

can be implemented as an executable Nial statement

Z' := Z iff ((A' isf A) andf (B' isf B))   (6)

where

iff IS min; isf IS max min; andf IS min;
orf IS max

The 'orf' can replace 'andf' if required. Alternative definitions are possible:

iff IS prod ; isf IS max prod

These do not violate the chain of simplifications in Fig. 3. It is possible, but trivial, to extend the proof in Fig. 3 to include more than two 'andf' or 'orf' connected inputs.

Evaluation

It is now possible to evaluate if an inference can be replaced by another in accordance with intuition. Fig. 4 is a list of useful implications. The symbolic form 'A => Z' represents an inference, in the sense of definition (6) above. The connective 'notf' is fuzzy negation, *notf A = 1 - A*, and 'veryf' is a fuzzy modifier that squares

Given	=>?	Consequence	id
A => Z A	yes	Z	(1)
A => B B => C	yes	A => C	(2)
(A andf (orf) B) => Z A, B from same universe	yes	A => Z andf (orf) B => Z	(3)
A => Z andf (orf) B => Z A, B from same universe	yes	(A andf (orf) B) => Z	(4)
A => (X andf (orf) Y) X, Y from same universe	yes	A => X andf (orf) A => Y	(5)
A => X andf (orf) A => Y X, Y from same universe	yes	A => (X andf (orf) Y)	(6)
A => (Z orf notf Z)	no	Z = 1	(7)
A => (Z andf notf Z)	no	Z = 0	(8)
A => Z notf Z	no	notf A	(9)
A => Z not A	yes	max Z below 0.5	(10)
A => Z veryf A	yes	Z	(11)

Figure 4. *Test results for some useful implications.*

membership values, *veryf A = A prod A* (Zadeh, 1973). All input sets are assumed normalized, such that the maximum item equals 1.

Implications 1 and 2 are the most important. Implication 1 ensures the consistency of the fuzzy inference (modus ponens), and implication 2 permits chaining of rules (hypothetical syllogism). Implications 7, 8, and 9, that hold for non-fuzzy sets, do NOT hold here (tautology, contradiction, and modus tollens). Implication 10 shows, that negation of the premise causes a very fuzzy consequence, if any, and implication 11 shows that the 'veryf' modifier does not cause modification to the output. All the tests can be verified using definition (6).

An IF-THEN-ELSE construct has not been implemented, because definition (6) has been sufficient. Consider the example

```
if level is high then clog is big, else
if level is not high then clog is not big
```

If the 'else' is interpreted as an 'orf', one could write

```
Clog := Big iff (Level isf High) orf (notf
        Big iff (Level isf notf High))
```

The diagnosis system consists of about 15 rules in the form of definition (6). The system detects clogs, leakages, and sensor problems (spikes, noise, outages, and jamming) based on certain indicators computed from the sensor measurements. Output is one or several diagnoses, each with a single fuzzy degree of belief attached. The fuzzy vectors are 21 points long. The implementation is satisfactory, mainly because it is simple. The rules are directly executable so there is no overhead from parsing. The rules can be mixed with ordinary Nial statements, so the inference is entirely under programmer control. Thus, an inference engine has not been needed.

Conclusion

The implementation of an IF-THEN inference, definition (6), is probably the simplest possible in Nial. It can very well be implemented in any other language, as a simple means for handling fuzzy uncertainty.

The fuzzy inference is an illustrative example of applied array theory. Array theory and fuzzy theory seem to fit each other well, both being theories of sets.

References

Holmblad, L.P & J.-J. Østergaard: "Control of a Cement Kiln by Fuzzy Logic". FUZZY INF. DECISION PROCESSES, 1982, 389-399.

Jenkins, M.A. and W.H. Jenkins: "Q'Nial Reference Manual". Kingston, Ontario, Canada: Nial Systems Ltd, 1985.

Mamdani, E.H.: "Application of Fuzzy Logic to Approximate Reasoning". IEEE TRANS COMPUTERS, 1977, 26 (12), 1182-1191.

Mizumoto, M., S. Fukami and K. Tanaka: "Some Methods of Fuzzy Reasoning". In Gupta, Ragade and Yager (Eds): ADVANCES IN FUZZY SET THEORY APPLICATIONS. New York: North-Holland, 1979

More, T.: "Notes on the Diagrams, Logic, and Operations of Array Theory". In Bjørke and Franksen (Eds): STRUCTURES AND OPERATIONS IN ENGINEERING AND MANAGEMENT SYSTEMS. Trondheim, Norway: Tapir,1981, 497-666.

Wenstøp, F.: "Application of Linguistic Variables in the Analysis of Organizations". Ann Arbour: University Microfilms, 1975 (Ph.D.thesis).

Wenstøp, F.: "Quantitative Analysis with Linguistic Values". FUZZY SETS AND SYSTEMS, 1980, 4 (2), 99-115.

Yamazaki, T.: "An Improved Algorithm for a Self-Organising Controller, and its Experimental Analysis". Queen Mary College, London: Dept. of Electrical and Electronic Engineering, 1982 (Ph.D. thesis).

Zadeh, L.A.: "Fuzzy Sets". INF. AND CONTROL, 1965, 8, 338-353.

Zadeh, L.A.: "Outline of a new Approach to the Analysis of Complex Systems and Decision Processes." IEEE TRANS SMC, 1973, 3, 28-44.

Index

MIX
Papier aus verantwortungsvollen Quellen
Paper from responsible sources
FSC® C105338

If you have any concerns about our products,
you can contact us on
ProductSafety@springernature.com

In case Publisher is established outside the EU,
the EU authorized representative is:
Springer Nature Customer Service Center GmbH
Europaplatz 3, 69115 Heidelberg, Germany

Printed by Libri Plureos GmbH
in Hamburg, Germany